U.S.

GOVERNMENT

LEADERS

———

U.S. Government Leaders

Volume 1
Dean Acheson–Ulysses S. Grant
1–308

edited by
Frank N. Magill

consulting editor
John Powell

SALEM PRESS, INC.
Pasadena, California   Englewood Cliffs, New Jersey

Original essays which appeared in *Great Lives from History: American Series*, 1987, and *Great Lives from History: American Women Series*, 1995, have been updated and reformatted; new material has been added.

∞ The paper used in these volumes conforms to the American National Standard for Permanence of Paper for Printed Library Materials, Z39.48-1984.

Library of Congress Cataloging-in-Publication Data
U.S. government leaders / edited by Frank N. Magill; consulting editor, John Powell.
p.   cm. — (Magill's choice)
Includes bibliographical references and index
ISBN 0-89356-954-2 (set : alk. paper). — ISBN 0-89356-955-0 (v. 1 : alk. paper). — ISBN 0-89356-956-9 (v. 2 : alk. paper). — ISBN 0-89356-957-7 (v. 3 : alk. paper)
1. Statesmen—United States—Biography—Dictionaries. 2. Politicians—United States—Biography—Dictionaries. 3. United States—Biography—Dictionaries.   I. Magill, Frank Northen, 1907-1997. II. Powell, John (John Douglas). III. Series.
E176.U23   1997
920.073—dc21   97-22519
                                                        CIP

First Printing

PRINTED IN THE UNITED STATES OF AMERICA

Table of Contents

Volume 1

Publisher's Note

U.S. Government Leaders surveys 124 of the most important government and political leaders in U.S. history: the most often taught and most often studied in the American library. Collected from two of Magill's *Great Lives from History* sets—the *American Series* (5 vols., 1987) and the *American Women Series* (5 vols., 1995)—and supplemented by eleven entirely new essays on leaders never before covered, this collection surveys the lives and achievements of more than one hundred of the nation's key figures in a uniform, easy-to-use reference format.

Every list of contents in a work such as this is subjective, and the inclusion of any one figure over another is open to debate. We have, however, made it our priority to cover those key personages of American history who appear time and again in the core curriculum, presenting at least those who are common to every basic discussion of American history, civics, and U.S. government. All U.S. presidents, from George Washington to Bill Clinton, are represented, as are such great colonial leaders as William Bradford, John Winthrop, and William Penn. Framers of the Constitution and leaders of the early republic appear, along with some who did not hold formal office but whose stature and contributions to U.S. government are equally great, among them Frederick Douglass and Martin Luther King, Jr. Leaders of Congress, presidential cabinets, and political parties will be found here—from Henry Clay to William Jennings Bryan to Tip O'Neill to Robert Dole—along with great political leaders who happened to be women, from Jeannette Rankin to Helen Gehagan Douglass and Margaret Chase Smith to Barbara Jordan and Janet Reno. Those who helped form government within the nation's expanding boundaries—such as Sam Houston, John C. Frémont, and Nellie Tayloe Ross—join those who articulated the American vision abroad, including Dean Acheson, Ralphe Bunche, Cordell Hull, and William Averell Harriman. Those whose focus was the nation's defense against foreign threats, from George Washington to George C. Marshall, join those who have encouraged government as defender against moral decay, from Increase Mather to Jesse Jackson.

To bring this collection of key leaders up to date, eleven essays have been added on leaders never before covered, including Madeleine Albright, George Bush, Bill Clinton, Robert Dole, Alan Greenspan, Jesse Jackson, Jr., Thomas "Tip" O'Neill, H. Ross Perot, Colin Powell, and George Wallace. In all cases, the persons presented here have left their mark on the government and governance of the United States.

The essays are arranged alphabetically by last name of leader, in three volumes, and each essay is chronologically organized, in a format that allows easy access to basic ready-reference data. Each essay begins with the leader's name, birth date and place, death date and place when appropriate, and a paragraph summarizing the leader's major achievements. The text of the essay is divided into three subsections: "Early Life" surveys the leader's youth and coming-of-age, including such formative influences as family, education, and early career; "Life's Work" focuses on the adult years and achievements for which the leader is known; and "Summary" surveys the leader's significance and long-term impact on the history of the United States.

The back matter of each essay includes a "Bibliography" that lists the basic texts and biographies about the leader. Each bibliography has been carefully updated with books and articles published during the 1980's and 1990's which are both significant additions to the literature and easy to find in most public libraries.

Volume 3 concludes with three reference tools that will assist students and general readers alike: The "Time Line" of U.S. leaders lists all leaders chronologically by birth year and will assist those interested in a particular period of American history. The "Index of Presidents" lists U.S. presidents in chronological order, by their ordinal ranking (from first through forty-second), with the years of their term or terms in office, their names, and the page numbers on which their essays appear. Finally, the "Name Index" lists all leaders covered as well as the page numbers on which their essays are located.

A list of the many scholars who contributed their time and knowledge to writing the articles, along with their academic affiliations at the time of writing, appears on the following page.

Contributors

John M. Allswang
California State University, Los Angeles
Stanley Archer
Texas A&M University
Mary Welek Atwell
Radford University
Betty Balanoff
Roosevelt University
Carl L. Bankston III
University of Southwestern Louisiana
Robert A. Becker
Louisiana State University, Baton Rouge
Robert L. Berner
University of Wisconsin at Oshkosh
Robert E. Bieder
Indiana University, Bloomington
David Warren Bowen
Livingston University
Gerhard Brand
California State University, Los Angeles
J. R. Broadus
Independent Scholar
Norman D. Brown
University of Texas at Austin
William H. Burnside
John Brown University
Donald Burrill
California State University, Los Angeles
Charles J. Bussey
Western Kentucky University
Light Townsend Cummins
Austin College
Paul E. Doutrich
York College of Pennsylvania
Charles Duncan
Atlanta University
Penelope J. Engelbrecht
DePaul University
Norman B. Ferris
Middle Tennessee State University
James E. Fickle
Memphis State University
Paul Finkelman
State University of New York at Binghamton
Roy E. Finkenbine
Florida State University
Richard G. Frederick
University of Pittsburgh, Bradford

Lynne M. Getz
Appalachian State University
Lewis L. Gould
University of Texas at Austin
Larry Gragg
University of Missouri, Rolla
C. L. Grant
Georgia State University
Lloyd J. Graybar
Eastern Kentucky University
D. Harland Hagler
North Texas State University
William I. Hair
Georgia College
David S. Heidler
Salisbury State College
Peter B. Heller
Manhattan College
Carlanna L. Hendrick
Francis Marion College
Ari Hoogenboom
City University of New York, Brooklyn College
Carlton Jackson
Western Kentucky University
Robert Jacobs
Central Washington University
Willoughby G. Jarrell
Kennesaw State College
Wm. Laird Kleine-Ahlbrandt
Purdue University, West Lafayette
Carl E. Kramer
Indiana University Southeast
James D. Lockett
Stillman College
Maxine N. Lurie
Rutgers University, New Brunswick
Arthur F. McClure
Central Missouri State University
Robert McColley
University of Illinois at Urbana-Champaign
Susan MacFarland
Wesleyan College
George McJimsey
Iowa State University of Science and Technology
Paul D. Mageli
Independent Scholar

Jo Manning
Independent Scholar
Marsha Kass Marks
Alabama Agricultural and Mechanical
University
Annette Marks-Ellis
Antelope Valley College
John F. Marszalek
Mississippi State University
Richard D. Miles
Wayne State University
Gordon R. Mork
Purdue University, West Lafayette
Michael R. Nichols
Texas Christian University
Frank Nickell
Southeast Missouri State University
Richard L. Niswonger
John Brown University
Keith W. Olson
University of Maryland at College Park
Gary B. Ostrower
Alfred University
Judith A. Parsons
Sul Ross State University
Thomas R. Peake
King College
William Pemberton
University of Wisconsin—La Crosse
Robert C. Petersen
Middle Tennessee State University
Donald K. Pickens
North Texas State University
Richard GidPowers
City University of New York College of
Staten Island
Verbie Lovorn Prevost
University of Tennessee, Chattanooga
Leo P. Ribuffo
George Washington University
Edward A. Riedinger
Ohio State University
Stephen P. Sayles
University of La Verne

J. Christopher Schnell
Southeast Missouri State University
Elizabeth A. Segal
Ohio State University
Robert W. Sellen
Georgia State University
David Curtis Skaggs
Bowling Green State University
C. Edward Skeen
Memphis State University
Jane Marie Smith
Butler County Community College
Joseph E. Suppiger
Limestone College
Patricia E. Sweeney
Independent Scholar
Sarah Thomas
Independent Scholar
Kenneth W. Townsend
Coastal Carolina University
Vernon L. Volpe
Texas A&M University
Harry M. Ward
University of Richmond
Donald V. Weatherman
Arkansas College
William C. Widenor
University of Illinois at
Urbana-Champaign
David L. Wilson
Southern Illinois University at
Carbondale
Major L. Wilson
Memphis State University
RaymondWilson
Fort Hays State University
Sharon K.Wilson
Fort Hays State University
Michael Witkoski
Office of Research, South Carolina
House of Representatives
James Edward Zacchini
Marquette University
Robert F. Zeidel
University of Nebraska at Lincoln

U.S.

GOVERNMENT

LEADERS

DEAN ACHESON

Born: April 11, 1893; Middletown, Connecticut
Died: October 12, 1971; Sandy Spring, Maryland

As secretary of state from 1949 to 1953, Acheson conducted negotiations leading to the establishment of the North Atlantic Treaty Organization and dealt with crises involving the victory of Communism in China and American participation in the Korean War; his policies determined the basic framework of the United States' security commitments in Europe and Asia during the Cold War.

Early Life

The son of a Canadian couple who had moved to the United States only the year before, Dean Gooderham Acheson was born on April 11, 1893, in Middletown, Connecticut. His father, Edward Acheson, had served with a Canadian militia regiment before settling upon a career as an Episcopalian minister. Eleanor Gooderham Acheson, the boy's mother, was from a prosperous and socially prominent family in Toronto. Margot and Edward, Jr., a sister and a younger brother, were born during the next ten years. Acheson recalled that his childhood was unusually happy, a golden age of games, pony riding, and Fourth of July celebrations. He never quarreled with his father until he was in college; he had a particularly fond and close relationship with his mother. During his adolescent years, Acheson was educated at the Groton School in southeastern Connecticut. After six languid years there, he spent the summer of 1911 in Canada, working on the Temiscaming and Northern Ontario Railroad; the experience of unrelenting physical labor among rough-hewn railway men left enduring memories of life in the wild that Acheson cherished in later life. That autumn, he enrolled at Yale University, and with only a modicum of effort he received passing grades and was graduated in 1915.

Acheson then entered the law school of Harvard University; he found academic demands there far more rigorous but also more challenging and stimulating. Particularly rewarding was his relationship with Professor Felix Frankfurter, who encouraged him in the study of constitutional law. For some time Acheson had seen his sister's roommate at Wellesley College, Alice Stanley, the daughter of a Michigan lawyer; in 1917 he married her. The following year, after he had earned his law degree, Acheson enlisted in the Naval Auxiliary Reserve, and for several months, until World War I ended, he served as an ensign at the Brooklyn Navy Yard. He then intended to pursue graduate studies in law, but after six months at Harvard, Professor Frankfurter obtained a position for him as secretary to Supreme Court Justice Louis D. Brandeis. In 1919, Acheson moved to Washington, D.C.; as he attended to the myriad details of cases brought before the high court, he received lasting impressions of Brandeis' unstinting standards of excellence. Devoted to the justice's work, Acheson provided needed assistance and support when Brandeis' wife suffered a nervous breakdown. In appreciation, Brandeis made an unusual offer, extending Acheson's appointment as his secretary for a second year.

Life's Work

At about this time, Acheson's life became more settled. A daughter, Jane Acheson, was born in 1919, followed by a son, David, and a younger daughter, Mary. In 1920, the family moved into a small house in Washington; later they acquired a quaint old farmhouse in Sandy Spring, Maryland, which Acheson regarded as a welcome refuge from legal and political cares. By his own account, Acheson was a liberal in politics, and the Republican ascendancy of the 1920's evidently deepened these convictions. In 1921, he joined Covington and Burling, a promising new law firm in the nation's capital. Although often aroused by political issues, he spent the next twelve years handling cases at law, some of which had international implications. In 1922, he represented Norway in proceedings arising from wartime shipping contracts; with others in the firm, Acheson argued this case before the Court of International Justice in The Hague. Other legal work concerned corporations or involved claims of water rights in the United States.

Dean Acheson was six foot three, with a spare but powerful build. His oval features were set off by a large protruding nose; he had brown hair, which he combed back in spite of its tendency to recede in later years. He had thick, bushy eyebrows which seemingly were underscored by the mustache he had cultivated since early manhood; to the delight of cartoonists, he often combed the ends upward, producing a curiously flamboyant effect. His manner perplexed many of those around him. He could be supercilious to the point of overt arrogance, but he could also act with a distinct stoicism, which possibly arose from his father's religious calling. He was able to endure direct affronts with quiet dignity. His style of speaking and writing, which was urbane and refined, bore the hallmarks of careful and discriminating reading; at times he would invoke great American or British thinkers or quote aphorisms in Latin.

In 1933, Franklin D. Roosevelt's Democratic administration assumed power, and Felix Frankfurter's intercession with the new president secured for Acheson an appointment as under secretary of the treasury. Major disagreements ensued, however, over the government's policy of manipulating the price of gold in an effort to stimulate economic growth. Acheson had misgivings about the legal basis for such action and believed that it was improper in view of existing gold contracts. After six months in office, he resigned and returned to his law practice. In 1939, Felix Frankfurter was nominated as a Supreme Court justice; Acheson served as adviser and representative to his old mentor during the Senate confirmation hearings. Acheson then became chairman of a committee advising the attorney general. During the next year, President Roosevelt considered means by which American destroyers might be sent to Britain, to aid in its war with Nazi Germany; Acheson assisted in legal work facilitating this transfer of military vessels. In 1941, Acheson was appointed assistant secretary of state for economic affairs. He played an important part in financial planning during World War II and aided in the establishment of such organizations as the World Bank and the International Monetary Fund. As under secretary of state from 1945 to 1947, he participated in deliberations leading to the European Recovery Program, or Marshall Plan. He was also the chairman of a special committee which considered problems surrounding proposals for the international control of atomic energy.

Although he had often expressed his wishes for a return to private life, and indeed left the State Department in 1947, President Harry S Truman appreciated his experience and his skill in coordinating administrative work. Accordingly, Acheson accepted his appointment to the nation's highest diplomatic post, in January, 1949. He had first to deal with proposals for mutual security arrangements, which had been considered among Western nations as a means to deal with Soviet expansionism. Enlarging upon projects that had already been advanced, involving Great Britain and several European states, Acheson carried out negotiations for a formal defense alliance. By reassuring hesitant states, such as Norway and Denmark, and encouraging those eager to join, such as Italy, the particular concerns of various governments were reconciled. In all, twelve original members joined the Atlantic alliance, which, while committed to maintaining peace, affirmed that an armed attack upon any signatory would be regarded as an attack upon all. Acheson also appeared before the United States Senate and adroitly dispelled the doubts of those who were wary of overseas commitments. In July, 1949, the Senate ratified the North Atlantic Treaty, and thus the nation embarked upon a military alliance in peacetime.

More intractable were problems in China, where for several years Communist insurgents steadily had won control of major provinces; in October, 1949, they entered the capital, whereupon their Nationalist opponents fled to the island of Formosa. The State Department and the Administration at large had come under criticism for their seeming inaction. Acheson, called upon to answer for the United States' China policy, firmly insisted that no reasonable measures could have prevented a Communist victory; he held to this position both in the State Department's official publications and in his testimony before the Senate.

Anxiety also had arisen about Communist influence in the United States. An alleged Communist, Alger Hiss, was a former State Department officer who at one time had worked under Acheson. When he was convicted of perjury, Acheson expressed his personal compassion for the man. The secretary of state's critics charged that he was doing little to oppose Communist inroads. Senator Joseph R. McCarthy later insinuated that Acheson was somehow subservient to international Communism.

In Korea, Communist forces launched a direct attack from across the demarcation line dividing the peninsula, in June, 1950; President Truman, upon consultation with Acheson and other members of his cabinet, authorized the use of American troops to drive back the invaders. During the crisis, Acheson coordinated efforts to obtain support from America's allies and the United Nations. By November, North Korean troops had been compelled to retreat, but Chinese Communist armies then entered the war and threatened the wholesale rout of United Nations forces. While insisting upon the stalwart defense of positions in Korea, Acheson resisted demands for direct action against China itself. Nevertheless, General Douglas MacArthur, the American and United Nations commander in Korea, called for expanded action and, in defiance of a standing directive from Washington, issued his own version of possible peace terms in a virtual ultimatum to the other side. President Truman consulted with other military leaders and members of his cabinet; they concluded that MacArthur had exceeded his authority and, in April, 1951, he was removed from his command. Acheson supported this measure; in June, 1951, he testified before the Senate for eight days in justification of Truman's decision. Throughout the Korean War, Acheson maintained that the peninsula had to be defended, but in a limited war that would avoid the risk of major confrontations elsewhere. Thus he supported the defense of Formosa but rejected proposals for involving Nationalist China in action against the Communists.

Diplomatic activity affecting other parts of the world was guided by Acheson's concerns for European security and the defense of Asia. He authorized American aid to support French forces fighting Communist guerrillas in Indochina; Middle Eastern concerns, such as a major government crisis in Iran in March, 1951, and the Egyptian revolution of July, 1952, he handled guardedly. In September, 1951, the United States concluded negotiations for a peace treaty with Japan, which Acheson endorsed as a means of strengthening the United States' security arrangements in the Far East.

When Republican Dwight D. Eisenhower became president in January, 1953, Acheson left the State Department. During the last eighteen years of his life he took on the role of elder statesman. He published seven books; two collections of essays and an anthology of his letters appeared posthumously. He did perform some legal work, and once again he was involved in international litigation at The Hague. Widely respected for his deftly conjoined views of politics and diplomacy, he was in some demand as a public speaker. Although he did not seek any permanent appointments, he was called back to Washington as an adviser during the Cuban Missile Crisis of 1962; Presidents Lyndon B. Johnson and Richard M. Nixon also consulted with him on means by which a resolution might be found for the Vietnam War. Late in life he was increasingly affected by physical ailments, which he bore with some fortitude; finally, on October 12, 1971, Dean Acheson died of a heart attack and was found slumped over his desk at his home in Sandy Spring, Maryland.

Summary
Having witnessed political upheaval on the international stage during the first half of the twentieth century, Dean Acheson became secretary of state during a critical period, when the United States' role in world politics awaited clear definition. After World War II, various responses were considered to meet challenges from the Soviet Union and its allies. Profoundly distrustful of the counsels of isolationism, which still appeared in certain guises, Acheson also was skeptical that international organizations such as the United Nations in and of themselves would ensure peace and security. His approach was to underscore the United States' commitment to international order, first and foremost by organizing the Atlantic alliance and involving the United States directly in the defense of Europe. Communist advances in Asia he took to be manifestations of Soviet ambitions in the Far East; nevertheless, he recognized the limitations of the United States' ability to act. It could not reverse the course of events in China, where massive political turmoil had engulfed the world's most populous nation; even while at war in Korea, the United States could not court wider and more dangerous confrontations. The course Acheson charted established commitments for the defense of Korea and Japan but left the United States with somewhat broader concerns about Communist penetration in other regions of the world as well.

Acheson's views of foreign policy were distinctively shaped by the temper of his times; he had seen the rise of dictators preceding World War II, and his dealings with the Soviet Union came during the most intransigent period of Stalinist diplomacy, when most other Communist parties monotonously echoed the Soviet line. Thus the measures Acheson took reflected certain assumptions about the postwar world; during his later years, he steadfastly maintained that the Soviet Union benefited from the efforts of Chinese and Vietnamese Communism. For a time he defended American involvement in Vietnam; only after several years of war did he conclude that victory there was not possible. Much in the world changed after he left the State Department, and many new concerns arose, but the basic structure of American foreign policy continued to rest on security alliances Acheson negotiated for the common defense of Western Europe and of major Asian nations in the Pacific region.

Bibliography

Acheson, Dean. *Among Friends*. Edited by David S. McLellan and David C. Acheson. New York: Dodd, Mead and Co., 1980. A group of letters selected from among those written between 1918 and the last month of his life, this collection often shows Acheson in various offhand moods, commenting on issues of the day to his family, friends, and public officials. Useful as a guide to his way of thinking over the years.

_____. *Morning and Noon*. Boston: Houghton Mifflin Co., 1965. Whimsical sketches of Acheson's first forty-eight years, which recapture childhood joys, assess his education, and point to the influence of great jurists, such as Felix Frankfurter and Louis D. Brandeis, in the development of his legal career. The formation of his political outlook and his brief but stormy period of service in the Treasury Department are also discussed.

_____. *Present at the Creation: My Years in the State Department*. New York: W. W. Norton and Co., 1969. Sweeping panoramic memoirs that trace the entire ambit of Acheson's formal diplomatic career, written with some regrets but no apologies. Acheson was forthright in his judgments of men and events, and his dry, mordant wit is often in evidence; particularly vivid and illuminating are his reflections on the Atlantic alliance, the Korean War, and Senator Joseph McCarthy's anti-Communist campaign. For this work, Acheson was awarded the Pulitzer Prize.

_____. *This Vast External Realm*. New York: W. W. Norton and Co., 1973. Acheson's unsentimental views of international power politics, and his unshaken conviction that Soviet influence must be kept in check, are set forth in this collection of articles and speeches. Also noteworthy are his piquant suggestions for instilling a greater sense of realism in American diplomacy.

Brinkley, Douglas. *Dean Acheson: The Cold War Years, 1953-71*. New Haven, Conn.: Yale University Press, 1992.

McGlothlen, Ronald L. *Controlling the Waves: Dean Acheson and U.S. Foreign Policy in Asia*. New York: Norton, 1993.

McLellan, David S. *Dean Acheson: The State Department Years*. New York: Dodd, Mead and Co., 1976. A careful scholarly examination of Acheson's diplomatic practice, this work delineates his approach to foreign policy from among the divergent standpoints that existed at the time in the State Department and in other branches of government. Due balance is assigned to the demands of Cold War crises abroad and domestic political pressures that affected Acheson's positions on issues that shaped the postwar world.

Smith, Gaddis. *Dean Acheson*. New York: Cooper Square Publishers, 1972. This thoroughgoing and thoughtful exposition of Acheson's work as secretary of state, volume 16 of the series "The American Secretaries of State and Their Diplomacy," sets forth the particular means by which his handling of European and Asian crises defined America's foreign policy objectives. Sympathetic though not uncritical, the author is incisive in conveying the historical context against which American diplomacy under Acheson was carried out.

Stupak, Ronald J. *The Shaping of Foreign Policy: The Role of the Secretary of State as Seen by Dean Acheson*. New York: Odyssey Press, 1969. A brief study of problems of organization and bureaucracy in the State Department, this work is studded with the terminology of political science and reaches no larger conclusions about the direction of American foreign policy under Acheson's stewardship.

J. R. Broadus

JOHN ADAMS

Born: October 30, 1735; Braintree, Massachusetts
Died: July 4, 1826; Quincy, Massachusetts

As a member of the Continental Congress, Adams helped bring the American Colonies to the point of independence in 1776. As one of the new nation's first diplomats, he helped negotiate the treaty that ended the American War of Independence. He was the second president of the United States.

Early Life

John Adams was born on October 30, 1735, in Braintree, Massachusetts, where his family had lived for nearly a century. His father was a farmer and a town constable who expected his eldest son, John, to become a Congregational minister. The young Adams attended the Free Latin School in Braintree and then enrolled at Harvard College in 1751. On graduation in 1755, he taught school for a while at Worcester before deciding to abandon the ministry to take up law instead. In 1758, the intelligent, studious Adams returned to Braintree to practice law in what was still a country town only ten miles from Boston.

Six years later, he married Abigail Smith of Quincy, Massachusetts, a woman who matched him in intelligence and ambition and perhaps exceeded him in practicality. Short and already stocky (colleagues later called him rotund), Adams seemed to be settling into the life of a successful country courthouse lawyer who might, in time, aspire to a seat in the legislature when, in 1765, Parliament altered American Colonial politics forever by passing the Stamp Act. The ensuing Stamp Act crisis offered to the ambitious Adams a quick route to popularity, influence, and public office. He did not miss his chance.

Life's Work

In 1765, Adams denounced the Stamp Tax in resolutions written for the Braintree Town Meeting. When they were reprinted around the colony, his reputation as an opponent of British arrogance began to grow. Those in Boston who led the opposition to English taxes (including John's distant relative, Samuel Adams) began to bring him more actively into their campaigns. He moved to Boston and won a seat in the

Massachusetts General Court. He became, in effect, the local antigovernment party's lawyer, writing some of its more important public papers for the Boston Town Meeting and defending its members in court against charges brought by the Crown.

When Parliament answered the Boston Tea Party with the Intolerable Acts in 1774, the General Court chose Adams as a delegate to the intercolonial congress scheduled to meet in Philadelphia that fall, to discuss what the Colonies should do. He wrote a "Declaration of Rights," which the First Continental Congress adopted, that based Colonial rights to self-government not only on their charters and on the inherent rights of Englishmen but also on "the immutable laws of nature." Those were the grounds on which many colonists would soon challenge not merely England's right to tax them, but England's right to govern them at all. In good part, those were the grounds that underlay the Declaration of Independence.

Before the Congress met again, war began at Lexington in April,

John Adams *(Library of Congress)*

1775. When Adams arrived at the Second Continental Congress in the spring of 1775, he already believed that the only true constitutional connection between the Colonies and England was through the king—a position he set out in newspaper essays signed "Novanglus." He had not yet, however, openly called for a severing of all ties to the mother country. He had seen the colonists' rage run out of bounds in the Stamp Act riots of 1765. He had been disturbed and angered by the joy with which some colonists greeted the closing of civil and criminal courts in Massachusetts when British authority collapsed in the colony. He was worried that a revolution might get out of hand and establish not liberty, but mob rule. Although such worries stayed very much in his mind, by the time the Second Continental Congress met, Adams realized that there were no practical alternatives left but armed resistance or submission to Parliament. At the Congress, therefore, he worked both openly and by guile to bring reluctant and sometimes timid delegates to accept the inevitability of independence. When the Congress finally agreed to act, after more than a year of war, it was Adams who wrestled Thomas Jefferson's declaration through to adoption on July 4, 1776.

Adams had applauded Thomas Paine's *Common Sense* when it appeared in January, 1776, but he disliked the very democratic plan of government advocated by Paine. The kind of government Adams favored can be seen most clearly in the plan he drew up for Massachusetts' revolutionary constitution. Adams thought the purpose of the Revolution was to preserve old liberties, not to establish new ones, and that the new Constitution ought to conserve as much of England's admirable constitutional heritage as possible. The constitution he drafted included relatively high property qualifications for voting and holding office (to ensure stability); it left the structure of Massachusetts' government much as it had been before independence, except for replacing English officials with elected American ones.

For more than a year after independence, Adams served on a variety of committees in Congress and in Massachusetts, doing work that was as exhausting as it was important. In October, 1777, he withdrew from Congress and returned to Massachusetts, but in November, Congress named him one of its emissaries to France, charged with raising loans for the Republic across Europe and with negotiating treaties of friendship, trade, and alliance, especially with the French nation.

That alliance was concluded before Adams arrived at Paris, but he stayed on and was immediately caught up in the roiling jealousies that were endemic at the American mission there. Adams especially disliked and distrusted Benjamin Franklin, whose demeanor, integrity, honesty, and morals he judged inferior to his own. Adams returned to Massachusetts in August, 1779, but by December, he was back in France to help negotiate a peace treaty with England. He feuded with Franklin almost constantly over which of them was responsible for what in conducting the Republic's diplomacy, but ultimately, all three peace commissioners (Adams, Franklin, and John Jay) agreed to negotiate a separate treaty between the United States and England, a treaty that did not directly involve France.

Though Franklin was responsible for the broad outlines of the agreement, Adams worked out some crucial compromises, without which the treaty may well have failed. Adams persuaded the English, for example, to concede to American fishing rights off the Newfoundland and Nova Scotia coasts in return for the new nation agreeing to open its courts to Loyalists. Adams stayed on for a year in France after the war ended in 1783, and then moved to London as the United States' first minister to the Court of St. James in 1785. He spent three years there, trying with little success to iron out problems between the United States and England (mostly involving noncompliance with the peace treaty).

While in London, he wrote the three-volume *A Defense of the Constitutions of Government of the United States of America* (1787), in which he explained his conservative and primarily English approach to the proper constitution of civil governments. The work was frank in its praise of the basic principles of the British constitution and earnest in its cautions about the risks of letting government rely too heavily on popular majorities to determine policy and law. Indeed, some Americans began to consider Adams soft on aristocracy and even monarchy. The first volume of *A Defense of the Constitutions of Government of the United States of America* appeared in time to influence the thinking of delegates at the Constitutional Convention.

Adams returned home in 1788, and he was chosen as George Washington's vice president under the new Constitution of 1787. He did not like the job. "My country," he wrote to his wife, "has in its wisdom contrived for me the most insignificant office that ever the invention of man contrived or his imagination conceived." For the next eight years, nevertheless, he served Washington loyally, presiding over the Senate and breaking tie votes in favor of Federalist policies. His reward came in 1797, when, as Washington's chosen successor, Adams defeated Jefferson and became the second president of the United States.

Adams' presidency was at best only a partial success. He had hoped, as Washington had in 1789, to become president of a united people. By the time he took office, however, the people had already divided themselves into two rival political parties: the Federalists (ostensibly led by Adams) and the National (or Jeffersonian) Republicans, led by Adams' vice president and old friend, Thomas Jefferson. Further, world affairs all but guaranteed that his presidency would be troubled. As Adams took office, for example, the United States was already dangerously close to war with France. The French, who had already fought their own revolution and created a republic of sorts, were at war with England and were angry that the United States had refused to aid France. By 1797, the French were beginning to seize American ships on the high seas. When American peace commissioners, whom Adams had sent to France to try to work things out short of war, reported that the French had demanded bribes to begin serious negotiations, Americans reacted angrily. Adams asked Congress to prepare for a war that seemed inevitable, but, at the same time, he refused to abandon his efforts to avoid it if possible. For the remainder of his presidency, Adams stuck to the same policy—prepare for war, but work for peace—until (just as he left office) it yielded a new treaty of amity between the United States and France.

In the meanwhile, the Federalist Party, influenced by Alexander Hamilton more than by Adams, forced through Congress very high (and very unpopular) taxes to pay for the war which they confidently expected to begin at any moment. Moreover, Federalist congressmen passed, and Adams signed, the unpopular Alien and Sedition acts in 1798. The first act raised the number of years an immigrant had to live in the country before becoming a citizen to fourteen and was evidently designed to prevent recent Irish immigrants from voting against Federalists, whom they rightly believed to be pro-English. The second, the Sedition Act, made the publication of virtually all criticism of federal officials a crime. Both laws lost whatever legitimacy they may have had in the eyes of the public when the supposedly imminent war, which might have justified them as national defense measures, failed to come. Federalist judges and prosecutors enforced the laws anyway, jailing, for example, several prominent Republican newspaper editors for violating the Sedition Act by criticizing Adams (though no Federalist editor ever went to jail for vilifying Jefferson). The partisan application of the law left Adams and the Federalists saddled with a reputation as opponents of free speech as the election of 1800 approached. Adams was further crippled by growing divisions in his own party (Hamilton actually campaigned against him) and by the slow pace at which his diplomacy worked. Most voters did not know, for example, until after they had voted, that Adams' policy had succeeded and that a lasting peace with France had been arranged.

In the election of 1800, Adams lost to Jefferson by eight electoral votes. Exhausted, bitterly disappointed, and tired as well of the constant bickering and criticism, public and private, of the last four years, Adams retired from public life on the day Jefferson was inaugurated. He returned to his home in Quincy to spend his time farming, reading, and writing an occasional essay on law or history. He died on July 4, 1826, a few hours after his great antagonist and greater friend, Jefferson, died in Virginia.

Summary
Throughout his life, Adams never got the praise he thought was his due. He was an important writer in the years preceding independence, but none of his writings had the broad impact of John Dickinson's *Letters from a Farmer in Pennsylvania, to the Inhabitants of the British Colonies* (1767-1768) or the great popular appeal of Thomas Paine's *Common Sense* (although in the long run, through his writings on government and constitutions, Adams contributed as much or more to the development of republican constitutional thought than all but two or three of the founders). His work in Europe negotiating the peace treaty of 1783 was at times brilliant, but it was the colorful and cunningly rustic Benjamin Franklin who caught the public's eye. Adams was president of the United States, but he immediately followed Washington in that office and inevitably Americans compared the two and found Adams the lesser president. Adams claimed that he did not seek the people's praises, but all of his life he watched men who were no more intelligent than he, no more dedicated to the Republic, and no

more successful in serving it, win the kind of warm public applause that seemed beyond his grasp. He was respected but not revered, and he knew it.

Broadly speaking, Adams made three major contributions to the Revolution and the new Republic. First, he worked in Massachusetts and in Congress to keep the Revolution from running amok and destroying what was good in the British political tradition. He demonstrated to skeptical Tories and doubtful rebels, by both his words and his work, that independence need not be an invitation to anarchy, despotism, or mob rule, and so he helped make independence an acceptable alternative to submission. Second, he (with Jay and Franklin) protected American interests in the double-dealing diplomatic atmosphere of Paris and London during the war, and won for the Republic a treaty that secured its independence as well as the vast undeveloped territories and other economic resources it needed to survive and develop. Third, as president, he kept the new Republic out of what would have been a bitter, divisive war fought under a new, untested Constitution; thanks to Adams' skillful foreign policy, the Republic did not have to face its first war under the Constitution for another twelve years. Yet Adams never completely accepted the more democratic implications of the Revolution, and so, by the end of his career, he was both one of the most important of the Republic's founders and one of the least appreciated.

Bibliography

Bowen, Catherine Drinker. *John Adams and the American Revolution.* Boston: Little, Brown and Co., 1950. As much novel as history: Much of the book's dialogue was created by Bowen. Nevertheless, the book is generally historically accurate and is beautifully written. Conveys a more rounded picture of Adams than most strictly historical biographies do.

Butterfield, H. L., et al., eds. *The Book of Abigail and John: Selected Letters of the Adams Family, 1762-1784.* Cambridge, Mass.: Harvard University Press, 1975. An excellent way to discover John and Abigail through their own words. Their letters to each other illustrate their remarkable relationship and the private and public worlds in which they lived.

Cappon, Lester J., ed. *The Adams-Jefferson Letters: The Complete Corre-*

spondence Between Thomas Jefferson and Abigail and John Adams. 2 vols. Chapel Hill: University of North Carolina Press, 1959. Covers the years 1777 to 1826. Excellent in conveying the revolutionary and early national periods through Adams' eyes. The letters following 1812 are remarkable. In them, the two aging rebels reminisce about the Revolution and their presidencies and speculate about the nation's future.

Ellis, Joseph J. *Passionate Sage: The Character and Legacy of John Adams.* New York: Norton, 1993.

Ferling, John E. *John Adams: A Life.* Knoxville: University of Tennessee Press, 1992.

Jensen, Merrill. *The Founding of a Nation: A History of the American Revolution, 1763-1776.* New York: Oxford University Press, 1968. One of the best accounts of the origins and events of the Revolution from the Grenville Program of 1763 to the Declaration of Independence. Narrative in form, scholarly, and nicely written.

Kurtz, Stephen G. *The Presidency of John Adams: The Collapse of Federalism, 1795-1800.* Philadelphia: University of Pennsylvania Press, 1957. Good basic account of Adams' term in office and its impact on the Federalist Party. More recent studies are less well written and add little except detail to Kurtz's account.

Morris, Richard B. *The Peacemakers: The Great Powers and American Independence.* New York: Harper and Row, Publishers, 1965. The best available account of the negotiations leading to peace in 1783. Highly detailed, but Morris writes well. Not all of his judgments about the motives of the men and governments involved are convincing, but most are.

Shaw, Peter. *The Character of John Adams.* Chapel Hill: University of North Carolina Press, 1976. Examines Adams' ideas in the light of his background (especially his Puritan background) and his personal experiences at each stage of his life and career. Controversial but interesting and insightful.

Smith, Page. *John Adams.* 2 vols. Garden City, N.Y.: Doubleday and Co., 1962. The most complete and detailed life of Adams available, although at times, oppressively detailed. Especially helpful as a source for a good, thorough chapter or two on particular incidents or periods of Adams' life.

Robert A. Becker

JOHN QUINCY ADAMS

Born: July 11, 1767; Braintree, Massachusetts
Died: February 23, 1848; Washington, D.C.

As diplomat, secretary of state, president, and member of the House of Representatives, in a career spanning the early national period to nearly the time of the Civil War, John Quincy Adams helped to shape America's major foreign and domestic policies, always in the direction of strengthening the nation as a unified whole.

Early Life

John Quincy Adams was born in Braintree (later Quincy), Massachusetts, on July 11, 1767, the second child and first son of John and Abigail (Smith) Adams. At such a time and in such a family, he was a child of both the Revolution and the Enlightenment, nurtured as well with a strong Puritan sense of duty and destiny, directed throughout his life toward politics (and its attendant sacrifices), always striving to fulfill the expectations and retain the approbation of his parents, especially the redoubtable Abigail. His unorthodox and irregular education was to produce both a scholar and a nationalist, unswerving in his principles and forever unsatisfied with his performance, always striving to increase his learning and improve his habits, and never able to mingle easily with others or develop satisfying personal relationships.

As a boy, John Quincy imbibed patriotism in the midst of the Revolution and then spent a number of years in Europe while his father was engaged in the nation's diplomatic business; in France, Holland, and Russia he learned languages, associated with important men of the time, studied sporadically, and began what was to be a lifelong diary. Returning to America in 1785 (while his father remained as minister to England), he became again a schoolboy and was graduated from Harvard in 1787. In his commencement address, he referred to this time as a "critical period." He then studied law in Newburyport with Theophilus Parsons until his admission to the bar in 1790. Uninterested in the legal profession yet reluctant to be drawn into the hardships of public service, John Quincy entered the newspaper battles with essays on the French Revolution (against Thomas Paine's

John Quincy Adams *(Library of Congress)*

Rights of Man, 1791) and the Genêt affair. His arguments in favor of American neutrality won for him the attention of President George Washington and the post of minister resident at The Hague, in 1794. He took up his position at this excellent listening post during the Napoleonic expansion over Europe, reporting in detail to Washington and to the secretary of state on its course, his ideas influencing Washington's foreign policy statements in the Farewell Address.

John Quincy Adams' appointment as minister to Portugal was changed before he took it up, and he and his wife, Louisa, whom he had married in 1797, traveled to Berlin, where the new minister plenipotentiary to Prussia negotiated a treaty, saw his wife successfully enter court society, and began a volume of descriptive letters about a visit to Silesia. Recalled by his father, John Adams, who had lost reelection to the presidency, Adams brought his wife and son (George Washington Adams, born April 12, 1801) to an America they had never seen in order to renew an interrupted law practice. Drawn inevitably to public service, Adams was elected to the Massachusetts Senate in April, 1802, and to the United States Senate in February, 1803. He immediately demonstrated the qualities that were to characterize and frustrate his political career: commitment to the nation rather than to any party, consistency of principle and attention to detail, and the inability to deal effectively with varied personalities and the social demands of the Washington political scene.

The young senator was five feet, seven inches tall, balding, with rather sharp and expressive features; he had always been careless in his dress, and despite his lifelong habit of exercise frequently suffered from dizziness, insomnia, stomach trouble, and attacks of anxiety and depression. Always introspective and self-critical, he was reserved and humorless; formally a Unitarian, he was well versed in the Bible, classical literature, science, and the humanities.

Although Adams opposed the Republican administration's acquisition of Louisiana for constitutional reasons, he soon demonstrated his differences from the Federalists on the important issues of the Aaron Burr intrigue, Judge John Pickering's impeachment, and the *Chesapeake* incident and embargo policy. His nationalism and independence in supporting Republican policies provoked Federalist hostility in both political and personal relations; he resigned his Senate seat before his Federalist replacement took over, and he experienced problems even in his lectures as Boylston Professor of Oratory and Rhetoric at Harvard. Without consulting Louisa, he accepted President James Madison's appointment as minister plenipotentiary to Russia; the two older boys remained with their grandparents in Quincy, and Adams, Louisa, and Charles Francis (born August 18, 1807) arrived in St. Petersburg late in 1809.

Despite inadequate funds, both Adamses established themselves with the diplomatic community and at the extravagant court of Czar Alexander I. John Quincy was able to achieve some diplomatic successes with the Russian government, attend to his youngest son, and maintain a correspondence with his older sons filled with stern expectations for their education and achievements—expectations which neither was ever able to fulfill.

As Alexander and Napoleon Bonaparte fell out over the Continental System and the War of 1812 opened, Adams was an obvious choice for the commission to negotiate peace with Great Britain. When its five members met finally in Ghent in 1814, they achieved a satisfactory treaty based on the prewar status quo. Adams then journeyed to Paris to meet Louisa, who had, by herself, wound up their affairs in Russia and traversed Europe with young Charles in the aftermath of war and during the Hundred Days. The Adamses then spent the next two years happily in London, as John Quincy had been appointed by President James Monroe as minister plenipotentiary to Great Britain. It became apparent that Great Britain was willing to negotiate and arbitrate the points still at issue after the Treaty of Ghent.

Adams' appointment as Monroe's secretary of state brought the family back to the United States late in 1817 and renewed the pattern of separation (the parents in Washington, the boys educated elsewhere) and family problems. Adams, at fifty, reentered domestic politics by becoming embroiled with the new generation of politicians. He was still and always a nationalist and an independent in a time of growing partisanship and sectional controversy and reserved and scholarly during the development of popular sovereignty and anti-intellectualism. For the rest of his long life, despite personal tragedy and bitter political disappointments, he was to shape much of America's domestic and foreign policy.

Life's Work

Adams became secretary of state as the Era of Good Feelings began to dissolve in personal and partisan contention for the presidency, and at a time when the State Department conducted both foreign and domestic affairs with one chief clerk and seven assistant clerks. Adams organized the department and its papers, did much of the office work himself during long days and nights (even cutting down on his reading), and attended to the census, congressional printing, extraditions, and commissions. He had, early in his career as a Federalist, demonstrated his political independence; he had received his appointments from Republican administrations; as secretary of state and son of John Adams, he was inevitably a presidential candidate. His foreign policy positions therefore developed as much in response to domestic political concerns as to the international situation. Yet his early principles dominated: He was a nationalist and an expansionist, cautious but determined to develop a hemispheric role for the United States.

Attempting to defend and expand American trade interests, Adams concentrated on the problem of discriminatory British customs duties in the West Indies trade. British interests and disturbed world conditions, however, meant the retention of those duties. Boundary problems with Great Britain and Russia in the Northwest presented less difficulty than those with Spain in Florida. The Treaty of 1818 settled United States-Canadian boundary and fisheries problems and provided for joint United States-British occupation of Oregon for ten years (the northern boundary fixed with Russia at 54°40′ in the Convention of 1824). When General Andrew Jackson's sensational raid into Florida threatened an international incident, Adams alone in the Cabinet supported the general and used the uncontrolled Florida situation as an effective point in the negotiations that led to the 1819 Adams-Onís (Transcontinental) Treaty. Acquisition of Florida and the demarcation of a clear southwestern boundary to the Pacific represented major gains for the United States, even though Adams' opponents then and later attacked him on certain details (in which he had been uncharacteristically careless) and charged him with deliberately giving up Texas. Although he was not directly involved in the Missouri Compromise, Adams was against slavery and fearful that the sectional controversy had the potential to dissolve the Union. Even more immediately threatening was the possibility of European powers acting in the Western Hemisphere to regain newly independent colonies. Adams urged a unilateral American statement and greatly influenced the formulation of the basic policies of nonintervention and noncolonization, and American noninvolvement in Europe, points which President Monroe incorporated into his December, 1823, message, later known as the Monroe Doctrine.

A presidential nominating system still in flux made social events crucial for politics: Protocol for formal calls was subject matter for

Senate resolutions and cabinet papers; Louisa Adams' entertaining was vital for the cold, unsocial, and ambitious John Quincy, who furthermore refused to pursue the nomination actively, preferring it unsought as recognition of his ability and service. Throughout his political career he was to spurn the idea of active campaigning directed at the mass of voters, seeing public service as properly in the hands of the dedicated and qualified rather than the "popular" politicians.

In the election of 1824, Adams received eighty-four electoral votes to Jackson's ninety-nine, but as there was no majority, the House was to decide between Jackson, Adams, and Henry Clay, the third runner-up. While Adams actively swayed some Federalists, it was Clay's influence that turned the tide; "Harry of the West" feared the rash general more than a fellow nationalist, and the two rivals realized their basic agreement on major issues. With Clay's influence added, the House chose Adams to be president; Adams' appointment of Clay as secretary of state (and therefore a potential next president) led the Jacksonians to open their presidential campaign almost immediately, based on the charge of "bargain and corruption." The accusation of an Adams-Clay collusion continued to affect American politics for many years.

President like his father, and like his father a single-term executive facing the more popular candidate, Adams was a minority president in a period of great partisan pressures, a nationalist in an era of deepening sectionalism, and an executive with a program at a time of legislative dominance. He never really controlled the National Republicans, nor could he prevent the development of the Democratic Republican Party. Determined to avoid party considerations in appointments, he kept many in his cabinet and other offices (such as Postmaster General John McLean) who worked actively against him. He proposed large-scale national government action for general improvement in both learning and scientific activity (a national university, national observatories) and in the specifics of the "American System," usually identified as Clay's program, but which Adams claimed as his own. Not surprisingly, Adams considered foreign affairs very important; he had a Jeffersonian view of developing American world trade, with an emphasis on reciprocity and neutral rights. The Administration's diplomatic failures, particularly Great Britain's closure of West Indies trade, were often a result of domestic politics and sectional interests. The same was true of Adams' concept of the United States' democratic mission vis-à-vis Latin America: Any possibility of United States leadership in the Western Hemisphere was broken on the reefs of partisan opposition. The Panama Congress and the sensitive status of Cuba overshadowed negotiations and consultations which often laid the foundations for later administrations' successes.

Adams delegated much domestic policy to his cabinet and was therefore not deeply involved in the sectional maneuvering which produced the Tariff of Abominations. He strongly supported internal improvements, regarded the public lands as a long-term national resource, and backed off from a confrontation with Georgia over states' rights stemming from the Indian removal policy. Despite his concept of interdependent sectional interests producing national unity, Adams was usually identified with the economic interests of the Northeast.

A large antiadministration majority in Congress after the 1826 midterm elections left Adams a lame-duck president, depressed, ill, and socially isolated in the White House, mourning his father (who had died on July 4, 1826) and attempting to come to terms with his wife's depression and illness and the total disappointment of his hopes for his two elder sons, George, a debt-ridden depressive, and John, something of a rake. A developing interest in botany was a diverting hobby, although the live-oak plantation he established in Florida (to benefit naval construction) was abandoned by the next administration. All of Adams' personal difficulties, combined with his political ineptitude, helped ensure his isolation in the campaign of 1828, one of the most bitter and vicious ever waged.

Adams was politically inept for a variety of reasons. The Adams family considered its members to be different from the general public, more principled and determined and therefore doomed to popular misunderstanding and lack of support. Adams preferred not to respond to public criticism or to explain and justify his actions; he refused to "electioneer," and his public speeches were scholarly, elaborate, and open to ridicule. His handling of the patronage (a difficult field complicated by factions within the parties) alienated his supporters and gave aid and comfort to his political enemies. He had not been able to rally support for a nonpartisan federal government program of wide-ranging improvements for the national benefit; he could not develop an effective party organization or even meld Federalists and nationalistic Republicans into a politically supportive bloc. His administration ignored the developing labor movement and the broadening popular base of voters and played into Jacksonian egalitarian propaganda. The well-organized Jacksonians easily set the cold Yankee aristocrat against the man of the people, concentrating on Jackson's personal popularity rather than his positions on issues (such as the tariff and internal improvements), which would alienate his disparate supporters.

John Quincy Adams, like his father before him, felt his defeat deeply, taking it as his country's repudiation, refusing (also like his father) to attend his successor's inauguration and moving into regular routines, exercise, and writing in order to make the transition to private life. On April 30, 1829, George Washington Adams jumped or fell from a steamboat and drowned in Long Island Sound, leaving a mass of debts and an illegitimate child. Adams at sixty-two was a failed president with his eldest son dead; nevertheless, mutual guilt brought him and Louisa closer (they had left George with others to rear; they had pushed him too hard) and helped them to concentrate on their two grandchildren and their youngest and favorite son. The latter soon married a wealthy and passive wife and began to produce a large family (Louisa Catherine II, John Quincy II, Charles Francis, Jr., Henry, Arthur, Mary, and Brooks). Political ambition (which Adams regarded as his chief character flaw) led him to agree (as usual, without consulting his wife) to represent his district in the House of Representatives. In 1831, he was elected by a large popular majority, a victory he regarded as the most satisfying of his entire political career. He missed politics and needed the salary, and for seventeen years and eight elections he carved out another and even more effective position in the service of the nation.

Still short, stout, and bald except for a fringe, Adams, as he had done all of his life, rose early, read his Bible and classical works regularly, swam, and walked; he developed into a connoisseur of wine and mellowed socially. He accepted Anti-Masonic support for a presidential nomination in 1832 (which did not eventuate) and lost the election for governor of Massachusetts in 1833 and Massachusetts (Whig) senator in 1835; none of this lessened his commitment to his House career. The House chamber had bad acoustics, as a result of which Adams at his desk could hear whispers from everywhere; his own high-pitched voice was to become a feared instrument in the coming House debates. After he spoke against Daniel Webster in connection with the "French Question" (of treaty payments) in 1836, he began to be called "Old Man Eloquent."

In the Nullification controversy, Adams recognized again the divisive potential of sectionalism, but in the next few years he focused more on the slavery issue as the greatest threat to the Union. He was neither an egalitarian nor an abolitionist per se; while Louisa began to acquaint herself with the problem, associating with the Grimkés and other abolitionists and coming to see the parallels between black slavery and the oppression of women, Adams viewed slavery in terms of principle: as morally reprehensible and politically dangerous to the continued existence of the nation. It was fitting, therefore, that he reacted first to the House's vote, in May of 1836, to table without reading all petitions dealing with slavery. The long battle against the "gag rule" invigorated Adams; the issue of the rights of petition and free speech gave him a broad ground on which to stand and aided him in debate when he dealt with slavery as a threat to the Union, a possible provocation of war with Mexico, a politically divisive question, and the source of the denial of basic rights of citizens. In this period also he began to examine the question of slavery in a broader context. Reading his mother's papers (Abigail Adams had died on October 28, 1818) and reacting to his wife's growing involvement with feminism, Adams came to support the concept of women's political rights, although without endorsing specific issues or deflecting his emphasis on the slavery question.

Always a political independent, Adams supported many of the Jackson Administration's policies, disagreeing, however, on bank policy. As an independent and a skilled parliamentarian, he was able in 1839 to effect the necessary organization of the House committees despite paralyzing partisan divisions. Southern members frequently opposed his actions and called for resolutions of censure. Although his early ponderous and erudite *Report on Weights and Measures* (1821) had never had any direct influence, Adams was able, from 1838 to 1846, to direct the use of the fund that established the Smithsonian Institution.

Despite bitter opposition, Adams maintained his battle in the House on all issues connected with slavery, although he believed that he could only begin what must be a long struggle. He opposed the 1838 attempt to annex Texas for constitutional reasons and because he believed that it would lead to a free-land policy to gain Western political support, thus dissipating a national resource. In 1841, he argued for the defense in the *Amistad* case before the Supreme Court, never submitting a bill for his legal services. In 1842, demonstrating great intellectual resources and physical stamina, he conducted a six-day, successful defense against a House resolution to censure him. He now received and enjoyed public adulation, and in December of 1844, on his resolution, the House rescinded the gag rule.

Feebler and somewhat absentminded, Adams continued to oppose the Mexican War, being reelected as a Conscience Whig in November of 1846. Nearing eighty, he had had to discontinue his daily early morning swims in the Potomac, and on November 20, 1846, he suffered a stroke but was able to resume his seat in early February, 1847. He spoke only once, in opposition to indemnifying the *Amistad* owners, and on February 21, 1848, had another stroke in the House. Carried to the Speaker's room in the Capitol, he died two days later without having regained consciousness. The national mourning ceremonies were like none since Washington's death. John Quincy Adams was buried in the family plot in Quincy. Louisa remained in Washington, keeping in touch with politics, buying and freeing a woman slave, and for much of the time suffering from ill health; she died on May 15, 1852.

Summary

President of a disintegrating party, politically impotent halfway into his only term, his personal life marred by an unsatisfying relationship with his wife and bitter disappointments with his two elder sons, Adams left—almost fled—the nation's highest political office, the lifelong goal of his great ambition and dynastic sense of duty and destiny. He seemed to be facing a lifetime in the ebb tide of politics and the treacherous shoals of financial insecurity and family disappointment. Even as his personal tragedy deepened with the death of his eldest son, he entered into a new phase, a time nearly as long as his life until then. He experienced a growing satisfaction, a greater harmony in relationships and decision-making within his own family: his remaining son, his growing brood of grandchildren, and his wife, finding her way to her own identity and a political role which could afford her a long-delayed satisfaction in contributing to and participating in the real life of the nation, rather than the confined, ornamental, subservient place expected by contemporary society.

During the course of his "two careers," John Quincy Adams contributed mightily to the basic elements of American foreign policy, influenced domestic issues, and stood as a beacon in the sectional controversy which, as he foresaw, was to lead the Union into civil war.

Bibliography

Bemis, Samuel Flagg. *John Quincy Adams and the Foundations of American Foreign Policy.* New York: Alfred A. Knopf, 1949. A detailed, scholarly, analytical work by a major authority on diplomatic history. Focuses on Adams' "first career" as diplomat and continentalist.

_____. *John Quincy Adams and the Union.* New York: Alfred A. Knopf, 1956. A companion volume, completing the biography, dealing with Adams' "second career." As effective as the preceding work; lacks details of Adams' personal life.

Clark, Bennett Champ. *John Quincy Adams: "Old Man Eloquent."* Boston: Little, Brown and Co., 1932. A rather popularized biography, not a panegyric but somewhat filiopietistic. Accurate and adequate; reads well.

East, Robert A. *John Quincy Adams: The Critical Years, 1785-1794.* New York: Bookman Associates, 1962. Deals with the early period of Adams' life, vital for shaping his basic concepts. Fulsome in spots; may read too much importance into the early years.

Falkner, Leonard. The President Who Wouldn't Retire. New York: Coward-McCann, 1967. Based on Bemis and various primary documents but chiefly on secondary works. Popularized; emphasizes Adams' congressional career.

Hargreaves, Mary W. M. *The Presidency of John Quincy Adams.* Lawrence: University Press of Kansas, 1985. Detailed and scholarly examination of Adams' presidency, including the political and economic background. Concludes that Adams' term was more positive in goals and action than many historians have judged it. Dense but readable.

Hecht, Marie B. *John Quincy Adams: A Personal History of an Independent Man.* New York: Macmillan Publishing Co., 1972. Provides political background, with good attention to various personalities. Admires

John Quincy, but is rather critical of Louisa. Lengthy but not dull.

Lipsky, George A. *John Quincy Adams: His Theory and Ideas*. New York: Thomas Y. Crowell, 1950. A good biographical chapter, but mainly concerned with Adams' intellectual system. Good analysis but a rather convoluted style. Unbounded admiration for a cold intellect. Adams seems a sanctimonious prig in some of the author's admiring references, somewhat more than he probably was.

Morse, John T., Jr. *John Quincy Adams*. Boston: Houghton Mifflin Co., 1882. Written in 1882 for and by the editor of the "American States-men" series. Brief (three hundred small pages), basic narrative.

Oliver, Andrew. *Portraits of John Quincy Adams and His Wife*. Cambridge, Mass.: The Belknap Press of Harvard University Press, 1970. Portraits, busts, silhouettes, including the later daguerreotypes. Accompanying text informative.

Russell, Greg. *John Quincy Adams and the Public Virtues of Diplomacy*. Columbia: University of Missouri Press, 1995.

Shepherd, Jack. *Cannibals of the Heart: A Personal Biography of Louisa Catherine and John Quincy Adams*. New York: McGraw-Hill Book Co., 1980. Extensive research in the primary sources. An insightful view of the private life of a very public man, with equal attention to the lives of his wife and children. Well written; the psychological analysis is not intrusive. Good blend also of political and social background.

Weeks, William Earl. *John Quincy Adams and American Global Empire*. Lexington: University Press of Kentucky, 1992.

Marsha Kass Marks

SAMUEL ADAMS

Born: September 27, 1722; Boston, Massachusetts
Died: October 2, 1803; Boston, Massachusetts

Strategically placed in Boston, the center of resistance to British colonial policies, Adams was one of the most significant organizers of the American Revolution.

Early Life

Samuel Adams' American ancestry began with Henry Adams, who emigrated from Devonshire, England, to Quincy, Massachusetts, in the early seventeenth century. One branch of the family included John Adams, who became second president of the United States. Samuel Adams' grandfather was a sailor, Captain John Adams. His father, Samuel Adams, Sr., lived his entire life in Boston, operating a malt house, or brewery, and was an active member of the old South Church in Boston. He was also active in local politics, establishing the first of the Boston "Caucus Clubs," which played a vital role in the early upheavals of the Revolutionary period.

Samuel Adams, then, was born into an active and influential civic-minded Boston family. He grew up with a familiarity with and keen interest in local politics and knew most Boston political leaders through their friendship with his father. Many of those leaders were prominent in Massachusetts colonial politics as well. Samuel absorbed the traditional independent-mindedness of Boston and thought of Massachusetts as autonomous and largely self-governing within the broader parameters of the British Empire.

Educated in the small wooden schoolhouse in the rear of King's Chapel, Samuel received a traditional grounding in Latin and Greek grammar, preparatory to entering Harvard College. When he received the A.B. degree in 1740 and the master of arts in 1743, his interest in politics was already clear. He titled his thesis, "Whether It Be Lawful to Resist the Supreme Magistrate, if the Commonwealth Cannot Otherwise Be Preserved."

Life's Work

Samuel Adams thus embarked upon his life's work in colonial politics, but he also had to make a living for his family. To that end, his father gave him one thousand pounds to help him get started in business. He promptly lent five hundred pounds to a friend (who never repaid the loan) and lost the other five hundred through poor management. His father then took him into partnership in his malt house, from which the family made a modest living.

Adams lived an austere, simple life and throughout his life had little interest in making money. At a time of crisis just before the war, General Thomas Gage governed Massachusetts under martial law and offered Adams an annuity of two thousand pounds for life. Adams promptly rejected the offer; "a guinea never glistened in my eyes," he said. A man of integrity, he would not be bribed to refrain from doing what he believed to be right. His threadbare clothing was his trademark, reflecting his austerity and lack of interest in material things.

In 1748 his father died, leaving him one-third of his modest estate. Adams gradually sold most of it during the busy years of his life and was rescued from abject poverty in his retirement years only by a small inheritance from his son. (During most of his life, his only income was a small salary as a clerk of the Massachusetts General Assembly.)

Adams married Elizabeth Checkley, the daughter of the minister of New South Congregational Church, in 1749. She died eight years later, survived by only two of their five children, a boy and a girl. Adams reared the children and managed alone for seven years but remarried in 1764 to Elizabeth Wells. He was then forty-two; she, twenty-four.

Adams was of average height and muscular build. He carried himself straight in spite of an involuntary palsied movement of his hands and had light blue eyes and a serious, dignified manner. He was very fond of sacred music and sang in the choir of New South Church. Personable, he maintained a close relationship with his neighbors and was constantly chatting with those he met along the street. He had a gift for smoothing over disputes among his friends and acquaintances and was often asked to mediate a disagreement. Adams was a hard worker, and through the years his candle burned late at night as he kept up his extensive correspondence, much of which does not survive today. His second cousin, John Adams, likened him to John Calvin, partly because of his deep piety but also because of his personality: He was "cool . . . polished, and refined," somewhat inflexible, but consistent, a man of "steadfast integrity, exquisite humanity, genteel erudition, obliging, engaging manners, real as well as professed piety, and a universal good character. . . ."

Samuel Adams was very interested in political philosophy and believed strongly in liberty and Christian virtue and frugality. He helped organize discussion clubs and the *Public Advertiser*, a newspaper to promote understanding of political philosophy. He served in political offices large and small, as fire ward, as moderator, and as tax collector. An orthodox Christian, he warned of the political implications of the "fallen" nature of man, susceptible as most men were to self-aggrandizement, if not corruption. Colonial Americans believed that power had the tendency to corrupt, and Adams was no exception. Speaking for the Boston Town Meeting, Adams said:

> [Such is] the depravity of mankind that ambition and lust of power above the law are . . . predominant passions in the breasts of most men. [Power] converts a good man in private life to a tyrant in office.

Despite mythology to the contrary, Adams was not a mob leader, though he was popular with the common workers of Boston. He was opposed to violence and sought to achieve his aims by political means. No evidence has ever been found placing Adams at any of the scenes in Boston involving mob violence such as the Boston Massacre, the wrecking of Lieutenant Governor Thomas Hutchinson's house, or the physical harassment of merchants. He has often been charged with "masterminding" these events, but only by conjecture, not on the basis of historical evidence.

In his early forties, Adams was well known in Boston politics when the Stamp Act crisis occurred in 1764-1765—the beginning of the revolutionary period. Along with his friend James Otis, Adams spoke out strongly and wrote much against the dangers of the Stamp Act. Before the Boston Town Meeting, Adams denied the right of the British Parliament to tax the colonists. The Massachusetts Charter gave Americans the right "to govern and tax ourselves." If Parliament could tax the Colonies, then the Englishmen living in America would become "tributary slaves" without representation. Adams called for a unified resistance to this "tyranny" throughout the Colonies. The Boston Town Meeting then elected Adams to a seat in the Massachusetts General

Assembly, where he was soon elected to the position of clerk, a position he held for ten years.

This principle of opposing taxation without representation became one of the most significant rallying points for resisting British control of the Colonies. Adams nevertheless stressed that he had no desire for colonial representation in the British Parliament. Since the colonists would be considerably outnumbered and since travel to England was so slow, it would be "impracticable for the subjects in America" to have a tiny voice in Parliament. Instead, Adams and most of his fellow American strategists wanted to be able to make their own laws in their own American "parliaments." "All acts," wrote Adams, "made by any power whatever other than the General Assembly of this province, imposing taxes on the inhabitants, are infringements of our inherent and unalienable rights as men and British subjects. . . ."

On November 1, 1765, the day the Stamp Act was to go into effect, Boston buildings were draped in mourning black and the church bells tolled slowly. Governor Francis Bernard ordered the Boston militia to muster as a precautionary peacekeeping measure. Yet the men would not respond; one drummer sounded the call only to have his drum promptly broken. The rest of the drummers preserved their instruments by not using them. In direct violation of the Stamp Act, the Massachusetts General Assembly voted 81 to 5 to open the law courts of the province without using stamped papers, as required by the act.

In 1772, Adams sought and received the authorization of the Boston Town Meeting to create a committee of correspondence to inform and consult with other towns in the province, with a view to concerted and coordinated action. This was not a new idea. It had been customary for many years in Europe and in America for legislative bodies to use committees to handle official correspondence with other such governing authorities. As early as 1768, Richard Henry Lee had suggested to the Virginia House of Burgesses the formation of an intercolonial system of correspondence among the provincial assemblies. It was in Boston, however, that the idea was finally implemented.

As clerk of the Massachusetts General Assembly, Adams expanded the circular-letter type of correspondence to include all the Colonies. In time, those letters contributed significantly to the unified action of the Colonies. Realizing the potential strength in such an arrangement, the British secretary of state for the Colonies, Lord Hillsborough, instructed the governor of Massachusetts to order the General Assembly to rescind a circular letter sent to other colonies. Instead, the General Assembly, in a heated debate, voted 92 to 17 to refuse to rescind the letter. The governor dissolved the legislature, but Adams—a pioneer in realizing the enormous importance of communication and information in sustaining any cause—published the names of the seventeen who had voted against the measure, impairing their political future. Britain now sought to obtain evidence to arrest and deport to England for prosecution those who resisted British law. Adams also published that letter, and the effect was electrifying, because it showed the clear intention of the British government to bypass the cherished English right of trial by jury of one's peers.

The political year of 1773 began with now-governor Thomas Hutchinson's opening speech to the Massachusetts General Assembly on the issue of parliamentary supremacy; did the British Parliament have authority over the elected assembly of Massachusetts, and, if so, to what extent? Adams headed the committee of the assembly designated to reply to the governor. He simply and cleverly took Hutchinson's own famous book, *History of Massachusetts Bay* (1760), and compared what he had written earlier with the current message. Adams found many inconsistencies and contradictions. The governor's book, for example, acknowledged that the founders of Massachusetts Bay Colony had been assured by the Crown that "they were to be governed by laws made by themselves" and not by Parliament.

Adams also had a hand in the Boston Tea Party later that same year. The British East India Company was partially owned by the British government but, because of mismanagement, had stockpiled a great quantity of tea that needed to be sold before it spoiled. The Tea Act of spring, 1773, gave the company a monopoly on tea sales in America but sharply cut the price of tea. The controversial tea tax (set by the Townshend Acts of 1767) would continue to be levied, but the actual price, including the tax, paid in America for tea would only be about one-half that paid by a Londoner for his tea.

This monopoly on the tea trade could be seriously damaging to American free enterprise. Without competition, merchant trade could not prosper, and the Americans would eventually pay unnecessarily high prices for imports. Moreover, a precedent would be set regulating trade excessively instead of following more of a free market system.

Adams, however, chose to focus on the taxation issue rather than the monopoly issue, because the former could be defended more emotionally and symbolically. When American patriots refused to allow the tea to be landed, the governor refused to allow the merchant ships to return with their cargoes of tea. The standoff ended when colonists destroyed thousands of pounds of tea by dumping it into the bay.

The response of the British government inflamed the angry Americans. The Boston Port Act closed the port of Boston and threatened to ruin Boston as a commercial center. Salem and Marblehead merchants responded by inviting the merchants of Boston to use their docks and warehouses free of charge. Contributions of food and supplies came from many colonies. Adams asked the people of Massachusetts to support a "Solemn League and Covenant" not to buy British goods. (The wording of the boycott was significant, reminiscent to American colonists of the English Civil War and of the heroism of the later Scottish Covenanters.)

General Gage in effect established martial law in Boston and even dissolved the General Assembly. The assembly, however, was in the process of selecting delegates to the First Continental Congress in Philadelphia. When General Gage's messenger arrived to order the assembly to disband, Adams, the clerk, locked the doors to keep the messenger out until the delegation process was completed. The elected delegates included both Samuel Adams and John Adams. General Gage considered arresting Samuel Adams but did not want to provoke a violent reaction, which such a measure would assuredly incite.

The three-hundred-mile trip to Philadelphia was the longest of Adams' life. Even there, however, he found himself influential politically, becoming the key member of the newly organized Committee of Safety, a coordinating group. Adams was also the chairman of the Donation Committee, which distributed gifts of food and supplies collected all along the Atlantic seaboard for the aid of the unfortunate people of the Boston area. The Committee of Safety began collecting weapons and supplies—and even stored cannon at Concord.

An active member of the Continental Congress, Adams played a significant political role throughout the Revolutionary War. After the war, he approved of the new Constitution of the United States—but only after assurances were given him that a bill of rights was to be added. Adams became lieutenant governor of Massachusetts in 1789 and governor in 1793, retiring from that office in 1797. On October 2, 1803, at the age of eighty-one, he died, having devoted his life to the cause of liberty and independence in a new nation, the United States of America.

Summary

It would be difficult to overestimate the importance of Samuel Adams to the American Revolution. Along with Virginia, New York, and Pennsylvania, Massachusetts led the way to independence. There was no center of power quite so volatile, however, as Massachusetts; it was there that the events which sparked the revolution occurred: resistance to the Stamp Act, the Boston Massacre, the *Liberty* incident, organized boycotts, letters of protest, and so on.

Samuel Adams was involved in all of these events. His importance, moreover, was recognized in the very highest echelons of the British government. When King George III ordered Governor Hutchinson to London for consultation, one of the questions he asked him was what accounted for the importance of Samuel Adams in the Colonies. Hutchinson's reply reflected his frustration with Adams: "A great pretended zeal for liberty and a most inflexible natural temper. He was the first that publicly asserted the independency of the colonies upon the kingdom."

It is true that Adams was a principal advocate of complete independence from Great Britain, but not until 1775. All that he had advocated for years following the Stamp Act crisis was self-government within the British system. He did not push for independence until it became obvious to him that the king was a "tyrant [with] an unalterable determination to compel the colonies to absolute obedience."

Bibliography

Adams, Samuel. *The Writings of Samuel Adams.* Edited by H. A. Cushing. 4 vols. New York: G. P. Putnam's Sons, 1904-1908. Indispensable primary material: Adams' ideas in his own words—in letters, newspaper articles, and official correspondence of the Massachusetts General Assembly.

Bailyn, Bernard. *The Ideological Origins of the American Revolution.* Cambridge, Mass.: The Belknap Press of Harvard University Press, 1967. Not much on Adams directly, but essential for understanding his ideological milieu. Bailyn finds, as did Adams, that the war was fought over constitutional issues.

Chidsey, Donald Barr. *The Great Separation: The Story of the Boston Tea Party and the Beginning of the American Revolution*. New York: Crown Publishers, 1965. Written in a popular novelist's style, this book brings to life the issues and actions surrounding the Boston Tea Party, including Adams' role.

Fowler, William M., Jr. *Samuel Adams: Radical Puritan*. Edited by Oscar Handlin. New York: Longman, 1997.

Galvin, John R. *Three Men of Boston*. New York: Thomas Y. Crowell, 1976. A retelling of the events leading to the Revolution in Boston through the significant parts played by Thomas Hutchinson, James Otis, and Samuel Adams. Galvin captures the complexity of the period and shows how the issues and events were interrelated.

Hosmer, James K. *Samuel Adams*. Boston: Houghton Mifflin Co., 1885. This is the standard nineteenth century biography of Adams.

Maier, Pauline. *The Old Revolutionaries: Political Lives in the Age of Samuel Adams*. New York: Alfred A. Knopf, 1980. Chapter 1, "A New Englander as Revolutionary: Samuel Adams," is a brilliant analysis of Adams' importance in history. Maier analyzes the interpretive data on Adams and introduces many fresh insights. Her subtitle indicates the absolutely dominant role that Adams played in the Revolutionary era.

Miller, John C. *Sam Adams: Pioneer in Propaganda*. Stanford, Calif.: Stanford University Press, 1936. A pioneer work analyzing Adams' propaganda warfare against the British. Adams' techniques in communications are described in detail.

Montross, Lynn. *The Reluctant Rebels: The Story of the Continental Congress, 1774-1789*. New York: Harper and Brothers, Publishers, 1950. The important role of the Continental Congress in the conduct and winning of the American Revolution, as well as Adams' contribution during that phase of his career.

Umbreit, Kenneth. *Founding Fathers: Men Who Shaped Our Tradition*. Port Washington, N.Y.: Kennikat Press, 1941. One useful chapter on Adams. He is ranked along with Thomas Jefferson, John Adams, John Hancock, Patrick Henry, and George Washington as a Founding Father.

William H. Burnside

MADELEINE ALBRIGHT

Born: May 15, 1937; Prague, Czechoslovakia

As ambassador to the United Nations and as the first woman to hold the office of secretary of state, Albright helped to shape a foreign policy emphasizing an activist role for the United States.

Early Life

Madeleine Korbel was born in Prague, Czechoslovakia, in 1937, shortly before Nazi Germany took control of the country. Her father, Josef Korbel, was an intellectual and a member of the Czech diplomatic corps. Her mother, Anna Speeglova Korbel, was the daughter of a prosperous family who gave birth to two other children, Katherine Korbel Silva and John Joseph Korbel. Madeleine's grandparents were Jewish, and three of them died in the Holocaust—a fact Albright revealed only after her appointment as secretary of state. Her parents converted to Catholicism, apparently to escape persecution, and Madeleine grew up celebrating Christian rituals such as Christmas and Easter.

Madeleine's earliest experiences were shaped by World War II. When German agents took power in Czechoslovakia in 1938, her father, an outspoken opponent of the Nazis, was targeted for execution. While Josef Korbel tried to get false diplomatic papers that would get his family out of the country, he and his wife walked the streets of Prague with the infant Madeleine, making sure they stayed in public places where the Nazis would not assault him. They were able to escape to England; Madeleine later recalled staying in London air-raid shelters and sleeping under a steel table during bombing raids. During her stay, she became fluent in English. After the war, the Korbel family returned briefly to Prague. Josef, though, soon resumed his diplomatic career, which took him to Belgrade, Yugoslavia, and then to New York when he was assigned a position at the United Nations.

While the Korbels were in New York, Czechoslovakia experienced another coup; the communists had taken charge, and Josef Korbel was once again a wanted man. The family was granted political asylum in the United States, and in 1949 they moved to Colorado, where Josef became a professor of international relations at the University of Denver. A respected scholar and the author of many books on diplomacy, Josef Korbel was Madeleine's first major intellectual authority; she has attributed many of her views to her father's influence.

In Colorado, Madeleine attended a small private high school. She won a scholarship to Wellesley College in Massachusetts, where she majored in political science, edited the college newspaper for a year, and campaigned for Democratic presidential candidate Adlai Stevenson. In 1959, she was graduated with honors.

Only three days after her graduation, Madeleine married Joseph Medill Patterson Albright, the heir of a prominent newspaper family. They moved to Chicago, where he was employed with the *Chicago Sun-Times*; Madeleine, however, was told that as a journalist's spouse, she would never be hired by a newspaper. Instead, she worked briefly in public relations for the *Encyclopædia Britannica* before the family moved to New York City in 1961. During the next six years, Madeleine gave birth to three daughters: twins, named Alice and Anne, and Katherine. She also enrolled in the graduate program in public law and government at Columbia University.

Life's Work
Madeleine Albright has credited her success to her willingness to work hard. While she pursued graduate study and reared a family, she typically awoke at 4:30 A.M. and worked late into the night. She earned a master's degree, a certificate in Russian studies, and, in 1976, a doctorate; her dissertation concerned the role of the press in the 1968 crisis in Czechoslovakia, during which dissidents had tried to end Soviet control of the country. Her dissertation, like much of her later career, would combine her fascinations with journalism and foreign policy. At Columbia, Albright studied with Professor Zbigniew Brzezinski, who directed the Institute on Communist Affairs. Along with her father, Brzezinski would be one of Albright's most important intellectual mentors.

In 1968, Madeleine's husband was transferred to Washington, D.C., where he became the bureau chief of *Newsday*. Madeleine became involved with her daughters' private school, for which she organized several successful fund-raising projects. As a result, a friend recommended her as a fund-raiser for Senator Edmund Muskie's campaign for the 1972 Democratic presidential nomination. Although Muskie did not win the nomination, he hired Albright to serve as the chief legislative assistant in his Senate office. She was especially involved in assisting Muskie with his duties as a member of the Senate Foreign Relations Committee.

Madeleine Albright *(Reuters/Robert Giroux/Archive Photos)*

When Jimmy Carter was elected president in 1976, he appointed Zbigniew Brzezinski to be his national security adviser. Brzezinski brought Albright onto the staff of the National Security Council, where she worked as congressional liaison. When Ronald Reagan became president in 1981, Albright moved from governmental service to a position as senior fellow in Soviet and Eastern European affairs at the Center for Strategic and International Studies.

In 1982, Albright and her husband separated, and she began to devote herself wholeheartedly to her career as a foreign-policy analyst and advocate. With the support of a fellowship from the Smithsonian Institution's Woodrow Wilson Center for Scholars, she published *Poland: The Role of the Press in Political Change* in 1983.

Also in 1982, Albright joined the faculty of Georgetown University, where she remained until 1993. Her experience as a university faculty member was a decided success. She served as a professor of international affairs and directed the school's Women in Foreign Service Program, and she was named the university's teacher of the year on four occasions. While on the Georgetown faculty, Albright began inviting a variety of guests from academia, the diplomatic service, journalism, and politics to her home for discussions of international issues. Among those who attended Albright's "salons" was the governor of Arkansas, Bill Clinton; among the topics was the shape that U.S. foreign policy might take if the Democrats regained the White House.

Albright coordinated foreign policy for Democratic presidential nominee Walter Mondale and vice presidential nominee Geraldine Ferraro during the 1984 campaign. Four years later, she was senior foreign-policy adviser and a major speechwriter for Democratic nominee Michael Dukakis. During the next four years, Albright served as president of the Center for National Policy, a Democratic think tank and a resource for members of Congress, where she dealt principally with Eastern European affairs. She was also involved with the Georgetown Leadership Seminar, an annual session for government officials, bankers, journalists, and military officers. Albright was a frequent guest on the public television program *Great Decisions*, which provided her with the chance to reach a larger audience with her views on international affairs.

When Bill Clinton ran for president in 1992, Albright helped to write the foreign-policy sections of the Democratic Party platform as well as position papers for the nominee. She was, therefore, an obvious choice for a diplomatic post in the Clinton Administration, and in December, 1992, the president-elect named her U.S. ambassador to the United Nations and made her a member of the Cabinet.

Albright brought great energy to her role at the United Nations. She traveled to the capital of every member nation of the Security Council, visited Somalia when U.S. troops were stationed there, and went to Bosnia, where she strongly advocated greater American involvement in the conflict with Serbia. In 1995, she attended the U.N. Conference on Women, held in China, where she spent a day escorting First Lady Hillary Clinton. She also led Mrs. Clinton on a tour of Prague in 1996.

Albright increased the visibility of the seven women ambassadors to the United Nations by organizing lunches for them, and she led the effort to oust Secretary General Boutros Boutros-Ghali from his leadership post. Boutros-Ghali was intensely unpopular with conservatives in the U.S. Congress, and her opposition to him later helped to win Senate approval of her appointment as secretary of state. While serving in the United Nations, moreover, Albright remained closely tied to the decision-making process in Washington, D.C., where she attended Cabinet meetings and sessions of the National Security Council's principals group.

After Clinton was reelected in 1996, it soon became apparent that Secretary of State Warren Christopher would step down from his post. The president considered several former senators and career diplomats to fill the position, but he eventually chose to nominate Madeleine Albright. She was easily confirmed by the Senate, which supported her nomination by a vote of 99-0.

Summary

Prior to Albright's appointment as secretary of state, no woman had held so high a position in the U.S. diplomatic service; moreover, only one woman, Jeane Kirkpatrick, had preceded her as ambassador to the United Nations. Albright assumed the secretary of state's post with a reputation for being candid, and she was also outspoken about affirming her identity as a woman. For example, she noted immediately that the secretary of state's office had been designed with a male occupant in mind. It was equipped with conveniences such as racks for men's suits and drawers for socks. Albright's occupancy of the office clearly defied the traditional image of a secretary of state.

With respect to foreign policy, Albright was an enthusiastic advocate of the assertive use of American power and influence. She stated that her "mind-set is Munich"; in other words, her view was formed by the experience of Czechoslovakia: At Munich in 1938, diplomats from Great Britain and France effectively handed control of her native country over to Adolf Hitler in return for his promise to cease aggression. Hitler promptly took Czechoslovakia, continued his conquests, and provoked World War II. The lesson of Munich that Albright described, therefore, was that one should not compromise with aggression.

As secretary of state, Albright was a severe critic of nations charged with violations of human rights, including Cuba, Iraq, and Iran. On the other hand, she had to find a way to balance disapproval of China's internal repression with efforts to promote trade with the world's most populous country. During her tenure, the Department of State also faced instability in Russia, conflicts in the Middle East, and tensions caused by expansion of the North Atlantic Treaty Organization (NATO). Madeleine Albright thus had an important influence in two areas of public life: both as a model of a woman's achievement in a nontraditional role and as a major architect of American foreign policy.

Bibliography

"Altered State." *The New Republic*, December 30, 1996, pp. 17.

Cooper, Matthew, and Melinda Liu. "Bright Light." *Newsweek*, February 10, 1997, pp. 22-29.

Gibbs, Nancy. "The Many Lives of Madeleine." *Time*, February 17, 1997, pp. 52-61.

_____. "Voice of America." *Time*, December, 16, 1996, pp. 32-33.

"Madeleine Albright." *Current Biography* 56 (May, 1995): 8-12.

Sciolino, Elaine. "Madeleine Albright's Audition." *The New York Times Magazine*, September 22, 1996, p. 63.

Weymouth, Lally. "As I Find out More, I'm Very Proud." *Newsweek*, February 24, 1997, pp. 30-32.

Mary Welek Atwell

JOHN PETER ALTGELD

Born: December 30, 1847; Niederselters, Prussia
Died: March 12, 1902; Joliet, Illinois

Altgeld furnished American political life with a high standard of moral courage and, during a crucial historical period, helped to establish the principle that maintenance of the welfare society is an obligation of government.

Early Life

John Peter Altgeld was born December 30, 1847, in Niederselters, in the Prussian province of Nassau, the eldest son of a wagon-maker, also named John Peter Altgeld, and his wife, Mary Lanehart. The family came to the United States in the spring of the following year, and Altgeld grew up on farms near Mansfield, Ohio. Because his father was against the idea of education for his children, Altgeld attended country schools for only three terms. When he was sixteen, he enlisted in an Ohio militia regiment and was sent to Virginia. There, he contracted a fever which permanently damaged his health, but he refused to be sent home and finished out the hundred days for which the regiment had been mustered.

When he returned to Ohio, Altgeld, much against his father's wishes, attended high school in Mansfield and a teacher-training school in Lexington, Ohio, and taught school for a time. Until he was twenty-one, he turned over all of his wages to his father, but in the spring of 1869, perhaps because the parents of Emma Ford would not permit her to marry him, he headed west on foot, working on farms as he went. He arrived finally in St. Louis with only fifteen cents, worked there for a time in a chemical plant, and later worked on a railroad that was being built in southern Kansas. When a recurrence of his fever forced him to quit, he went to northwestern Missouri, most of the way on foot. Dressed in rags, he collapsed at a farm near Savannah, Missouri, and was taken in by a farmer who restored him to health and gave him work. Later, he taught school and read law, and in April, 1871, was admitted to the bar and began legal practice in Savannah. He had not revealed any interest in politics until this time, beyond a devotion to the ideals of Thomas Jefferson, but he served as city attorney for Savannah for a year and ran successfully as the Populist candidate for prosecuting attorney of Andrew County in 1874.

For reasons which remain obscure, Altgeld resigned this office after a year and, with only one hundred dollars, moved to Chicago. There he established a law practice, and in 1877, on a visit to his parents in Ohio, he married Emma Ford. During the next years, Altgeld achieved great success investing in Chicago real estate and in 1890 held property valued at a million dollars.

Life's Work

In 1884, Altgeld was the unsuccessful Democratic candidate for Congress in the traditionally Republican Fourth District. At this time, he was an apparent conservative in politics and part of the Chicago economic establishment. In the same year, however, he published *Our Penal Machinery and Its Victims*, which revealed many of the ideas for reform that he sought to implement later in his political career. The book pleaded for the elimination of the causes of crime and the rehabilitation of criminals, and it condemned police brutality against vagrants. In 1886, in the immediate wake of the Haymarket Riot, he wrote a newspaper article in which he argued for the compulsory arbitration of strikes.

That year, he ran successfully for judge of the Cook County Superior Court, serving for five years. Apparently Altgeld regarded the judgeship as the first step toward his ultimate goal—a seat in the United States Senate, the highest office possible for him because of his foreign birth. When he resigned his judgeship and failed to win election to the Senate, he embarked on his greatest project in real estate—the construction of the sixteen-story Unity Block, at that time one of Chicago's greatest buildings.

In 1892, he was nominated by the Democrats for the Illinois governorship, probably more for his success as a businessman than for any stand he had taken on social issues. In this campaign, he revealed the strict ethics and liberal instincts for which his followers admired him, mixed with a real hunger for power and an occasional tendency to political chicanery. As the first Democratic governor of Illinois in forty years, Altgeld cleared out all the Republicans in state government, and though many of his replacements were brilliant, he fired some able Republicans and appointed some incompetent Democrats.

In the aftermath of the Haymarket Riot, when a bomb killed several policemen, eight anarchists had been sentenced to death; one of them committed suicide in prison, and four others were hanged. The sentences of the other three—Samuel Fielden, Michael Schwab, and Oscar Neebe—had been commuted to life imprisonment. Altgeld's supporters expected him to pardon these three men and assumed that he would be motivated only by feelings of mercy. Yet when the pardons were issued on June 26, 1893, it was clear that though he detested anarchism, he was convinced that the eight men had been convicted not for their deeds but for their opinions, that the jury had been impaneled improperly, that the judge was prejudiced, and that five of the accused were, in effect, the victims of judicial murder. Altgeld issued a pamphlet of eighteen thousand words in which he presented his arguments with great clarity and logic, but this explanation could not allay the storm of abuse which fell upon him for his act. Those who had favored the sentences now raged at him in virtually every newspaper in the country, and those who had favored a pardon were angered that he had issued an absolute pardon and that the pamphlet exposed the errors of the judicial system itself. Altgeld was accused of being an anarchist; this was said by many editorialists to be the result of his foreign birth.

The charge that he was an anarchist seems absurd when one considers his use of the Illinois militia during the labor troubles of his term as governor. Only two weeks before he issued the pardons, he sent the militia to Lemont in response to a plea from local authorities that they could not maintain order in a labor dispute. In June, 1894, he sent the militia to Mount Olive, where striking miners were interfering with mail trains. These affirmations of the power of the state did not satisfy his enemies, because, unlike his predecessors, Altgeld used the militia only to maintain order, not to break the strikes.

This was one of several issues that led to Altgeld's break with President Grover Cleveland. In July, 1894, when the Pullman Company had locked out its employees and federal troops had been dispatched by Cleveland to break the "strike," Altgeld, in a letter to the president, condemned his action on the grounds that sufficient Illinois militia were available on the scene to preserve order. The Chicago newspapers, still harping on Altgeld's supposed anarchism, wildly denounced him for this protest, but in fact violence did not occur until the federal troops arrived, and then Chicago police and the state militia put it down. In fact, the disorder actually ended when a company of Altgeld's militia killed seven men by firing point-blank into a mob.

This dispute was only one of Altgeld's quarrels with the president. Altgeld saw Cleveland as an unquestioning supporter of "government by injunction," the use of the courts to rule strikes illegal, and he condemned the Supreme Court when it struck down the federal income tax in 1894, in an opinion written by Cleveland's appointee, Chief Justice Melville Fuller. Altgeld saw little difference between Republicans and Cleveland Democrats on the tariff question or on the silver issue. By thorough study, he made himself the outstanding authority on the latter question in American public life, and he embraced the silver issue in 1895, calling for the coinage of silver to increase the money supply. By this time, in spite of the campaign of vilification against him in the press for the Haymarket pardons and his stand on the Pullman dispute, Altgeld was the most influential Democrat in the country. With the laboring class throughout the country, he enjoyed an affection which verged on idolatry, and his stand on silver gave him a large following in the West and South. As a result, there is little reason to doubt that, had it not been for his foreign birth, he would have been the Democratic nominee for president in 1896.

As it was, he was clearly the master of the Democratic convention of that year. The platform reflected his views—free coinage of silver and gold at a ratio of sixteen to one, opposition to government by injunction, arbitration of labor disputes involving interstate commerce, protection of the rights of labor, and an income tax. While he did not favor the nomination of William Jennings Bryan, Altgeld worked mightily for his election, even at the expense of his own reelection campaign. He did not want another term as governor—his finances had suffered from the economic depression of the time, and his health was bad—but he bowed to the party's wishes. The Republican strategy, in the face of a national trend away from the gold standard, was to depict Bryan as the tool of the "anarchist" and communist Altgeld. Not for the last time in the nation's history, political profit was made from calling an opponent a communist. On October 17, 1896, in a great speech at Cooper Union, Altgeld took the fight to the enemy, arguing against government by injunction and against federal interference in the rights of states to maintain order within their own borders.

Throughout the campaign, he literally rose from a sickbed to speak, sometimes seven or eight times a day.

In the Bryan debacle, Altgeld's defeat for reelection was probably inevitable, and he was defeated in the legislature as a candidate for the United States Senate. He returned to Chicago to attempt to rebuild his shattered finances, but he lost control of the Unity Building and returned to the practice of law. As governor, he had rejected a bribe of a half-million dollars from the Chicago traction magnate Charles Yerkes, and he had always favored public ownership of monopolies. On this platform, he ran unsuccessfully as an independent for mayor in 1899.

In the 1900 presidential campaign, Altgeld was still a powerful influence, as was evident in the Democratic Party's repetition of its 1896 stand on the silver issue, and he campaigned with great energy for Bryan. At this time, he was also condemning American policy in the Philippines. He died suddenly on March 12, 1902, a few hours after making a speech which condemned the treatment of Boer women and children in British concentration camps in South Africa.

Summary

During his governorship, John Peter Altgeld achieved much for Illinois in the improvement of existing state institutions and the building of others, and his use of the state's police power to preserve order reflected a deep conservative respect for the rights of property, contrary to the charge of anarchism leveled against him by journalistic hacks and by politicians who must have known better. His pardoning of Samuel Fielden, Michael Schwab, and Oscar Neebe, an act of courage with few parallels in American political life, was consistent with his stands on social and economic issues—stands which have been vindicated by history. In 1896, he forced the Democratic Party to commit itself for the first time to social reform, and the achievements of the Progressive era and the New Deal were the fruits of the seeds he planted. Indeed, it is an irony of history that Altgeld is forgotten by most Americans, while Theodore Roosevelt, who once in a foolish speech called him an apologist for wholesale murder, is a hero of American Progressivism because he enacted much of Altgeld's program. Altgeld remains what Vachel Lindsay called the "wise man, that kindled the flame."

Bibliography

Barnard, Harry. *Eagle Forgotten: The Life of John Peter Altgeld*. Indianapolis: Bobbs-Merrill, 1938. The definitive biography of Altgeld, not likely to be superseded, and the basic source for information on his early years.

Browne, Waldo R. *Altgeld of Illinois*. New York: B. W. Huebsch, 1924. The first biography of Altgeld, written out of profound respect for its subject and informed by a deep sense of social justice. Lacks a thorough account of Altgeld's pre-Chicago years. Valuable, though superseded by Barnard's biography.

Christman, Henry M., ed. *The Mind and Spirit of John Peter Altgeld*. Urbana: University of Illinois Press, 1960. Includes a useful though brief biographical account and a representative selection of Altgeld's writings, including the Cooper Union speech of 1896 and "Reasons for Pardoning Fielden, Neebe, and Schwab."

Ginger, Ray. *Altgeld's America*. New York: Funk and Wagnall's Co., 1958. A thorough study of Altgeld's achievements in developing a progressivism which would adapt American political idealism to modern industrial conditions.

Whitlock, Brand. *Forty Years of It*. New York: D. Appleton and Co., 1925. Whitlock served in the Illinois government during Altgeld's governorship and was his close associate. This autobiography provides a firsthand account of events surrounding the Haymarket pardons and the Pullman dispute.

Wish, Harvey. "Altgeld and the Progressive Tradition." *American Historical Review* 46 (July, 1941): 813-831. Emphasizes the progressivism of Altgeld's social and economic beliefs. Puts his career in perspective which is frequently lacking in those accounts which concentrate on his role in the Haymarket case.

Robert L. Berner

CHESTER A. ARTHUR

Born: October 5, 1829; Fairfield, Vermont
Died: November 18, 1886; New York, New York

Arthur's presidency, virtually free of corruption, comforted a nation grieving over the death of President James A. Garfield, maintained peace and order, promoted economic growth, and demonstrated the stability and adaptability of the American political system, particularly during emergencies.

Early Life

Chester Alan Arthur was born October 5, 1829, in Fairfield, Franklin County, Vermont, the oldest of seven children. His mother, Malvina Stone, was a Canadian whose ancestors immigrated from England and were Baptist; his father, William Arthur, was an Irish immigrant turned Baptist minister as well as a respectable scholar. Under the tutorship of his father, Arthur showed an intense interest in learning and a high aptitude in the subjects he studied, matriculating at Union College in Schenectady, New York (at that time, one of the best known colleges in the East), on September 5, 1845, at the age of fifteen. He became a member of the Psi Upsilon Society, taught in the local schools to help defray the cost of his education, and in July, 1848, at the age of eighteen, was graduated with high honors, including membership in the Phi Beta Kappa honor society.

After his graduation from college, Arthur pursued his ambition to become a lawyer by enrolling in the law school at Ballston Springs, New York, where he studied for a few months, continuing his studies at home and teaching. In 1851, he became principal and teacher at the North Pownal Academy in Bennington County, Vermont, ten miles from his family across the border in Hoosick, New York. During Arthur's tenure as principal there, James A. Garfield served for a time as a faculty member, teaching business and penmanship—a circumstance that was to be fully exploited in the presidential campaign of 1880. In 1852, Arthur became principal of an academy at Cohoes, New York; in 1853, he continued his legal studies in the office of the prestigious firm of Erastus D. Culver.

On May 4, 1854, after having been certified to the Supreme Court of

New York by the Culver firm that he had satisfactorily completed his studies, Arthur was admitted to the bar. He joined Culver's firm and began practicing law. In 1856, upon becoming a judge of the Civil Court of Brooklyn, Arthur formed a partnership with an old friend, Henry D. Gardiner. For three months, Arthur and his friend tried to

Chester A. Arthur *(Library of Congress)*

establish a practice out West but returned to New York City after becoming disillusioned by widespread lawlessness. Two of Arthur's first and most celebrated cases involved the Fugitive Slave Law and discrimination against black people on New York City streetcars. As a staunch abolitionist, Arthur found in these two cases an opportunity to make a significant contribution to the antislavery movement.

As a Whig delegate from Brooklyn, dedicated to the abolitionist movement, Arthur participated in the convention that met at Saratoga in August of 1854, for the purpose of developing methods for combating the Kansas-Nebraska Act, which repealed the Missouri Compromise of 1820. The action of the convention led to the birth of the Republican Party. In the party's first campaign for the presidency, Arthur wholeheartedly supported and campaigned for the first presidential nominee of the Republican Party, John C. Frémont. During the campaign, Arthur served on an executive committee that worked for the election of Frémont. On election day, Arthur served as an inspector of elections at the polls.

In October, 1859, Arthur married Ellen Lewis Herndon, a member of a distinguished Virginia family and sister of a good friend, Dabney Herndon. Their union produced two sons (one son died at the age of four) and one daughter. Arthur's wife died in January, 1881.

Life's Work
After joining the state's militia, Arthur gained extensive knowledge of military science especially concerning strategy and logistics. His highly rated performance led to his appointment as Judge Advocate-General of the Second Brigade of the New York Militia. Having fully assisted him in his bid for reelection, the governor of New York appointed Arthur as engineer-in-chief and charged him with the responsibility of drawing plans to protect the state. After the Civil War began, the governor promoted Arthur to the position of inspector general of New York troops in the field. Later, he was appointed assistant quartermaster general, then quartermaster general of New York, responsible for raising regiments to fight on the battlefields and maintaining the troops. While serving in the post of quartermaster general, Arthur got his long-awaited chance to participate in direct combat on the battlefields; on two occasions, he was elected first by the Ninth Regiment of the New York Militia and, second, by the Metropolitan Brigade

of New York City to lead them in battle. Both times, the governor successfully dissuaded Arthur, convincing him to remain in his post as quartermaster general, wherein he ably carried out his responsibilities for the cause of the Union.

After he resigned his position following the election of a Democrat as governor of the Empire State, Arthur spent much time in Albany and Washington working on war claims and drafting important bills that required quick action, soon becoming one of the best lawyers in New York. In 1866, Arthur helped Roscoe Conkling get elected to the United States Senate, then became his chief henchman until he became president.

In 1867, Arthur was elected to the Century Club, a prestigious intellectual and social organization, and was elected chairman of the executive committee of the New York Republican Party. In 1871, Arthur established one of the most outstanding law firms in New York; in the same year, President Ulysses S. Grant appointed him collector of the Port of New York—the most important political position outside Washington, D.C. Impressed with Arthur's management of the Port of New York, Grant reappointed him to the collectorship, and the Senate confirmed the reappointment unanimously.

In 1878, however, President Rutherford B. Hayes dismissed Arthur from the collectorship on the grounds that his positions in the government and the Republican Party were incompatible with respect to civil service reforms. The outrageous scandals of Grant's two administrations had convinced Hayes of the dire need for an appreciable reform program in government designed to take politics out of the bureaucracy. The removal of Arthur was therefore not based on his competence but on the fact that, as a consummate politician, he had manipulated his position in a way that made him the undisputed "boss" of the Republican Party of New York City as well as chairman of the Central Committee of the Republican Party of the state. Upon his removal, a petition signed by some of the most reputable persons of the time, asking that Arthur be retained, was suppressed by Arthur. Like Garfield, Arthur never sought a position; he wished to retain the collectorship on his own merit, but as a result of a bitter struggle between the Hayes Administration and the Conkling machine, he chose to return to practicing law.

In 1879, as chairman of the Republican Central Committee, Arthur worked hard to strengthen the Republican Party of his state—particularly the Stalwarts (1869-1880), the "regular" or machine wing of his party, who were opposed to the reform program of Hayes's administration—and, disregarding the two-term tradition honored by all the presidents since George Washington, strongly advocated and worked to secure a third term for Grant. In Chicago in June, 1880, at the Republican National Nominating Convention, destiny brought Garfield and Arthur together again as it had twenty-six years earlier at the North Pownal Academy in Vermont. This time their relationship was reversed: Arthur worked under Garfield. The nomination of Garfield and Arthur as candidates for president and vice president of the Republican Party startled the nation, including the candidates themselves.

Both men went to Chicago to do everything within their power to help get the leader of their wing nominated. A bitter struggle was expected between the Stalwarts and the Half-Breeds (a wing of the Republican Party, 1876-1884, which supported Hayes's conciliatory policy toward the South, opposed a third term for Grant, and supported the nomination of Garfield), but there were those who believed that the leaders would find a way to resolve the struggle with some kind of compromise. Finally, in order to end the deadlocked convention, the Half-Breeds turned to Garfield on the thirty-sixth ballot and nominated him to lead the Republican Party to victory in 1880. Because they knew that they had no chance of winning the presidency without the support of the Stalwarts, they offered the nomination for vice president to the second most powerful boss of the New York political machine, Chester A. Arthur.

Arthur's nomination was based on political strategy designed to produce some semblance of unity within the Republican Party. On the basis of his experiences of all the candidates available in 1880, Arthur was one of the least qualified to serve as vice president and had no qualifications that would have justified his nomination for the office of the president. Arthur was chosen because he was Conkling's right-hand man. Without the support of the New York political machine, the Republican Party could not win the election. At the outset, Conkling squawked at Arthur's decision to join the Garfield forces, but before the campaign ended, he gave some support.

As the campaign got under way in 1880, the jockeying by the

various factions for control left the Republican Party in a state of disarray, and consequently, the opposing forces expediently closed ranks. One of the most thrilling national political conventions in American history produced one of the most unusual tickets in the history of presidential nominating conventions: The presidential candidate thoroughly qualified, with seventeen years of yeoman's service in the House of Representatives on behalf of the people of his district and the nation; the vice presidential candidate was a skilled politician deeply tied to a powerful political machine, with all of his work experience limited to his home state, and with no experience that equipped him to serve as president. The ticket that had surprised the party, the nation, and the candidates themselves succeeded in achieving a narrow victory at the polls in November.

Only a few months after his inauguration, however—on July 2, 1881—Garfield was shot by a deranged office-seeker, Charles J. Guiteau, in a Washington railroad station. Eighty days later, Garfield died, and the agonizing wait of the people who had prayed so hard for his recovery came to an end. Arthur remained extremely apprehensive throughout the lingering death struggle, hoping that somehow Garfield would survive, recover, and resume his duties as president. When Arthur accepted the invitation to run on the ticket with Garfield, he did so on the basis that it would give him the opportunity to escape the continual and perplexing problems associated with his management of the political machine. After his removal from his position as collector of the New York Customhouse by the outgoing President Hayes, Arthur regarded his selection as vice presidential candidate as a vindication of his integrity.

Garfield's tragic death cast the nation into a state of shock that for a while quelled the political discord that to an appreciable degree remained constant in the wake of the presidential campaign of the previous year. As the shock gradually subsided, however, consternation gripped the nation, for the office and power of the president had devolved on the second most powerful political boss in the country, who himself was the chief lieutenant of the most powerful boss in America. To allay such fears, Arthur gradually dissolved his relationship with Conkling and his machine.

During his term as president, Arthur fought hard for a canal in Nicaragua, owned and operated by the United States; advocated a program of reciprocal trade agreements; developed America's first modern steel navy; prosecuted those who defrauded the Post Office Department; and vetoed the Chinese Exclusion Act, changing the suspension of Chinese immigration from twenty to ten years. Possibly Arthur's greatest achievement was his strong support of the act that became the foundation of civil service reform—the Pendleton Act of 1883.

In addition, Arthur recognized the significance of issues which, while not resolved during his presidency, were later to confirm the soundness of his judgment. Among the recommendations Arthur proposed were statehood for Alaska, a building for the Library of Congress, a law determining who should count the electoral votes in order to avoid the type of dispute that occurred in 1876, and the regulation of interstate commerce. In order to avoid another presidential succession crisis, Arthur strongly recommended a constitutional amendment that would provide for the expedient resolution of questions pertaining to presidential succession. Arthur's proposal concerning presidential succession was ultimately realized with the ratification of the Twenty-fifth Amendment to the Constitution on February 10, 1967.

Arthur's long bout with Bright's disease (he had it at the time he assumed the presidency) failed to affect his administration significantly; it did, however, to a large extent, prevent him from succeeding himself, which was an eventuality he very much desired. After his unsuccessful efforts to obtain the nomination of his party in 1884, his supporters in the Republican Party of New York tried to urge him for a seat in the United States Senate in their efforts to repair their badly damaged "machine." Because of his infirmity and lack of interest (after having been president, he considered campaigning for the Senate to be improper), he rejected the idea. He attended ceremonies opening the Brooklyn Bridge in May, 1883. Just before his term expired, Arthur dedicated the Washington Monument, on February 22, 1885.

After Arthur left office, he was elected president of his fraternity, Psi Upsilon, and elected the forerunner of the subway system of New York City, the New York Arcade Railway. Arthur died on November 18, 1886, at his home in New York City.

Summary
Arthur showed that the aura of the office and power of the presidency

can transform a politician wedded to a political machine into a president who dissociates himself from the machine and bases his policies and programs on what he deems best for the people and the nation. Under the leadership of President Arthur, the intense perturbation of the American people caused by the assassination of Garfield was greatly alleviated. Arthur demonstrated that a man of limited experience could be inspired by prestige, office, and authority of the presidency to exploit his talents and experience to the fullest extent possible, to become an effective president.

When the leading historians in the United States were polled to rate the presidents, they evaluated their subjects as great, near great, above average, average, or below average, with a final slot reserved for outright failures. The historians assigned Arthur to the average class, along with seven other presidents: William McKinley, William Howard Taft, Martin Van Buren, Rutherford B. Hayes, Benjamin Harrison, Zachary Taylor, and Jimmy Carter. Arthur's rating indicates that he overcame his political handicaps and commendably performed his responsibilities as president.

Bibliography

Brisbin, James S. *From the Tow-path to the White House: The Early Life and Public Career of James A. Garfield, Including Also a Sketch of the Life of Honorable Chester A. Arthur*. Philadelphia: Hubbard Brothers, 1880. A classic work containing a readable story of the life of Arthur.

Doenecke, Justus D. *The Presidencies of James A. Garfield and Chester A. Arthur*. Lawrence: University Press of Kansas, 1981. This is a revisionist work inspired by the renewed examination occurring during the centennial of the Gilded Age (1870-1896). Includes brilliant notes and bibliographical essays.

Howe, George Frederick. *Chester A. Arthur: A Quarter-Century of Machine Politics*. New York: Dodd, Mead and Co., 1934. One of the most significant biographical studies of Arthur. This was the only major scholarly biography of Arthur until the publication of Thomas C. Reeves's study in 1975 (see below). Howe's major thesis is that Arthur filled a place of power and responsibility far above his aspirations, bravely and adequately, if not with greatness.

Levin, Peter R. *Seven by Chance: Accidental Presidents*. New York: Farrar, Straus and Co., 1948. This work is a study of the seven men who became president because of the death of a president. The most valuable section of Levin's work is that in which the author assesses the method of choosing a vice-presidential candidate. The author mentions a number of ways to improve the vice presidency. An erudite work that provides an excellent source for studying the vice presidency.

Reeves, Thomas C. *Gentleman Boss: The Life of Chester Alan Arthur*. New York: Alfred A. Knopf, 1975. The author covers Arthur's career in New York politics before he became president, showing that Arthur was a more skillful political organizer and manager than previous accounts indicate. Reeves's work provides a fresh view of Arthur and has become the standard biography.

Sievers, Harry J., ed. *Six Presidents from the Empire State*. Tarrytown, N.Y.: Sleepy Hollow Restorations, 1974. This volume is a scholarly study of the impact on the presidency of the six presidents from New York. They are divided into three pairs whose terms in office correspond broadly to three major eras in the history of the presidency: Martin Van Buren and Millard Fillmore, pre-Civil War; Chester A. Arthur and Grover Cleveland, the Gilded Age; and Theodore Roosevelt and Franklin Delano Roosevelt, the modern presidency. Includes the Schlesinger polls on presidential greatness, a selected bibliography of the Empire State presidents and their contemporaries, splendid illustrations of the six presidents, and sketches of the thirteen outstanding contributors and the editor.

James D. Lockett

STEPHEN FULLER AUSTIN

Born: November 3, 1793; Wythe County, Virginia
Died: December 27, 1836; Columbia, Texas

Austin established the first Anglo-American colony in Texas and played a significant role in the Texas Revolution, which resulted in that province securing independence from Mexico.

Early Life

Stephen Fuller Austin was born on November 3, 1793, in Wythe County, Virginia. His father, Moses Austin, was a mine owner who came from a family of Connecticut merchants. His mother, née Maria Brown, had a New Jersey Quaker heritage. The Austin family moved to the province of Spanish Louisiana in 1798 to seek better lead deposits for mining. Moses established and operated a lead mine south of St. Louis. There young Stephen passed his childhood until the age of eleven years. In 1804, his family sent him to Connecticut to begin his formal education. He spent several years as a pupil at Bacon Academy and then entered Transylvania University in Kentucky. In 1810, the youth returned to Missouri, which had become part of the United States because of the Louisiana Purchase. The young man worked at a bank in St. Louis and, for a time, engaged in storekeeping. In 1814, his neighbors elected him as a delegate to the Missouri Territorial Legislature, a post he held until 1820.

In 1817, Austin took charge of the financially troubled family mining operation at Potosi. He was, however, unable to make it a profitable business. In 1820, he therefore followed his brother-in-law James Perry to the Arkansas Territory. There he established a farm near Long Prairie on the Red River. The governor of Arkansas appointed him a district judge in July of 1820.

By early adulthood, it had become obvious that Austin had natural leadership ability. He had a pleasing personality along with a mature outlook. He was a physically small person of slight build, only five feet, six inches in height. Dark haired and fine featured, Stephen was no doubt a handsome youth who inspired confidence in all whom he met. His greatest strengths, however, were his moderate personal

Stephen Fuller Austin *(Archives Division, Texas State Library, Austin)*

habits. A well-educated man, he was charitable, tolerant, and loyal in his relationships with others. Also, although he never married, he seldom lacked companionship from the many friends he made throughout his life. It is not surprising, therefore, that Austin decided upon the practice of law as his career. In 1821, he went to New Orleans to study for the bar.

Events set in motion about this time by his father, however, changed forever the course of Austin's life. Moses Austin decided to found a colony in the Spanish province of Texas. The fertile and unsettled land there had rich agricultural potential. Many Anglo-Americans from the United States, especially cotton farmers from the South, would probably be glad to immigrate to Texas. They would exploit the land, something the Spanish had never done. Moses went to San Antonio, where he secured a colonization career from the Spanish governor in 1821. This grant permitted him to settle three hundred families in the province. These immigrants would agree to become Spanish subjects in return for grants of land. Moses Austin, however, died in 1821, before he could begin his colonization venture. With his dying breath, he asked that Austin carry through this enterprise and bring it to successful conclusion. This his son agreed to do.

Life's Work

The summer of 1821 found Austin in San Antonio. There he secured a reconfirmation of his father's colonization grant from the Spanish authorities. Unfortunately, however, Mexico became independent from Spain in early 1822, and, consequently, the grant was no longer valid. Austin, who could not secure a renewal from the incoming Mexican authorities in Texas, decided to travel to Mexico City to speak about his grant directly with the newly independent government. He arrived there on April 29, 1822, in the hope that meeting with the Mexican leaders would restore his concession. In the meantime, various Anglo-American farmers began moving to Texas in anticipation of Austin's success in Mexico City.

Austin remained in Mexico for a year while he witnessed the turmoils and instabilities of the new Mexican government. Because of problems related to establishing a workable form of government, Austin could not immediately secure a confirmation of his Texas concession. He did use this time in Mexico City to personal advantage, however, learning to speak and write Spanish with marked fluency. He also made many friends among the Mexican leaders, including Miguel Ramos Arispe, who authored the Mexican Constitution of 1824. Austin furnished Arispe with a translated copy of the United States Constitution and made recommendations concerning the contents of the Mexican document.

The Mexican government confirmed the Austin grant in early 1823. Austin returned to Texas and assumed direction of the colony, which grew rapidly. By the end of 1824, almost all three hundred colonists permitted by the colonization charter had received grants. The Austin colony centered along the rich land of the Brazos River. Most colonists settled in a region called "the bottom," several leagues inland from the Gulf coast. The small town of San Felipe became its chief settlement. A formal census of the colony taken in 1825 showed eighteen hundred residents, of whom 443 were slaves.

During the summer of 1824, the Mexican government approved the establishment of additional Anglo colonies in Texas. Any prospective colonizer could apply for an *empresario* contract, the Spanish term used to describe these concessions. In all, Mexico issued several dozen such contracts to various individuals during the following decade. Most of them did not enjoy success, although Austin continued to do so. His original contract fulfilled, he applied for additional colonial grants under the *empresario* provisions. The additional settlements which he sponsored brought hundreds of families into Texas. By 1830, Austin had attracted some five thousand people into Texas. This influx, added to the families who came under the leadership of the other *empresarios*, resulted in a considerable Anglo population in the province by the end of the 1820's.

Austin became involved in Mexican politics which, during this period, was chaotic and complicated by factions. The Anglo-Texans increasingly came to identify with the Federalists, a Mexican political group whose beliefs seemed similar to their own. The Centralists, the opposing faction, thus began to identify Austin and the Anglo-Texans as members of the Federalists by the early 1830's. Therein lay one of the causes of the Texas Revolution.

In addition, the Mexican government was concerned that too many Anglo-Americans had immigrated to Texas. As a result, it passed the law of April 6, 1830, which (among other restrictions) ended all future immigration into Texas from the United States. Austin worked hard to secure a repeal of this law. He once again went to Mexico City to lobby for measures favorable to Texas. Although he failed to secure all the concessions he wanted, he did convince the government to repeal some of the most objectionable aspects of the law. By the time he returned to Texas in late 1831, events during his absence had made it increasingly difficult for Anglo-Texans to reconcile themselves to con-† nued Mexican rule.

The actions of the post commander at Anahuac on the Texas coast had caused great dissatisfaction among Anglo residents. During the summer of 1832, the colonists took to arms to force his removal. The military commander in Texas eventually removed the offensive garrison commander at Anahuac. For a time, this forestalled additional armed confrontations with the increasingly unhappy Anglo population. By then, however, the crisis had begun. The town council of San Felipe issued a call for a convention of Anglo colonists to discuss common problems and desires. The fifty-eight delegates who composed this group assembled in October, 1832, and elected Austin the presiding officer.

This Convention of 1832, as it subsequently came to be called, drafted a long list of concessions which the Anglo-Texans wanted from the Mexican government. It also created a standing committee of correspondence in each area of Texas for the purpose of monitoring additional problems with Mexico. The delegates also agreed that another convention would be held the following year. This second convention met in 1833 and drafted a provincial constitution for Texas as a separate state within the Mexican government. The Convention of 1833 delegated Austin to deliver this document to the central government. Austin left Texas in May, 1833, on a journey which would result in a two-year absence from Texas. He spent much of this time in a Mexican prison.

Austin arrived in Mexico City, where he presented the proposed constitution to government officials. He also wrote a letter to the town council in San Antonio which complained about the political situation in Mexico. A government official intercepted this letter en route to Texas and believed that it contained treason. Austin, arrested for this in early January of 1834, remained in prison until December of that year. He did not return to Texas until July 11, 1835. Austin's confinement in Mexico City, much of it in the harsh Prison of the Inquisition, permanently ruined his health. During his absence from Texas, dissatisfaction there with Mexico continued. By late 1835, many Anglo-Texans, including Austin, had come to favor a break with Mexico.

The Texas Revolution began on October 2, 1835, with a skirmish between Anglo and Mexican troops near Gonzales, Texas. A committee of colonists issued a call for a provincial convention which appointed Austin commander of the revolutionary army. He held this position for only a few months. The Texas government then appointed him as an agent to the United States, charged with finding materials and supplies for the revolt. Austin spent much of the Texas Revolution in the United States, visiting Washington, D.C., Richmond, Philadelphia, and other cities. He returned to Texas during the summer of 1836 after the Texas Revolution had ended in an Anglo-American victory. Austin permitted his supporters to place his name in candidacy as president of the Republic of Texas. When Sam Houston won election to this office, Austin looked forward to retiring to private life. Houston, however, prevailed upon him to become secretary of state in the new government, which Austin reluctantly agreed to do. He served only a few months. His health broken by the imprisonment in Mexico, Austin died on December 27, 1836.

Summary

Stephen Fuller Austin played a significant role in the westward expansion of the United States. Although credit for the Anglo colonization of Hispanic Texas belongs to his father, Austin carried out the dream, and its success belongs to him. He approached the colonization of Texas with a single-minded determination which consumed all of his efforts. In fact, he had time for little else from 1821 until the events of the Texas Revolution. Although he initially believed that Texas should remain a part of Mexico, Austin had become a vocal advocate of independence by 1835. His activities during the revolt materially assisted the Texan victory. It had been his intention to retire from public life after the success of the revolt. He had earlier selected a picturesque, unsettled location—on the lower Colorado River in Texas—as the site for his home. It is fitting that the modern city of Austin, the state capital, occupies that location. It is there Stephen Fuller Austin rests, in the State Cemetery.

Bibliography

Barker, Eugene C. *The Life of Stephen F. Austin, Founder of Texas, 1793-1836: A Chapter in the Westward Movement of the Anglo-American*

People. Nashville: Cokesbury Press, 1925. Standard scholarly biography from original sources, mainly the Austin family papers. This is the most detailed and complete study of Austin and his impact on American history. It is the only full-length biography and provides a solid history of the entire Austin colony.

_____. "Stephen F. Austin." In *Handbook of Texas*, vol. 1, edited by Walter P. Webb. Austin: University of Texas Press, 1952. Provides highlights of Austin's career in a short biography. It offers a concise, short treatment of Austin's life in a factual manner.

_____, ed. *The Austin Papers*. 3 vols. Washington, D.C.: American Historical Association, 1919-1926. Collection of personal papers and letters of Moses and Stephen F. Austin. Covers the early years of the Austin family in Missouri, with the major part of the collection dealing with the period from 1822 to 1836.

Cantrell, Gregg. "The Partnership of Stephen F. Austin and Joseph H. Hawkins." *Southwestern Historical Quarterly* 99, no. 1 (July, 1995).

Glascock, Sallie. *Dreams of Empire: The Story of Stephen Fuller Austin and His Colony in Texas*. San Antonio, Tex.: Naylor, 1951. Well-written biography designed for the general reader or for young readers. Good starting place for those unfamiliar with Austin's life.

Holley, Mary Austin. *Texas: Observations, Historical, Geographical, and Descriptive*. Baltimore: Armstrong and Plaskett, 1833. Holley was Austin's cousin. Provides a firsthand account of life and events in the colony and useful insights into the Austin settlement.

Tracy, Milton, and Richard Havelock-Bailie. *The Colonizer: A Saga of Stephen F. Austin*. El Paso, Tex.: Guynes Printing Co., 1941. Concentrates on the *empresario* career. Makes few improvements on the Barker biography of Austin but is a solid, general assessment of Austin's life, placing him in historical perspective.

Light Townsend Cummins

THOMAS HART BENTON

Born: March 14, 1782; near Hillsboro, North Carolina
Died: April 10, 1858; Washington, D.C.

A prominent United States senator from 1821 to 1851, Benton was a great champion of Western expansion, public land distribution, and "hard money." He was a leading supporter of President Andrew Jackson and his policies.

Early Life

Thomas Hart Benton, the son of Jesse and Ann Gooch Benton, was born near Hillsboro, North Carolina, in 1782. His father was a lawyer who had been a secretary to the British governor of Colonial North Carolina, a member of that state's legislature, and a speculator in Western lands. His mother was reared by her uncle, Thomas Hart, a prominent Virginia political and military leader with extensive wealth in land. Another uncle of Ann Gooch had been a British governor of Virginia.

Although his father died when he was eight, Benton's mother was able to keep the large family together. He attended local grammar schools and in 1798 enrolled at the recently established University of North Carolina, but was forced to leave in disgrace after one year when he was expelled for having stolen money from his three roommates. When he was nineteen, his mother moved the family of eight children and several slaves to a large tract of land south of Nashville, Tennessee, which had been claimed by Jesse Benton prior to his death. After three years on the family farm, young Benton left to teach school and study law. In 1806, he was admitted to the Tennessee bar and rather quickly became a successful attorney whose philosophy and practice reflected the rural frontier environment. Benton specialized in land cases, and he began to pursue the reform of the Tennessee judicial system, an issue that helped him to a seat in the state senate and wide recognition.

During the War of 1812, Benton joined Andrew Jackson in raising volunteers for the military effort against England. For this work he received an appointment as a colonel of a regiment, but Jackson apparently did not trust him enough to place him in a field command, and Benton therefore saw no action in the war. In 1813, Benton's relationship with Jackson was interrupted by a wild tavern fight in which his brother, Jesse Benton, was severely stabbed, Jackson was shot, and Thomas Benton was cut with a knife and either pushed or thrown down a flight of stairs.

In the fall of 1815, when Benton was thirty-three years of age, he moved to Missouri Territory, settling in the small riverfront village of St. Louis. He rapidly involved himself in the affairs of the city. Between 1815 and 1820, he established an active law practice, ran for local political offices, bought a house and property to which he relocated his mother and family, killed another St. Louis attorney in a duel, and for two years served as the editor of the *St. Louis Enquirer*. At this point in his life, he was clearly an imposing figure who seldom backed away from a quarrel or a fight. He was a large and physically powerful person with a wide and muscular upper body, a large head, a short, thick neck, and wide shoulders. He possessed a long nose, high forehead, and dark, wavy hair which was often worn long in the back and at the temples.

Benton used the pages of the *St. Louis Enquirer* to address current political issues. He concentrated upon the development of the West, banking and currency, and national land distribution policies, and he vigorously advanced Missouri statehood. By 1820, he was clearly established as a leader in Missouri politics. When Missouri entered the Union as a result of the great compromise of 1820, David Barton and Thomas Hart Benton were selected to represent the new state in the United States Senate.

Life's Work
After a four-week horseback ride from St. Louis, Benton reached Washington, D.C., in mid-November of 1820 to begin a celebrated thirty-year career in the Senate. En route to the capital, he stopped at the Cherry Grove Plantation, near Lexington, Virginia, and proposed marriage to Elizabeth McDowell, whom he had met in 1815. She accepted the offer and the marriage took place in March of 1821.

Once in the Senate, Benton moved quickly to an active involvement in national issues. He first pressed forward those items with a Missouri base and about which he had written in the *St. Louis Enquirer*: the opening of government mineral lands, the development of the Oregon country, federal support of the Western fur trade, and the revision of the national land distribution policy. In the early months of 1824, he introduced two proposals which became closely identified with him and which he would continue to promote throughout his senatorial career: the elimination of the electoral college and the graduated land distribution system. In the former, his goal was to amend the Constitution so that the president and vice president could be directly elected by the people; in the latter, he pursued legislation to reduce the price of public lands by twenty-five cents per acre per year until the land was available at no cost. This practice, he argued, not only would broaden the base of the new democratic system but also would effectively serve to increase the prosperity of the entire nation.

As a result of the controversies surrounding the presidential election of 1824, Benton and Jackson established a close personal and political relationship as a result of which the Missouri senator was elevated to a leadership position in the Democratic Party. When Jacksonian Democracy carried Jackson into the presidency in 1828, Benton became the leading Jacksonian in the Senate and one of the most powerful men in American government in the first half of the nineteenth century. He was often mentioned as a possible candidate for the presidency himself, but he quickly rejected such promotion. As a member of Jackson's famous Kitchen Cabinet, he led the fight to oppose the rechartering of the Bank of the United States and successfully expunged from the record the Senate resolution censuring Jackson for his role in the famous bank struggle. Benton also became the most ardent champion of hard-money policies—that is, those favoring a money system based upon the circulation of gold and silver only. It was his view that such a policy would best serve the common people, as paper currency was too easily manipulated by people of privilege. To this end, he prepared Jackson's famous 1836 Specie Circular, which required that public land purchases be made only with gold or silver coin. Because of his dedication to this issue, he received the nickname "Old Bullion."

Benton also played a key role in the Texas and Oregon annexation controversies. Although he was an ardent expansionist and Westerner, he opposed the acquisition of Texas in 1845 out of concern that it was unfair to Mexico and would lead to war between the two new nations. He was successful in his efforts to establish the northern boundary of Oregon at the forty-ninth latitude rather than the 54-40 line favored by many Americans in 1844 and 1845. His position on these two issues lost him much support in his home state, and he only narrowly won reelection to the Senate in 1844. In spite of his opposition to the Texas annexation and resulting war with Mexico, Benton supported the American war effort and served as chairman of the Senate Military Affairs Committee and as an important military adviser to President James K. Polk. In fact, Polk, who was suspicious of the leading field generals who were members of the Whig Party, extended to Benton the unprecedented position of joint military-diplomatic leader of the American war effort with a rank of major general. Benton considered the offer but rejected it when he could not receive from Polk the pledge of authority that he believed should cohere to such a position.

The American victory in the Mexican War and the subsequent annexation of vast new territories raised the issue of slavery to the forefront of the national political scene in 1848-1850. Although Benton was a slaveholder all of his adult life, he opposed slavery's expansion and expressed contempt for both secessionists and abolitionists. He reacted vigorously to John C. Calhoun's resolutions for noninterference with slavery in the new territories and was angered by the Missouri legislature's 1849 endorsement of the action. The Missouri resolutions assumed a strong proslavery position and directed the two Missouri senators to act accordingly. Benton spent most of 1849 in Missouri campaigning against this legislative policy and directive, and conducted a statewide speaking tour in an effort to reverse the action. This was a turbulent affair marked by name-calling, charges, counter-charges, and threats of violence.

The 1850 session of the United States Senate was one of the most famous in its history. For Thomas Hart Benton, it was one of the most crucial. He was a vigorous opponent of the slavery sections of the great compromise of that year as he believed there was too much sympathy for proslavery interests and secessionist threats. His rhetoric of opposition to Henry Clay's resolutions was direct and critical and elicited a strong response from Southern senators. On one occasion, Senator Henry S. Foote of Mississippi drew and aimed a loaded revolver at the Missouri senator on the Senate floor. Benton's strong and highly publicized opposition to sections of the 1850 compromise left him with a severely weakened political base at home, and when the Missouri legislature in January of 1851 moved to the senatorial election, Benton lost to the Whig and anti-Benton candidate Henry S. Geyer, bringing his thirty-year Senate career to a close.

Frustrated by his defeat in the Missouri legislature for reelection to the Senate, the sixty-nine-year-old Benton launched a campaign for election to the House of Representatives. Few people have ever pursued a House of Representatives seat with as much to prove as Benton did in 1852—and, for the moment, victory was his. From 1853 to 1854, he returned to Congress as a member of the House of Representatives, where he took the lead in opposing the Kansas-Nebraska Act as well as all other attempts to extend slavery into the territories. Because of his determined position on this issue, he lost further support in his home state, and his effort to win reelection to the House seat failed in 1854. Undaunted by this reversal, he developed an unsuccessful campaign for the governorship of Missouri in 1856 and worked nationally for the election of James Buchanan and the Democratic Party, refusing to vote for John C. Frémont, who headed the newly formed and sectional Republican Party, even though Frémont was his son-in-law, having married his daughter, Jessie.

With his political defeats in 1854 and 1856 and the death of his wife in 1854, Benton retired to his Washington, D.C., home to work on a number of writing projects. He continued an active schedule of appearances at political rallies and public speeches. He published a large two-volume summary of his thirty-year Senate career in 1854-1856, a sixteen-volume *Abridgement of the Debates of Congress from 1789 to 1856* (1857-1861), and a historical and legal examination of the Dred Scott decision, *Examination of the Dred Scott Case* (1857). His work in this direction was hampered by the increasing pain and complications of cancer and a fire that destroyed his home and personal records. The final page of his collection of the debates in Congress was completed on April 9, 1858. He died early the next morning, April 10, 1858, at the age of seventy-six. His wife and two sons had preceded him in death; four daughters survived.

Summary

Thomas Hart Benton reflects, in many ways, the character and nature of America in the first half of the nineteenth century. An Easterner who became a Westerner, he was tough, bold, aggressive, egotistical, talkative, shrewd, self-educated, and fiercely independent. He found his career and gained a reputation on the frontier. He moved easily into law, banking, land investment, newspapers, the military, and politics.

He extolled the strength and virtues of the common man in a society struggling with the issue of whether the elite or the common man should govern. As a leading proponent of Jacksonian democracy, Benton became the voice of union, a supporter of nationalism in an age of nationalism, and a builder of the nation in an era of change.

Benton believed that the great American West held the promise of the American future. He pressed for the development of the area from Missouri to Oregon and California and believed this region would provide unparalleled opportunity for the common man and unparalleled prosperity for the nation. To this end, more than anyone in American history, Benton stands as the champion of cheap land, developing policies and procedures that anticipated the great homestead movement later in the century.

To remove the benefits of privilege in a democratic society, he fought vigorously against the use of paper currency. It was his view that a financial system based upon the use of specie would protect "the people" from exploitation by people of influence. He was, thus, the leader of Jackson's war against the Bank of the United States and was the author of Jackson's famous and controversial Specie Circular.

In order to advance the cause of Union and American nationalism, Benton sought to suppress the issue of slavery on the national political scene. He believed that this could best be accomplished by preventing the extension of slavery into the territories. His great emphasis upon this may have had much to do with keeping Missouri in the Union when the great crisis of nationalism came in 1861.

Bibliography
Benton, Thomas Hart. *Thirty Years' View: Or, A History of the Working of the American Government for Thirty Years, from 1820 to 1850*. 2 vols. New York: D. Appleton and Co., 1854-1856. An autobiographical summary of Benton's senatorial career. A valuable political commentary for insight into Benton and all American politics of the era.
Chambers, William Nisbet. *Old Bullion Benton: Senator from the New West*. Boston: Little, Brown and Co., 1956. A well-researched biography of Benton based upon extensive manuscript material. Follows Benton's life in chronological order and provides numerous quotations from his speeches and writings. This is the most widely used biography of Benton.

Doss, Erika Lee. *Benton, Pollock, and the Politics of Modernism: From Regionalism to Abstract Expressionism.* Chicago: University of Chicago Press, 1991.

Kennedy, John F. *Profiles in Courage.* New York: Harper and Brothers, 1955. This well-known book contains a laudatory chapter on Benton, clearly emphasizing his great individualism and political independence. Kennedy finds Benton's opposition to the extension of slavery in the face of Missouri's perspective to be a courageous act of principle.

Meigs, William M. *The Life of Thomas Hart Benton.* Philadelphia: J. B. Lippincott Co., 1904. An early biography of Benton that depends much upon Benton's autobiography and the memoirs of his brilliant daughter Jessie and her husband John C. Frémont. Now outdated by the research of Chambers and Smith.

Oliver, Robert T. *History of Public Speaking in America.* Boston: Allyn and Bacon, 1965. A good analysis of Benton's oratorical skills with several examples of his most striking comments and most famous speeches. Incorporates the observations from several doctoral and masters' analyses of Benton's speaking methods.

Roosevelt, Theodore. *Thomas Hart Benton.* Boston: Houghton Mifflin Co., 1900. A biography in the American Statesmen series by President Theodore Roosevelt. Badly dated but reflects the interpretation of Benton held at the end of the nineteenth century. Roosevelt viewed Benton not as a great intellect but as a person unique for his hard work, determination, and speaking abilities.

Smith, Elbert B. *Francis Preston Blair.* New York: Macmillan Publishing Co., 1980. An excellent biography of Francis Blair, who was a Jacksonian editor and close personal friend of Benton. Provides good insight into Benton from the perspective of his closest friend and friendly biographer.

_____. *Magnificent Missourian: The Life of Thomas Hart Benton.* Philadelphia: J. B. Lippincott Co., 1958. A very well-written biography of Benton based exclusively upon manuscript and original sources. Provides excellent coverage of Benton's senatorial career and his role on the national political scene. Especially good coverage of Benton's role in the bank war.

Frank Nickell

JAMES G. BLAINE

Born: January 31, 1830; West Brownsville, Pennsylvania
Died: January 27, 1893; Washington, D.C.

Blaine was the most popular Republican politician of the late nineteenth century. Through his personal appeal and his advocacy of the protective tariff, he laid the basis for the emergence of the Republican Party as the majority party in the 1890's.

Early Life

James Gillespie Blaine was born January 31, 1830, in West Brownsville, Pennsylvania. His father, Ephraim Lyon Blaine, came from a Scotch-Irish and Scotch-Presbyterian background. Blaine's mother, Maria Louise Gillespie, was an Irish Catholic. Blaine was reared a Presbyterian, as were his brothers, while his sisters followed their mother's faith. In later life, Blaine became a Congregationalist but was tolerant of all creeds and avoided the religious issue in politics. Blaine's maternal background gave him an electoral appeal to Irish-Catholic voters.

Ephraim Blaine was a lawyer who was elected to a county clerk position in Washington County, Pennsylvania, in 1842. His son entered Washington and Jefferson College, a small school in the area, and was graduated in 1847. Blaine then taught at the Western Military Institute in Georgetown, Kentucky, from 1848 to 1851. He admired the policies of Henry Clay, the Whig leader, during his stay in the state. He also found time to court and then marry a teacher at a woman's seminary, Harriet Stanwood, on June 30, 1850. Leaving Kentucky in late 1851, Blaine taught at the Pennsylvania Institute for the Blind from 1852 to 1854. He also pursued legal studies while in Philadelphia.

Mrs. Blaine's family had connections in Maine. When a vacancy occurred for editor of the *Kennebec Journal* in 1853, her husband was asked to take over the management of this Whig newspaper. Money from his brothers-in-law helped this arrangement succeed. By November, 1854, Blaine was at work in Augusta, Maine, as a newspaperman, not a lawyer. His growing family eventually reached seven children, four of whom outlived their father. From this point onward, he became known as Blaine of Maine.

Over the next decade, Blaine became identified with the young Republican Party in his adopted state. He was elected to the Maine legislature in 1858, was reelected three times, and became Speaker of the House of Representatives during his last two terms. He was named chairman of the Republican State Committee in 1859, a post he held for two decades. Blaine attended the Republican National Convention in 1860 as a delegate. In 1862, he was elected to the United States Congress and took his seat in the House of Representatives in 1863.

As he entered the national scene at the age of thirty-three, Blaine had already shown himself to be a gifted politician. He had a charismatic quality that caused some who knew him to be loyal to him for life, becoming "Blainiacs." His speeches were received enthusiastically in an age that admired oratory. Blaine knew American politics intimately and could remember faces and election results with uncanny accuracy. Yet there was another side to him. His health and temperament were uncertain, and his illnesses often came at moments of crisis. In his private affairs, Blaine gained wealth without having a secure income, and he would not reveal information about his finances to the public. Enemies said that he was corrupt. That went too far, but he lacked, as did many of his contemporaries, a clear sense of what constituted a conflict of interest. In fact, James G. Blaine was a diverse blend of good and bad qualities—a truth reflected in the Gilded Age quip that men went insane about him in pairs, one for, and one against.

Life's Work

Blaine spent thirteen years in the House of Representatives, serving as its Speaker between 1869 and 1875. He was a moderate on the issues of the Civil War and Reconstruction, endorsing black suffrage and a strong policy toward the South without being labeled as a "radical." He became known as a "Half-Breed" in contrast to such "Stalwarts" as New York's Roscoe Conkling. Blaine and Conkling clashed on the House floor in April, 1866. His description of Conkling as having a "majestic, supereminent turkey-gobbler strut" opened a personal and political wound that never healed for the egotistic Conkling. His opposition proved disastrous to Blaine's presidential chances in 1876 and 1880.

By 1876, Blaine had left the House of Representatives to serve in the Senate. He was a leading candidate for the Republican presidential nomination in that year. Then a public controversy arose over whether Blaine had acted corruptly in helping to save a land grant for an Arkansas railroad in 1869. The facts about favors done and favors repaid were allegedly contained in a packet of documents known as the Mulligan Letters, named for the man who possessed them. The letters came into Blaine's hands, he read from them to the House, and his friends said that he had vindicated himself. Enemies charged that the papers proved his guilt, and the reform element of the time never forgave him.

Shortly before the Republican convention, Blaine fell ill. Nevertheless, his name was placed in nomination as Robert G. Ingersoll called him the "Plumed Knight" of American politics. The Republican delegates decided that Blaine was too controversial to win, and they turned instead to Rutherford B. Hayes of Ohio. Four years later, after Hayes's single term, Blaine led the opposition to a third term for Ulysses S. Grant and again was seen as a contender for the nomination. Blaine was more interested in his party's success than in his own advancement in 1880, and he was pleased when James A. Garfield of Ohio became the compromise nominee. In the fall campaign, Blaine stumped widely for the national ticket and developed the arguments for the protective tariff that he would advance in the 1880's.

After Garfield's narrow victory, he asked Blaine to be his secretary of state. In his first brief tenure at the State Department, Blaine pursued his concern for a canal across Central America, the fostering of Pan-American sentiment, and greater trade for the nation. Garfield's assassination in the summer of 1881 ended his presidency and led to Blaine's resignation at the end of the year. The administration of Chester A. Arthur that followed did not cut into Blaine's popularity with the Republican rank and file. He received the Republican nomination on the first ballot in 1884. John A. Logan of Illinois was his running mate.

Blaine wanted to make the protective tariff the central theme of his race against the nominee of the Democrats, Grover Cleveland, the governor of New York. Instead the campaign turned on the personal character of the two candidates. Republicans stressed Cleveland's admission that he had had an affair with a woman who had given birth to an illegitimate son. Democrats attacked the legal validity of Blaine's marriage and revived the charges of the Mulligan Letters. These sensational aspects overshadowed Blaine's campaign tour, one of the first by a presidential aspirant. The election was close as the voting neared. All accounts of the election of 1884 note that on October 29, Blaine heard the Reverend Samuel Burchard say in New York that the Democrats were the party of "rum, Romanism, and rebellion." These words supposedly alienated Catholic voters, swung New York to the Democrats, and thus cost Blaine the victory. This episode, however, has been given too much importance. In fact, Blaine improved on Garfield's vote in the state and ran stronger than his party. The significance of 1884 was not that Blaine lost in a Democratic year but that he revived the Republicans and laid the groundwork for the party's victory in 1888.

Over the next four years, Blaine continued to speak out for the tariff. He set the keynote for the 1888 campaign when he responded publicly to Cleveland's attacks on tariff protection in his 1887 annual message to Congress. "The Democratic Party in power is a standing menace to the prosperity of the country," he told an interviewer. Blaine stayed out of the presidential race and supported strongly the party's nominee, Benjamin Harrison of Indiana. After Harrison defeated Cleveland, it was logical that Blaine should again serve as secretary of state.

Blaine faced a variety of diplomatic issues, including Canadian fisheries and a running argument with Great Britain over fur seals in Alaska. He summoned the initial Pan-American Conference to Washington in October, 1889, sought to achieve the annexation of Hawaii, and was instrumental in obtaining reciprocal trade authority in the McKinley Tariff of 1890. In many ways Blaine foreshadowed the overseas expansion of the United States that occurred later in the decade. His working relationship with President Harrison deteriorated as the Administration progressed and Blaine's own health faltered. The death of two children in 1890 added to his personal troubles. Shortly before the Republican convention, on June 4, 1892, Blaine resigned as secretary of state. It is not clear whether Blaine was actually a candidate for the presidency this last time. He received some support when the Republican delegates met, but the incumbent Harrison easily controlled the convention and was renominated on the first ballot. Blaine made one speech for the Republicans in the 1892 race as Harrison lost to Grover Cleveland. In the last months of his life, Blaine gradually wasted away. He died of Bright's disease and a weakened heart on January 27, 1893.

Summary

When Blaine died, a fellow Republican said, "His is a fame that will grow with time." In fact, he is now largely a forgotten historical figure who is remembered only for a vague connection with "rum, Romanism, and rebellion." That impression does an injustice to one of the most popular and charismatic political leaders of the Gilded Age. Blaine embodied the diverse tendencies of the Republican Party in the formative stages of its development. In his advocacy of economic nationalism and growth, he spoke for a generation that wanted both to preserve the achievements of the Civil War and to move on to the fresh issues of industrial development. He was an important participant in the affairs of the House of Representatives in the early 1870's, and his tenure as Speaker contributed to the growing professionalism of that branch of government.

Blaine also symbolized the popular unease about the ethical standards that public servants should observe. In the Mulligan Letters episode and in his own affairs, he raised issues about conflict of interest and propriety that clouded his historical reputation. He became the epitome of the "spoilsman" who lived on patronage and influence. Blaine correctly understood these attacks as being to some degree partisan, but he failed to recognize the legitimacy of the questions that they posed.

Despite these failings, Blaine was a central figure in the evolution of the Republican Party during the 1870's and 1880's. His conviction that tariff protection offered both the hope of party success and an answer to the issue of economic growth laid the foundation for the emergence of the Republican Party as the majority party in the 1890's. In the 1884 presidential race, he improved the Republican performance and prepared the party for later success. As secretary of state, he was a constructive spokesman for the national interest. He educated his party on the tariff issue and, in so doing, fulfilled the essential function of a national political leader. For a generation of Republican leaders and voters, James G. Blaine came to stand for inspiration and commitment in politics. Although he failed to reach the presidency, Blaine was the most significant American politician of his era.

Bibliography
Blaine, James G. *Twenty Years of Congress: From Lincoln to Garfield.* 2 vols.

Norwich, Conn.: Henry Bill Publishing Co., 1884-1886. Blaine's memoir of his service in Congress does not contain any striking personal revelations.

Dodge, Mary Abigail. *The Biography of James G. Blaine.* Norwich, Conn.: Henry Bill Publishing Co., 1895. A family biography which is most useful for the many private letters of Blaine that it contains.

Morgan, H. Wayne. *From Hayes to McKinley: National Party Politics, 1877-1896.* Syracuse, N.Y.: Syracuse University Press, 1969. The best analytic treatment of American politics during the heyday of Blaine's career. Morgan is sympathetic and perceptive about Blaine's role as a Republican leader.

Muzzey, David S. *James G. Blaine: A Political Idol of Other Days.* New York: Dodd, Mead and Co., 1934. The best and most objective biography of Blaine. Argues that he was not consumed with the desire to be president.

Stanwood, Edward. *James Gillespie Blaine.* Boston: Houghton Mifflin Co., 1905. A short biography by a scholar who was related to Blaine.

Thompson, Margaret Susan. *The "Spider Web": Congress and Lobbying in the Age of Grant.* Ithaca, N.Y.: Cornell University Press, 1985. An innovative and interesting treatment of the House of Representatives and the Senate in the years when Blaine was Speaker. Reveals much about the political system in which he operated.

Tyler, Alice Felt. *The Foreign Policy of James G. Blaine.* Minneapolis: University of Minnesota Press, 1927. An older but still helpful examination of Blaine as a diplomat and shaper of American foreign policy.

Lewis L. Gould

WILLIAM E. BORAH

Born: June 29, 1865; Jasper, Illinois
Died: January 19, 1940; Washington, D.C.

For more than three decades in the United States Senate, Borah was a leading nationalist who spoke and voted courageously for his idealistic view of American democracy.

Early Life

William Edgar Borah was born on June 29, 1865, in Wayne County in southern Illinois. The seventh child in a family of ten, he grew up in a household where hard work and religious devotion were stressed. His father, William Nathan Borah, was a strict disciplinarian and lay preacher at the local Presbyterian church. His mother, Elizabeth, moderated her husband's sternness. Grammar school, reading at home, and the tedium of farm chores marked the early life of young Borah. He attended the Cumberland Presbyterian Academy at nearby Enfield but left after only one year, largely because of insufficient family finances.

At the invitation of his sister, Sue Lasley, Borah moved to Kansas to continue his education, entering the University of Kansas in the fall of 1885. He left in 1887, after contracting tuberculosis, but not before developing an interest in the history and economics courses of Professor James H. Canfield and demonstrating proficiency at debate. He studied law in the office of his brother-in-law, Ansel Lasley, passed the bar examination in September, 1887, and entered practice with Lasley in Lyons, Kansas. Both men found the legal profession less profitable as poverty spread throughout Kansas in the late 1880's; when the Lasleys moved to Chicago in 1890, Borah set out for the developing West to make his mark.

Although associated with Idaho for his entire political career, he landed in the state almost by accident. He allegedly traveled to the Northwest until his money ran out, near Boise, which he saw as a fertile area for a young lawyer. He quickly built a solid reputation there. At the age of twenty-five, Borah was powerfully built, with a thick neck, a broad face, and a deeply cleft chin which denoted honesty and forthrightness; these physical attributes, combined with his oratorical abilities and a capacity for hard work, made him a forceful figure in the courtroom. He built a large practice and a statewide reputation as a criminal lawyer before 1900; thereafter, he mainly practiced corporate law, which earned for him an annual income of thirty thousand dollars.

Borah entered Boise politics in 1891 and was chairman of the Republican State Central Committee the next year. In 1895, Borah married Mary McConnell, the daughter of the state's Republican governor, William J. McConnell, for whom Borah worked as secretary. Following his bolt from the Republican Party for William Jennings Bryan and "free silver" in 1896, Borah returned to lead Idaho's Progressive Republicans to statewide victories in 1901-1902. He campaigned for the United States Senate in 1906, as a vigorous supporter of President Theodore Roosevelt, and was selected by the state legislature early in 1907.

Before taking his seat in the Senate later that year, Borah was involved in two significant trials in Idaho; the first helped establish him as a national figure of importance, while the second threatened to end his public career as it was beginning. In the earlier case, Borah was appointed special prosecutor against William D. Haywood and two other leaders of the Western Federation of Miners, who were charged with conspiracy in the bombing death of former Governor Frank Steunenberg. While the jury voted to acquit the three, Borah was nevertheless outstanding in the fairness and clarity of his nine-hour summation for the prosecution. Borah was himself the defendant in the second case, in which he was charged with timber fraud while serving as attorney for the Barber Lumber Company. Although the incident was an ordeal for Borah, the evidence presented against him at the trial was flimsy, substantiating his charge that the affair was devised by his enemies to kill his political future. The jury acquitted him after less than fifteen minutes of deliberation. He was now free to assume the office in Washington which he would hold through five more elections, until he died.

Life's Work

Borah entered the Senate at a favorable time. The Progressive viewpoint was ascendant in national political affairs, and Borah was closely aligned with the Senate Progressive bloc on a number of issues. Furthermore, he was especially fortunate in being in a position to act, since Senate leader Nelson W. Aldrich assumed that Borah's former position as a corporate attorney meant that he shared Aldrich's pro-business, anti-labor outlook; consequently, Aldrich assigned Borah to choice committee appointments, including the chairmanship of the Committee on Education and Labor.

It was mainly during his first term that Borah earned his reputation for Progressive leadership. He sponsored bills for the creation of the Department of Labor and a Children's Bureau, and pushed for an eight-hour day for government-contracted labor. In addition, he was a mainstay in the fight for the direct election of United States Senators (which became the Seventeenth Amendment in 1913) and for the income tax (the Sixteenth Amendment, 1913). In the latter struggle, his major early contribution was his effective argument for the constitutionality of the income tax, contrary to the Supreme Court's finding in an 1895 case.

Borah also proved to be an effective representative of Idaho and other Western states on several key issues. He favored President William Howard Taft's proposal for a reciprocal trade agreement between the United States and Canada, involving free trade in some raw materials and agricultural products, an agreement favored by Western farmers. (The agreement passed in Congress but failed in the Canadian legislature.) He successfully promoted a plan for government-issued reclamation bonds, mainly used to finance irrigation projects in the Western states. He was the cosponsor of the Borah-Jones Act (1912), which reduced, from five years to three years, the period required for residence before homesteaders could acquire patents to the land they claimed. Finally, he managed to free, for private development, some Western land which the federal government had set aside for conservation.

Borah was not included in the roll call of other Progressives on all these issues, especially in regard to conservation matters. He was critical of the federal government's administration of conservation policy, believing that the individual states should play a greater role. In the *cause célèbre* over Interior Secretary Richard Ballinger's removal of Chief Forester Gifford Pinchot, Borah broke with the Progressives in supporting Ballinger and the Taft Administration; he also supported the Administration on the controversial Payne-Aldrich Tariff. In the election of 1912, Borah led the Theodore Roosevelt forces in the National Republican Convention but refused to bolt from the Republican Party when Roosevelt's followers formed the Progressive Party. During Woodrow Wilson's first term, Borah continued to be a selective Progressive, as he voted against legislation such as the Federal Trade Commission Act, the Clayton Antitrust Act, and the creation of the Federal Reserve system. Although opposition to some of these bills was based on partisan political considerations, Borah generally opposed federal centralization and often referred to states' rights in explaining his votes against measures supported by other Progressives.

Borah began to change the focus of his interests to international affairs with the onset of World War I; in the decades following the war, he became the acknowledged Senate spokesman on foreign policy for his party. He supported preparation for war in 1916, backed Wilson's breaking of diplomatic relations with Germany in February, 1917, and voted for the declaration of war in April. Like other Progressives, however, he became disillusioned with the war effort, which severely limited reform achievements, and stated that, if it were possible, he would change the vote he had cast in favor of war. At the end of World War I, he led the Senate irreconcilables in the fight against the Treaty of Versailles and the League of Nations, stating that it was not in the best interests of the United States to become entangled in the affairs of Europe.

As a nationalist in foreign affairs, Borah opposed any international agreements that would restrict the country's freedom of choice to act in world affairs. While he opposed American membership in the World Court as well as in the League of Nations, he was a strong proponent of disarmament plans. He was instrumental in organizing the Washington conference on disarmament in 1921 and, as Chairman of the Senate Committee on Foreign Relations after 1924, he supported plans for the international outlawry of war, which culminated in the Kellogg-Briand Pact of 1928. In the face of the international crises of the 1930's, Borah became increasingly isolationist, favoring the restriction of American trade and diplomatic involvement abroad.

Borah differed with the Republican Party on major political issues during the 1920's, but he refused to leave the party in 1924 to support his longtime political ally, Robert M. LaFollette, the Progressive Party candidate for president. He was a leading campaigner for Herbert Hoover in 1928, although he became a consistent critic of Hoover policies after the election. He supported most of the major legislation of the New Deal, with the exception of the National Industrial Recovery Act, which he criticized for its suspension of antitrust laws. Following his sixth consecutive election to the Senate, in 1936, he concentrated most of his energy on opposing the foreign policies of Franklin D. Roosevelt's administration. In January, 1940, he suffered a cerebral hemorrhage and died three days later. Following a funeral in the Senate chamber, he was buried in Boise.

Summary

In 1936, journalist Walter Lippmann wrote a trenchant description of Senator Borah as "an individualist who opposes all concentration of power, who is against private privilege and private monopoly, against political bureaucracy and centralized government." Lippmann was describing Borah the Jeffersonian Democrat, who believed in an ideal vision of the United States, with a relatively uncomplicated political system based on direct democracy, with guarantees for the freewheeling expression of rights by the individual, and without favoritism for special interests. These were the essential beliefs of Borah's political life, formed in his youth by family guidance and by reading authors such as Ralph Waldo Emerson, reinforced by his rural environment in Illinois, Kansas, and Idaho, and forged by his contacts with the Populists in the 1890's. Such beliefs formed the underpinnings of Borah's Progressive leadership.

Borah attempted to apply these principles throughout his public career. In his speeches and actions, he made it clear that his conscience and convictions served as his guide on major national issues, rather than considerations of party loyalty or personal popularity. In writing to a constituent about his religious ideals in opposition to the Ku Klux Klan, Borah averred, "If the time ever comes when I shall have to sacrifice my office for these principles, I shall unhesitatingly do so."

Borah's idealistic conception of the United States, while not always based on a realistic appraisal of modern conditions, influenced the nation during his career in the Senate because of his brilliance as an orator. He shared the belief of many other Progressives in the power of public opinion as a moral force and sought to mobilize that force through scores of well-researched and well-rehearsed addresses in Congress and the nation. His oratorical abilities, as well as the courageous pursuit of his convictions, placed him in the front rank of public men of his time.

Bibliography

Ashby, LeRoy. *The Spearless Leader: Senator Borah and the Progressive Movement in the 1920's.* Urbana: University of Illinois Press, 1972. Treats Borah's involvement in domestic affairs from 1920 to 1928, while most other accounts concentrate only on his foreign policy views as chairman of the Senate Committee on Foreign Relations. Valuable not only for Borah's viewpoints but also as a consideration of the fate of Progressivism in the 1920's.

Borah, William Edgar. *Bedrock: Views on Basic National Problems.* Washington, D.C.: National Home Library Foundation, 1936. Includes speeches and a few articles from 1909 to 1936, organized by topic. Introduces the reader to the flavor of Borah's speeches on a wide range of topics and presents Borah's viewpoints on what he considered to be paramount issues.

Cooper, John M., Jr. "William E. Borah, Political Thespian." *Pacific Northwest Quarterly* 56 (October, 1965): 145-153. A stimulating discussion of Borah's career, in which the author maintains that Borah's decision to deliver moral exhortations on issues, rather than to take bolder actions in the Senate, limited his effectiveness in public life. The article is followed with comments by two other Borah scholars and a reply by Cooper.

Godfrey, Donald G., and Val E. Limburg. "The Rogue Elephant of Radio Legislation: Senator William E. Borah." *Journalism Quarterly* 67, no. 1 (Spring, 1990): 214-225.

Horowitz, David A. "Senator Borah's Crusade to Save Small Business from the New Deal." *Historian* 55, no. 4 (Summer, 1993): 693-709.

Johnson, Claudius O. *Borah of Idaho.* New York: Longmans, Green and Co., 1936. Reprint. Seattle: University of Washington Press, 1967. The reprint edition includes a section on Borah's last years and the author's reevaluation of his career. Based largely on interviews with Borah, as well as the Borah papers, the book is thorough (to 1936) but often partial in its advocacy of Borah's views.

McKenna, Marian C. *Borah*. Ann Arbor: University of Michigan Press, 1961. The most complete and balanced biography of Borah. A well-written book, it is based, in part, on papers relating to Borah's early career, which the Idaho State Historical Society received in 1956.

Maddox, Robert James. *William E. Borah and American Foreign Policy*. Baton Rouge: Louisiana State University Press, 1969. Evaluates Borah's positions on major foreign policy issues from World War I until the eve of World War II. Maddox asserts that Borah's seemingly paradoxical (for an isolationist) interest in international conferences and treaties was actually a smoke screen for obstructing meaningful United States involvement in international organizations.

Vinson, John Chalmers. *William E. Borah and the Outlawry of War*. Athens: University of Georgia Press, 1957. Treats Borah's growing interest, from 1917, in the movement to "outlaw" war, which resulted in the 1928 Kellogg-Briand Pact. A thoroughly documented account based primarily on Borah's papers in the Library of Congress.

Richard G. Frederick

WILLIAM BRADFORD

Born: March, 1590; Austerfield, England
Died: May 19, 1657; Plymouth, Massachusetts

Bradford was the leader of the Pilgrims once they settled in America, and he was the author of a history of Plymouth colony, one of the great works of early American literature.

Early Life

William Bradford was born in March, 1590 (baptized on March 29), at Austerfield, Yorkshire, England, one of three children and the only son of William Bradford, a yeoman farmer, and Alice Hanson. His father died when he was sixteen months old. Upon his mother's remarriage when Bradford was four, he was put into the custody of his grandfather, after whose death in 1596 he went to live with his uncles, Robert and Thomas Bradford. "Like his ancestors," William Bradford pursued "the affairs of husbandry." At age twelve, Bradford started attending religious services conducted by Richard Clyfton, at Babworth, eight miles from Austerfield. The group was made up of Separatists, who believed in the sovereign authority of the Scriptures and the autonomy of each church. The Separatists had spun off from the Puritan movement, which sought reform toward greater simplicity in the worship and practices of the Church of England. When Clyfton's own congregation split, he took part of the original group to hold services at the bishop's manor house in Scrooby. William Brewster, who became a mentor and tutor for Bradford, was the local bailiff and postmaster and resided at the bishop's decaying mansion. John Robinson, who later would be the leader of the group when they went to Holland, was teacher of the congregation. Bradford had only to walk three miles to attend services at Scrooby, which was in Nottinghamshire, 150 miles north of London.

The Scrooby Separatists, completely at odds with the national church and fearing further persecution after King James I ascended the throne, sought refuge in the Netherlands. Failing in their first attempt to leave England in 1607, having been betrayed by the ship's captain, the following year via a Dutch vessel they went to Amsterdam, where they stayed briefly, and then moved to the university town of Leyden. The Netherlands offered the refugees full freedom of conscience. Their new home proved a relief, as Bradford said, from the situation which the Pilgrims (as they were to be called) had faced in England, where they were "hunted and persecuted on every side, so that their former afflictions were but as flea-bitings in comparison of those which now came upon them."

At Leyden the Pilgrims worked as artisans, with Bradford becoming a maker of fustian (a twilled cloth of cotton and linen). While in Leyden, Bradford learned some Latin and Hebrew. Coming of age in 1611, he gained an inheritance from his uncles, which he applied to buying a house; he also became a Dutch citizen. In December, 1613, Bradford married Dorothy May. The Pilgrims were unhappy in their new home for a variety of reasons, but chiefly for that of being an alien people in a strange land. In 1617, Bradford was one of a committee to make arrangements to take the congregation to America.

With the expedition financed by a joint stock company formed by English merchants and a patent from the Virginia Company (which was invalid because of where the Pilgrims had settled and was replaced a year later with one from the Council of New England), the Pilgrims set out for America. Shares in the company were ten pounds each, with an actual settler receiving one free. Bradford was among the 102 persons who crossed the Atlantic in the *Mayflower*, and was a signer of the Mayflower Compact in November of 1620 as the ship anchored off the tip of Cape Cod. This document, as John Quincy Adams observed, was "the first example in modern times of a social compact or system of government instituted by voluntary agreement conformably to the laws of nature, by men of equal rights and about to establish their community in a new country." Bradford led exploring parties, and the colonists chose a site at what is now Plymouth, Massachusetts. On December 17, 1620 (N.S.), Bradford's wife fell overboard and drowned, possibly a suicide. In August, 1623, he married Alice Carpenter, widow of Edward Southworth.

Life's Work
Upon the death of John Carver in 1621, William Bradford was elected governor of the colony, remaining in that office until his death in 1657, with the exception of the years 1633 to 1634, 1636, 1638, and 1644. He

received no salary until 1639, when he was paid twenty pounds annually. Bradford virtually dominated the colony's government, which had no standing under English law and had no charter from the king. Bradford, however, shared executive, legislative, and judicial powers with a court of assistants, which by the 1640's numbered eight people. The governor and assistants were elected annually by the freemen at large. Beginning in 1638, legislative powers were divided with a lower house of two representatives from each town, starting with those from Plymouth town, Duxbury, and Scituate. Bradford assisted in the codification of the Plymouth laws in 1636, significant as the first such embodiment of statutes in the Colonies, also noteworthy for setting forth basic rights.

Bradford and his colony faced many hardships. The people who emigrated to the settlement were poor, and for the most part the land was of poor quality. Lacking means for capital investment, the Pilgrims made little progress in establishing shipping and fishing industries. For a while they enjoyed success in the fur trade, but had to compete with the Dutch, the French, and the English in that pursuit. The colony struggled to pay off its indebtedness. Bradford, realizing that the communal system discouraged initiative, had it abandoned in 1623. In 1627, he and seven other colonists and four Londoners associated as "Undertakers" to pay off the eighteen-hundred-pound debt to the English members of the joint stock company, which was now dissolved. Bradford and the other "Undertakers" were given a monopoly of the fur trade and offshore fishing. Still, it was not until the 1640's that the debt was paid. Also at the time of dissolving the connection with the English merchants, all property in the colony, real and personal, was divided equally among heads of families and free single men.

Bradford and the Pilgrims fortunately had scant troubles with the Indians. The Patuxet Indians, who had lived in the vicinity of Plymouth town, had died off from the white man's diseases, principally the plague (typhus) brought over by English fishermen. Two Indians, Samoset and Squanto, who had themselves been to Great Britain and spoke the English language, served at the outset as a vital liaison with other Indians. Bradford was successful in keeping the friendship of Massasoit, chief of the Wampanoags, the only strong tribe in close proximity to the colony.

Indeed, though troops were mustered on several occasions to be sent against the Indians (for example, during the Pequot War of 1637), the colony under Bradford's administration contended with no large Indian hostility. Miles Standish's butchery of several Massachusetts Indians at Wessagusett can, however, be charged to Bradford's blame.

Amazingly, the latitude of freedom at Plymouth was great, in contrast to the Puritan colonies. At first seeking to oust dissenters, Bradford came to favor a policy of tolerance, allowing persons of other faiths to settle in the colony. Yet Bradford was thin-skinned with those who put the Pilgrims in a bad light in England, and once, upon intercepting the letters of two such individuals, forced them to return to England. A major blotch on Bradford's career was his overreaction to the "wickedness" of the times, namely during the alleged sex-crime wave of 1642. During this brief hysteria, induced largely by anxiety over an Indian crisis, a teenager was hanged for buggery. Otherwise, to the Pilgrims' credit, there were only executions for murder. In addition to serving as governor, Bradford was a commissioner of the Puritan defensive confederation, the United Colonies of New England, in the years 1647 to 1649, 1652, and 1656.

Of Plimmoth Plantation is Bradford's masterpiece. Probably intended only for the enlightenment of his family, it was not published in its entirety until 1856. For a long time, the manuscript was lost, probably taken out of the country by a British soldier during the Revolution; it surfaced at the Bishop of London's Library at Fulham Palace. In the late nineteenth century, as a goodwill gesture, it was returned to the United States. Bradford worked on it at various times, from 1630 to 1650, writing from notes, correspondence, and memory. The history traces the whole Pilgrim story from their English exile to 1646. Other writings of Bradford include admonitory poems and two dialogues between "some Younge-men borne in New-England" and "Ancient men which came out of Holand and Old England." Bradford was also the coauthor of the promotional tract, *Mourt's Relation* (published in London, 1622), and letters, printed as *Governor Bradford's Letter Book*, in the *Collections of the Massachusetts Historical Society*, first series, volume 3 (1794; reprinted in 1968).

Besides his home in Plymouth, Bradford had a three-hundred-acre farm on the tidal Jones River and scattered real estate elsewhere, which made him the largest landowner in the colony. Bradford, during the evening of the day in which he dictated his will, died, on May 19, 1657

(N.S.). He was buried on the hills overlooking Plymouth. He left four children: John (by his first wife), William, Mercy, and Joseph.

Summary

William Bradford's life epitomized the plain and simple virtues of a people longing to be free. From yeoman farmer in England to artisan in Leyden to immigrant in a primitive land, he displayed the courage and faith of one who believed that there was a better way. With skill, a sense of fair play, and an open-mindedness, he guided his people to founding a successful community, which would eventually grow into some twenty towns. Bradford's colony was unable to secure a charter, largely because of the lack of resources needed to support a lobbying effort in England. Plymouth Colony would later be incorporated into the royal colony of Massachusetts Bay, an event that Bradford probably would not have been too happy about, considering the differences between the Puritans and the Pilgrims. While Bradford discouraged people from hiving off and forming new settlements, he himself became a suburbanite, tending his farm outside of Plymouth.

Bradford's administration brought peace and stability to Plymouth, and the Pilgrim experience in founding government served as a model for the establishment of other colonies. In Plymouth Colony, under Bradford, there was a rigid separation of church and state, as to office-holding, though between them there was a mutuality of action.

Bradford's history of Plymouth exemplifies highest standards of clarity and straightforward prose; at the same time, it is enlivened by an understated humor that belies the popular image of the Pilgrims. It is regarded as one of the major works of Colonial American literature.

Bibliography

Bartlett, Robert M. The Pilgrim Way. Philadelphia: United Church Press, 1971. Sponsored by the Pilgrim Society, Plymouth, Mass. Discusses the Pilgrims only through the early years in America. Though emphasizing the role of John Robinson and religious issues, it probes the thinking and actions of the Pilgrim leaders, including Bradford.

Bradford, William. *Of Plimmoth Plantation*. Edited by Charles P. Deane. Boston: Massachusetts Historical Society, 1856. Reprint. New York: Random House, 1952. This work has undergone a number of editions since it was first published. Samuel E. Morison's 1952 reprint with the modernized title *Of Plymouth Plantation* is the most readable of the various editions. Morison lists all the previously published editions.

Dillon, Francis. *The Pilgrims*. Garden City, N.Y.: Doubleday and Co., 1973. Popularly written but well researched, this narrative traces the Pilgrim story to the time of the death of Bradford. Views the Pilgrim experience through Bradford's eyes.

Langdon, George D., Jr. *Pilgrim Colony: A History of New Plymouth, 1620-1691*. New Haven, Conn.: Yale University Press, 1966. A scholarly and perceptive examination of the Plymouth colony until its union with Massachusetts Bay Colony. Emphasis is on the government and institutions.

Runyan, Michael G., ed. *William Bradford: The Collected Verse*. St. Paul, Minn.: John Colet Press, 1974. Contains the seven items of verse attributed to Bradford. Places the poems in their historical context and in the context of Bradford's life as well as discussing their literary qualities.

Sargent, Mark L. "William Bradford's 'Dialogue' with History." *New England Quarterly* 65, no. 3 (September, 1992): 389-422.

Shurtleff, Nathaniel B., and David Pulsifer, eds. *Records of the Colony of New Plymouth in New England*. Boston: Press of W. White, 1861. Reprint. 11 vols. New York: AMS Press, 1968. All of Bradford's service as governor can be discerned from this collection, which contains the records of the General Court (governor, assistants, and deputies). Volume 11 is a compilation of the colony's laws.

Smith, Bradford. *Bradford of Plymouth*. Philadelphia: J. B. Lippincott Co., 1951. The only full-scale biography of Bradford. It is well researched but glosses over many topics.

Westbrook, Perry D. *William Bradford*. Boston: Twayne Publishers, 1978. Examines all of Bradford's writings from the point of view of literary criticism. Contains a chronology of Bradford's life.

Willison, George F. *Saints and Strangers*. New York: Reynal and Hitchcock, 1945. This is a lively and thorough narrative of the Pilgrim experience to 1691, stressing the early years. On small points the reliability and interpretations of the author are questionable. An appendix identifies all members of the "Pilgrim Company" who arrived in the colony during the formative period.

Harry M. Ward

WILLIAM JENNINGS BRYAN

Born: March 19, 1860; Salem, Illinois
Died: July 26, 1925; Dayton, Tennessee

With his crusader's zeal for righteousness and a determination to champion the cause of the common man, Bryan used his dramatic oratorical skills to gain the leadership of the Democratic Party from 1896 to 1912. Three times he won the Democratic nomination for president, but he lost all three elections.

Early Life

William Jennings Bryan was born March 19, 1860, in Salem, Illinois. His mother, née Mariah Elizabeth Jennings, was reared as a Methodist; his father, Silas Lillard Bryan, of Scotch-Irish descent, was a devout Baptist and became a frontier lawyer, judge, and politician in south central Illinois. As a trial lawyer, Silas was known for his habit of quoting Scripture to the jury. William Jennings Bryan grew up on a large farm which his father had purchased. The nearby town of Salem had an economy based primarily on agriculture, and Bryan's roots were in an agrarian environment that valued hard work, individualism, and religious faith. Especially influential in the Salem area were those churches stressing the necessity of a conversion experience. The revivalistic emphasis of the evangelicals in southern Illinois had a profound effect on young Bryan. Indeed, in later years, he would become what one historian has described as a "political evangelist," a politician whose oratory resembled that of a revival preacher and whose political faith contained a strong moralistic tone. Bryan the politician saw himself as God's warrior sent to destroy the Philistines, and he tended to see his own political concepts as baptized in light while those of his opponents as covered with darkness.

Bryan's father sent him to Whipple Academy for two years and then to Illinois College in Jacksonville for four years, where he was graduated in 1881. During his college days, Bryan showed little interest in physical exercise or athletics, but he did demonstrate at least modest ability as a debater. For two years, he studied law in Chicago, graduating from the Union College of Law in 1883. He then returned to Jacksonville, where he practiced law from 1883 to 1887. While still a

Witness for the prosecution William Jennings Bryan, right, faces American Civil Liberties Union lawyer Clarence Darrow at the Scopes "monkey trial" in Dayton, Tennessee, in 1925. *(AP/Wide World Photos)*

struggling young lawyer, Bryan married Mary Baird on October 1, 1884. During the first month of marriage, he gave a major share of his time to the campaign to elect Grover Cleveland as president. Mary Baird Bryan defied the conventions of her time by studying law and gaining admission to the bar in 1888.

In his early years, Bryan had an excellent physique and a handsome appearance. He was six feet tall, with a strong muscular frame. His clear baritone voice was resonant and pleasing. Age, lack of exercise, and gluttonous eating habits would in later life create a more corpulent figure.

In 1887, Bryan moved to Lincoln, Nebraska, and sought to establish a law practice there, but he quickly became involved in politics. Lincoln was a rapidly growing town that could afford opportunities for a young lawyer. The staunch Republican district that included Lincoln had recently sent a Democrat to Congress. Perhaps Bryan's decision to move to Nebraska was motivated in part by hopes of getting in on the ground floor of the growing Democratic structure in Nebraska.

Life's Work

In 1890, although he lived in a normally Republican district, Bryan won election to Congress as a Democrat. His district reelected him in 1892, but in 1894, when he sought a United States Senate seat, the Nebraska legislature chose his opponent. During his congressional years, Bryan gradually espoused the Free Silver movement. Those who favored the gold standard, he believed, would force debtors to pay back their debts with a dollar more valuable than the one they borrowed. The Populist Party, silver-mining interests, farmers, and silver state Republican senators were forming a coalition to fight for a bimetallic standard. In Congress, Bryan voted against repeal of the Sherman Silver Purchase Act, and he began vociferously condemning his own Democratic president, Cleveland, who sided with the "goldbugs." After his congressional career's sudden end, Bryan intensified his prosilver lecture campaign and became the most popular orator for the cause. The silver advocates were gaining control of the Democratic Party and were turning out Cleveland's supporters.

In 1896, Bryan managed to secure an opportunity to speak before the Democratic National Convention in Chicago. In his deeply moving and moralistic "Cross of Gold" speech, he mesmerized the delegates. Speaking to the "sound money" men he laid down the challenge, "You shall not press upon the brow of labor this crown of thorns, you shall not crucify mankind upon a cross of gold." When Bryan used this closing metaphor, he dramatized the crucifixion scene by holding his fingers to his head so that his hearers actually visualized the thorns piercing the brow of the working man. When he spoke of the cross, he held his arms extended horizontally for a full five seconds as the audience sat in a transfixed and reverent silence. The hush continued until he walked off the platform: Then came a wild outburst of enthusiasm as state banners were carried to the Nebraska delegation. The next day, the convention nominated him for the presidency. The more radical agrarian People's Party (the Populists) also took him up as their presidential candidate: For them to reject Bryan would have split up the prosilver advocates in the nation and possibly ensured defeat.

During the 1896 campaign, Bryan's opponent William McKinley conducted a quiet, dignified campaign, staying at his home in Canton, Ohio. While McKinley seemed a safe, sane candidate who would not upset business conditions in the country, Bryan seemed to many a dangerous demagogue whose radical views on the currency system would destabilize the economy. Bryan traveled eighteen thousand miles by train during his campaign, speaking up to nineteen times a day and sleeping only a few hours each night. In 1896, it was not yet considered tasteful for a presidential candidate to solicit votes in such a frenetic manner. McKinley's well-organized campaign won for him the presidency.

Bryan supported McKinley's decision to go to war against Spain in 1898 in support of Cuban independence. The governor of Nebraska appointed Bryan a colonel, and the "Great Commoner" recruited a regiment, but he never succeeded in leaving his base in Florida to take a hand in the fighting. After the conflict, Bryan stood with the anti-imperialists in opposing the acquisition of the Philippine Islands. Yet surprisingly, he encouraged Democratic senators to vote for ratification of the Treaty of Paris of 1898, which gave the Philippines to the United States. Bryan believed the matter could be settled later. The next election could become a referendum on both "free silver" and "free Cuba."

In 1900, Bryan gained his party's nomination a second time. Yet the depression that had plagued Cleveland's second term (1893-1897) gave way to prosperity in McKinley's administration (1897-1901). Farm prices rose, unemployment decreased, and the amount of gold being mined increased, causing a needed moderate inflation of the currency. Since Bryan's early popularity had been based on an appeal to those who were enduring hard times, he failed to compete successfully against McKinley's "A Full Dinner Pail" slogan. Bryan received fewer votes in 1900 than he had received in 1896.

In January, 1901, Bryan began editing a weekly newspaper, the *Commoner*, and was actively involved in its publication until he became secretary of state in 1913. He also spent his years lecturing on the Chautauqua circuit. He did not seek the 1904 Democratic nomination, but in 1908 he did become the nominee and lost again, this time to William Howard Taft. Bryan's choice as the nominee demonstrated that he was once again the acknowledged leader of the Democratic Party. This leadership continued until the election of a Democratic president in 1912, Woodrow Wilson.

Wilson chose Bryan to be secretary of state primarily because of the latter's political influence within the party. As secretary of state, Bryan turned his energies toward peacemaking. He secured "conciliation treaties" between many nations, treaties which included the promise to submit differences to arbitral commissions rather than seek military solutions. When war did come to Europe in 1914, Bryan diligently sought to prevent American entry. When Wilson sent a remonstrance to Germany for sinking a passenger liner (the Second Lusitania note), Bryan resigned in protest rather than approve what he thought an overly provocative message.

In his final years (1920's), Bryan spoke on college campuses against the theory of evolution. He defended the right of taxpayers to determine what should be taught in the public schools. In Tennessee, he supported Baptists in their drive to establish an antievolution law. When John Scopes, a Tennessee high school teacher, tested the constitutionality of the law, Bryan came to Dayton, Tennessee, to argue for the prosecution. The so-called Monkey Trial was held in an almost carnival-like atmosphere and received media attention across the nation. Clarence Darrow, attorney for the defense, subjected Bryan's defense of creationism to a withering barrage of ridicule and criticism. The ordeal of the trial, the heat of summer, Bryan's unfortunate habit of overeating, along with diabetes, all hastened his death, which came only five days after the trial.

Summary

Bryan's greatest achievement was his leadership of the Democratic Party during the years 1896 to 1912. During this time, he moved the Democrats toward progressive reformism. He failed to win the presidency because he did not succeed in uniting the farmer's protest crusade and the laborer's interests into a single movement. The Democratic Party was too diverse to be controlled by a single ideology in Bryan's time. Yet Bryan did press for reforms (many inherited from the Populists and others) which became legislative and constitutional realities in the twentieth century. These include the graduated income tax, popular election of United States senators, woman's suffrage, stricter railroad regulations, currency reform, and, at the state level, adoption of the initiative and referendum.

Bryan is also remembered as a peace activist. He was almost, though not quite, a pacifist. He opposed Wilson's neutrality policy before the United States' entry into World War I as too pro-British. In

1915, he supported Henry Ford's effort to settle the European troubles by sending a peace ship to Europe with leading peace advocates aboard. He frequently gave lectures on the "Prince of Peace." He crusaded also against imperialism and the liquor traffic.

His role as an influential voice for conservative Christianity is well known. He helped the Fundamentalists win a temporary victory when they took leadership positions in the Presbyterian Church in 1924; Bryan himself became vice-moderator of the denomination. Although lacking biblical scholarship, he willingly took part in the Scopes trial, casting himself in the role of a defender of the Genesis creation story.

Bibliography

Cherny, Robert W. *A Righteous Cause: The Life of William Jennings Bryan.* Boston: Little, Brown and Co., 1985. A readable, brief biography that covers not only the life of the man but also the social and political context. A final chapter offers an evaluation of Bryan's contribution.

Clements, Kendrick A. *William Jennings Bryan: Missionary Isolationist.* Knoxville: University of Tennessee Press, 1982. Clements views Bryan as a microcosm of the average man and his foreign policy views, creating a sample of how the typical American would approach foreign affairs. He thought Bryan sought a balance between the escapism of traditional isolationism, on the one hand, and a missionary impulse to give aid, on the other.

Coletta, Paolo E. *William Jennings Bryan.* 3 vols. Lincoln: University of Nebraska Press, 1964-1969. Because of its thorough research and detailed coverage, this is the most important biography of Bryan. The title of volume 1, Political Evangelist, suggests Coletta's interpretation of Bryan. He sees him as more of a moralist than a statesman, as a humanitarian who tried to encourage others to be guided by righteousness and ethics in their conduct of economic and political affairs.

Glad, Paul W. *The Trumpet Soundeth.* Lincoln: University of Nebraska Press, 1960. This volume concentrates on the era of Bryan's Democratic Party leadership (1896-1912). It attempts to understand Bryan in the context of Midwestern society. Glad views Bryan's later years (1920-1925) as a tragic era when the "Great Commoner's" views no longer suited the intellectual climate of the United States. Yet Glad sees him, during the earlier era, as a constructive leader of the political opposition.

Koenig, Louis W. *Bryan: A Political Biography of William Jennings Bryan.* New York: G. P. Putnam's Sons, 1971. This is the most complete one-volume biography. To Koenig, Bryan's career is extremely significant because he was a champion of causes that were far advanced for his day. He fought for economic and social justice in the same manner that mid-century Democratic liberals would do later. Although Koenig views Bryan as intellectually shallow, he portrays him as a brilliant politician.

Levine, Lawrence W. *Defender of the Faith.* New York: Oxford University Press, 1965. Levine concentrates on the last decade of Bryan's career (1915-1925). The book represents an attempt to understand the "change" in Bryan from his early to later career, how he was transformed from a crusader for economic justice and social reform into an ultraconservative champion of lost causes. Levine's answer: No such change ever took place. Bryan continued to be what he had always been, a paradoxical figure, one who could champion reform and reaction at the same time.

Springen, Donald K. *William Jennings Bryan: Orator of Small-Town America.* Foreword by Halford R. Ryan. New York: Greenwood Press, 1991.

Stone, Irving. *They Also Ran.* Garden City, N.Y.: Doubleday and Co., 1943. Stone's chapter on Bryan, in a book about defeated presidential candidates, is a good example of the more negative approach to Bryan. Liberals have found it difficult to forgive Bryan for his defense of Fundamentalist Christianity. Stone's colorful chapter portrays Bryan as a psychopath, a religious fanatic, and an intellectual dolt.

Richard L. Niswonger

JAMES BUCHANAN

Born: April 23, 1791; Mercerburg, Pennsylvania
Died: June 1, 1868; Lancaster, Pennsylvania

Buchanan worked hard to preserve the Union. His presidency was devoted to trying to maintain the Democratic Party's North-South coalition.

Early Life

James Buchanan was the second child of James and Mary Buchanan, both of whom were from strong Northern Irish-Scottish Presbyterian families. The year James was born, his elder sister died, so, understandably, James received an unusual amount of attention and affection. After James, the Buchanans had nine more children: five girls followed by four boys. One of the girls and one of the boys did not live to be one year old. The arrival of so many brothers and sisters, however, did not diminish the special place James held in the Buchanan household.

James's formal education began at the Old Stone Academy in Mercerburg. In the autumn of 1807, he entered the junior class at Dickinson College. Although he was expelled once for disorderly conduct, he still managed to be graduated in 1809. James's personality was the source of most of his difficulties in college: He had a high opinion of himself and was quite obnoxious at times.

Buchanan's self-confidence was at least partially justified. He was an able student who became an extremely successful lawyer. Along with his intellectual ability, Buchanan was distinguished in appearance. He was tall with broad shoulders, had wavy blond hair, blue eyes, and fine features. He walked in a distinctive manner, with his head tilted slightly forward. His size, appearance, and mannerisms made him stand out, even in large crowds. After college, Buchanan studied law in the office of James Hopkins of Lancaster and was admitted to the Pennsylvania bar in 1812. He quickly established a successful law practice. The two main ingredients of his success were his knowledge of the law and his talent for oral presentation.

Life's Work

The political career of James Buchanan began with his election to the Pennsylvania House of Representatives in 1813. As a Federalist, he opposed the war with England, but once war was declared, he became a volunteer in a company of dragoons. In 1815, he was reelected. During this period, he spent considerable time and energy trying to

James Buchanan *(Library of Congress)*

delay the return of specie payment to protect the United States Bank.

Buchanan emerged on the national political scene in 1820, as a member of the United States House of Representatives. In 1824, with the demise of the Federalist Party, he found himself increasingly at odds with President John Quincy Adams. By 1826, Buchanan was working on a new Amalgamation Party in Pennsylvania, a mixture of Federalist Congressmen and old-line Democrats. What held the group together was its desire for a new political party and its support of Andrew Jackson. The main result of the creation of this new, vaguely defined party was that Buchanan became the primary dispenser of patronage in Pennsylvania.

After ten successful years in the House of Representatives, Buchanan was offered and accepted the ministry to Russia. Before taking this post, he had been giving serious thought to leaving public life and returning to private law practice.

Buchanan stayed in St. Petersburg (now Leningrad) until August of 1833, returning home to run for the United States Senate. By that time, Buchanan was clearly identified with the Democratic Party, and he realized that this meant supporting President Jackson, which included following Vice President Martin Van Buren's lead in the Senate.

Buchanan was quickly recognized as a loyal and principled partisan. Although the United States Bank was located in his home state, Buchanan remained true to the Jackson Administration's commitment to getting the federal government out of the banking business. Everyone knew that destroying the bank would move the United States' financial center from Philadelphia to New York; still, Buchanan believed that the interests of the nation should come before the interests of his home state. Buchanan's ability to place the nation's interests above those of his state or region were motivated, at least in part, by his political ambitions. In 1838, many of his friends encouraged him to run for the office of governor of Pennsylvania; he chose instead to remain in the Senate and focus his attention on national issues.

President James K. Polk appointed Buchanan to serve as his secretary of state in 1844. Buchanan shared Polk's desire to expand the territory of the United States, but negotiating treaties for the rigid Polk was difficult at times. Buchanan's skills at settling disputes and striking compromises were perfected during his tour of duty at the State Department.

Buchanan's friends were surprised to learn that he was considering retirement as the 1848 presidential race approached. Whether it was the bitter division in the Democratic Party or the heightened concern over sectional rivalry, Buchanan sensed that 1848 would not be a good year for the Democratic Party. His instincts were correct. Buchanan's retirement from the State Department left him time to take care of some private affairs. He purchased his country estate, Wheatland, and began the groundwork for the 1852 presidential race. Buchanan's four years of retirement were some of the happiest he had known: He pursued the life of a gentleman farmer and spent time with the niece and nephew he was rearing. Unfortunately, his presidential ambitions were not well served by his temporary retirement.

The 1852 Democratic Convention was greatly divided. After some political maneuvering, much heated debate, and many caucuses, Franklin Pierce received the party's nomination. Pierce defeated Winfield Scott in the general election and then persuaded Buchanan to end his political retirement and serve as minister to Great Britain. Though Buchanan accepted this assignment reluctantly, it proved to be a good decision for him politically.

The Kansas-Nebraska Act was passed in 1854, repealing the Missouri Compromise and leaving both the nation and the Democratic Party bitterly divided. Buchanan's chief rivals for the 1856 Democratic presidential nomination were damaged by the sectional strife. When Buchanan returned home from London, many believed that he was the only candidate who could mend the Democratic Party's wounds and save the Union.

The 1856 party nomination did not come easily. Only after Stephen A. Douglas withdrew from the race was Buchanan able to acquire the sixty percent of the vote needed for the nomination. Fortunately for Buchanan, it was a transitional year for those who opposed the Democratic Party. Buchanan did not get a majority of the popular votes but was able to secure enough electoral college votes to win the presidency.

Buchanan's long journey to the White House was over. His quest for the presidency had been difficult, and so were his years in the White House. Buchanan's administration was haunted by the question of slavery in the United States territories. He hoped that the Supreme Court's Dred Scott decision would settle the issue once and for all, but his hopes were in vain. In many respects the Court's decision complicated the issue. Stephen Douglas found the Court's ruling to be a thorn in his side throughout the Lincoln-Douglas debates of 1858. The battle raging within the Democratic Party was over the same issue. Douglas believed that "popular sovereignty" was the solution to the slavery controversy. Buchanan, like Abraham Lincoln, did not accept Douglas' solution. Unlike Lincoln, Buchanan believed that the Dred Scott decision denied the federal government authority over the institution of slavery in the territories and that only states had the authority to prohibit slavery within their boundaries. The end result was that Buchanan, the great compromiser and diplomat, could not settle the controversy.

Buchanan believed that the Democratic Party had held the Union together for the past decade; as president, he believed that it was his job to unite the party before 1860. Yet Buchanan was unable to unify his party, and the Democrats lost the 1860 presidential campaign; then, as he expected, the Union came to face its greatest threat ever: civil war.

Summary

Buchanan realized that the nation's strength was its ability to strike a compromise among conflicting interests. The Constitutional Convention of 1787 succeeded because it was able to forge a consensus among the different groups represented at the Convention. The Democratic Party's success had been built upon its ability to rise above sectional disputes and focus on national issues. The United States, according to Buchanan, was a compromise republic that had succeeded in bending when necessary so that it would not break. Buchanan's unswerving commitment to the Union kept him from seeing that many Americans were tired of compromises. The old North-South coalition had been pushed to the breaking point, and the westward expansion had given the North a decided advantage. Those in the North knew this; those in the South knew this; but Buchanan seemed not to know.

What are often interpreted as Buchanan's Southern sympathies were really little more than his sense of fair play coupled with his sincere desire to preserve the Union. One of the nation's great compromisers had the misfortune of being president at a time when compromise was no longer possible. Unfortunately, James Buchanan is remembered not for his thirty-eight successful years in politics but for his four unsuccessful years. Buchanan, like most other politicians in the United States, is remembered for what he did last.

Bibliography

Auchampaugh, Philip G. *James Buchanan and His Cabinet: On the Eve of Secession*. Lancaster, Pa.: Author, 1926. As the title indicates, this work deals with the Buchanan Administration. Special emphasis is placed on Buchanan's handling of the slavery issue.

Binder, Frederick M. *James Buchanan and the American Empire*. Selinsgrove, Pa.: Susquehanna University Press, 1994.

Curtis, George Ticknor. *The Life of James Buchanan*. 2 vols. New York: Harper and Brothers, 1883. By far the most comprehensive work on the life of James Buchanan.

Jaffa, Harry. *Crisis of the House Divided*. New York: Doubleday and Co., 1959. The best work on the theoretical issues involved in the Lincoln-Douglas Debates of 1858. Provides a good perspective for the issues that dominated American politics at that time.

Klein, Philip. *President James Buchanan: A Biography*. University Park: Pennsylvania State University Press, 1962. A comprehensive study that covers some secondary literature that was not available to Curtis.

Moore, John Bassett, ed. *The Works of James Buchanan*. 12 vols. Philadelphia: J. B. Lippincott Co., 1908. A complete collection of Buchanan's public addresses and selected private papers. Includes a fine biographical essay by Moore.

Nichols, Roy F. *The Disruption of American Democracy*. New York: Macmillan, 1948. A careful examination of the Democratic Party from 1856 to 1861. Deals extensively with the differences between Douglas and Buchanan.

Reisman, David A. *The Political Economy of James Buchanan*. College Station: Texas A&M University Press, 1990.

Smith, Elbert B. *The Presidency of James Buchanan*. Lawrence: University Press of Kansas, 1975. This work argues that Buchanan's actions were motivated by strong Southern sympathies.

Donald V. Weatherman

RALPH BUNCHE

Born: August 7, 1904; Detroit, Michigan
Died: December 9, 1971; New York, New York

Bunche played a major role in making Americans conscious of the contradictions between their racial policies and their democratic aspirations. He helped bring better understanding between nations, participating in the drafting of the United Nations Charter, and through diplomatic negotiations helped to maintain peace in the Middle East and Africa, winning the Nobel Peace Prize for his efforts.

Early Life

Ralph Johnson Bunche was born in Detroit, Michigan, on August 7, 1904. His father, Fred Bunche, was a barber. His mother, Olive Agnes Johnson Bunche, named him for his grandfather, Ralph Johnson, who was born a slave. The family moved frequently during Ralph's early life, and he remembered that in each community a different ethnic group was singled out for contempt: the Italians in Detroit; the blacks in Knoxville, Tennessee, where he spent a winter when he was six; the Mexicans in New Mexico, where the family moved because of his mother's poor health; and the Chinese and the Japanese in California, where he and his younger sister, Grace, lived with their grandmother after their mother's death. These early memories of the different faces of prejudice clearly influenced his later interests and outlook on life.

In the fall of 1916, Bunche's father left home, never to be heard from again. The following February, his mother, who suffered from rheumatic fever, died. His maternal grandmother, Lucy Johnson, kept the family together, but within a few months, his favorite uncle, who suffered from tuberculosis, committed suicide. In less than a year, Bunche had lost three of the most significant adults in his life. His grandmother, widowed early in life, had reared her children alone and now became his anchor. A light-skinned woman who could have passed for white, she was a dominant influence in her family. Her husband, Ralph's grandfather, had been a schoolteacher, and education was a value she continued to uphold for her grandchildren.

Even as a child, Bunche was accustomed to hard work. By the age

Ralph Bunche *(The Nobel Foundation)*

of seven he was selling newspapers, and before his mother died he worked in a bakery after school until nearly midnight every day. In Los Angeles, where he went to live with his grandmother, he was graduated as valedictorian from Jefferson High School. He attended the

University of California at Los Angeles (UCLA) on an athletic scholarship, where he was also a teaching assistant in the political science department, and was graduated magna cum laude in 1927. He received an M.A. degree from Harvard in 1928 and in June, 1930, married Ruth Ethel Harris, one of his students, with whom he had three children: two daughters, Jean and Jane, and a son, Ralph.

A handsome man of medium height and build, Bunche was destined to attract favorable attention for his accomplishments and pleasing personality. On a Rosenwald field fellowship, he toured Europe, England, and North and West Africa in 1931-1932 and in 1934 received a Ph.D. from Harvard, winning the Tappen Prize for the best doctoral dissertation in the social sciences for that year. His dissertation was a study of colonial administration in French West Africa; the transition of the former African colonies to independent statehood was one of his abiding concerns through the remainder of his life. His Harvard years were followed by postdoctoral work in anthropology and colonial policy at Northwestern University, the London School of Economics, and the University of Capetown, South Africa, in 1936-1937. A Social Science Research Council postdoctoral fellowship allowed him to visit Europe, South and East Africa, Malaya, and the Netherlands East Indies between 1936 and 1938.

During these years, Bunche was also teaching. He began teaching political science at Howard University in 1928 and served as chairman of the department from 1929 to 1950, when he left Howard to teach government at Harvard. He codirected the Institute of Race Relations at Swarthmore in 1936 while on leave from Howard. By his early thirties, his brilliance, hard work, and breadth of interests made him one of the most highly educated, well-informed men in the United States.

Life's Work

In 1939, Bunche became a member of the staff of the Carnegie Corporation Survey of the Negro in America. This project was headed by a Swedish economist, Gunnar Myrdal, and resulted in a two-volume work, *An American Dilemma: The Negro Problem and Modern Democracy* (1944). Bunche was one of a half dozen staff men who helped Myrdal with this massive project, based primarily on hundreds of interviews and personal observations of the participating scholars. He toured the

South by automobile in 1939 with Myrdal, and most of the interviews were conducted by his assistants in 1939 and 1940.

Bunche's part of the study dealt mainly with black organizational life, leadership, and ideology. He emphasized the extent to which disfranchisement of black voters had corrupted politics in the South, cutting off reform possibilities at the grass roots. He castigated the use of the poll tax and the white primary and pointed out the lack of secrecy in voting, which made political independence unlikely for poor people of either race in the South. Bunche emphasized the glaring inconsistencies between democracy and discrimination, stating,

> If democracy is to survive the severe trials and buffetings to which it is being subjected in the modern world, it will do so only because it can demonstrate that it is a practical, living philosophy under which all people can live the good life most abundantly. It must prove itself in practice or be discredited as a theory.

His work on race relations in the United States was followed by work for the United States government, in which he dealt with race relations on a global scale. In 1941, he was asked to work as a senior social science analyst on Africa and the Far East areas of the British Empire section of the Office of Strategic Services. He became chief of the African section in 1943 and then became a territorial specialist in the Division of Territorial Studies of the United States State Department in 1944-1945. In 1945, he was the first black division head in the State Department. He also helped draft the United Nations Charter.

Bunche was made director of the Division of Trusteeship of the United Nations from 1946 to 1948, then principal director of the Department of Trusteeship from 1948 to 1954. In 1947, he became special assistant to representatives of the secretary general of the United Nations Special Committee on Palestine. Tensions were very high in Jerusalem as the question of the partition of Palestine was being considered. The Arab high command forbade Arabs to testify before the special United Nations commission, so Bunche and others met with them secretly in Syria and Lebanon. After meeting separately with both sides, Bunche composed both the majority and minority reports to the satisfaction of both parties. His ability to grasp the problems involved and his empathy for the opposing factions made him a unique diplomat, trusted and acceptable to both Jews and Arabs.

When the Arabs declared war on Israel in 1948, Bunche was sent as the chief representative of the secretary general of the United Nations to help mediate the dispute, along with Count Folke Bernadotte, the head of the Swedish Red Cross. Bernadotte was shot and killed just before the two were to leave the Middle East to meet in Paris, and Bunche became the acting mediator through 1948 and 1949, finally achieving a peaceful settlement. In 1950, he received the Nobel Peace Prize for his peacemaking success in the Middle East. In 1957 he again successfully negotiated a peaceful settlement between Egypt and Israel.

In 1960, Bunche was a special representative of the secretary general of the United Nations in peacemaking efforts in the Congo. Dag Hammarskjöld had planned to take Bunche back to the Congo with him on the last trip he made, which ended in a fatal plane crash, but had decided against it at the last minute. The new secretary general of the United Nations, U Thant, appointed Bunche deputy secretary general, making him the highest-ranking American to serve under three secretary generals of the United Nations. He resolved the dispute between Prime Minister Cyrille Adoula of the Congo Republic and President Moise-Kapenda Tshombe of the Katanga province. He was sent to Yemen in 1963 to help contain another civil war. In 1964, he was sent to Cyprus to mediate Greek-Turkish hostilities, and, partially as a result of his efforts, peace was preserved there for another ten years until the Turks invaded in 1974.

In 1965, Bunche turned his attention once again to racial problems at home. In the 1930's and 1940's, he had been much involved in efforts to improve the racial situation in the United States. He served on the national executive board of the National Association for the Advancement of Colored People (NAACP), helped organize a National Committee Against Discrimination in Housing, helped organize the National Negro Congress in 1935, and served as a member of President Franklin D. Roosevelt's "Black Cabinet" of advisers. When he joined the Security Council of the United Nations, he had taken an oath, as an international civil servant, to refrain from activity in domestic problems. Nevertheless, he joined the march led by Martin Luther King in Selma, Alabama, in 1965 and addressed the crowd of thirty-five thousand Americans gathered there, remarking that his wife's father had made civil rights speeches in that same city at the turn of the century and apologizing to the crowd for having to speak from the capitol steps, where Dixie's flag still waved.

By that time, his health was beginning to fail. In 1951, he discovered that he suffered from diabetes. When he returned home from Selma, he had hepatitis, but he continued to work until he developed heart failure in 1970. He recovered from a heart attack and pneumonia, only to suffer a fall at home and die the following year on December 9, 1971. He was buried in Woodlawn Cemetery, Bronx, New York, next to his daughter Jane, who had preceded him in death.

During his lifetime, he received thirty-nine honorary degrees, the Nobel Peace Prize in 1950, the Presidential Medal of Freedom in 1963, and other honors too numerous to mention. He remained a modest man, finding more pleasure in work than in fame and firm in his commitment to build a more truly democratic society.

Summary

Ralph Bunche presents both a model and a challenge to all Americans. Facing poverty, discrimination, and a family broken through death in his early life, he became one of the most highly educated men in the United States. He used that education to serve his people and his nation, to sound the alarm about the state of democracy in America, forcing others to deal with the contradiction between racial discrimination and democracy. He demonstrated the potential for peace in the world when intelligence and perseverance are applied to achieve it. Through his work with the United Nations, he helped to contain several disputes, any one of which could have escalated into a third world war.

Bibliography

Bunche, Ralph J. *The Political Status of the Negro in the Age of FDR*. Edited by Dewey W. Grantham. Chicago: University of Chicago Press, 1973. Consists of the notes Bunche made for the Carnegie-Myrdal report. Gives a good sketch of Bunche's life and career.

Cornell, Jean Gay. *Ralph Bunche: Champion of Peace*. Champaign, Ill.: Garrard Publishing Co., 1976. One of a series, Americans All Biographies, written especially for young people. Balanced but brief.

Franklin, John Hope. *From Slavery to Freedom: A History of American Negroes*. 3d ed. New York: Alfred A. Knopf, 1967. An overview of

American black history with scattered references to Bunche, placing him in the context of major events.

Franklin, John Hope, and August Meier, eds. *Black Leaders of the Twentieth Century*. Urbana: University of Illinois Press, 1982. Contains a brief sketch of Bunche.

Haskins, James. *Ralph Bunche: A Most Reluctant Hero*. New York: Hawthorn Books, 1974. Small, compact biography written by a young freelance black scholar. Includes information on Los Angeles black community support for Bunche in his youth.

Johnson, Ann Donegan. *The Value of Responsibility: The Story of Ralph Bunche*. San Diego, Calif.: Value Communications, 1978. A good biography for young children. Emphasis is on character building.

Keppel, Ben. *The Work of Democracy: Ralph Bunche, Kenneth B. Clark, Lorraine Hansberry, and the Cultural Politics of Race*. Cambridge, Mass.: Harvard University Press, 1995.

Kugelmass, Joseph Alvin. *Ralph J. Bunche: Fighter for Peace*. New York: Julian Messner, 1952. The first biography of Bunche, written for older children and teenagers. Well-balanced coverage of his life.

Mann, Peggy. *Ralph Bunche: UN Peacemaker*. New York: Coward, McCann and Geoghegan, 1975. Best, most accurate biography available. The Bunche family, Roy Wilkins, and United Nations coworkers assisted the author. Major emphasis is on Bunche's work at the United Nations.

Urquhart, Brian. *Ralph Bunche: An American Life*. New York: W. W. Norton, 1993.

Betty Balanoff

GEORGE BUSH

Born: June 12, 1924; Milton, Massachusetts

As forty-first president of the United States (1989-1993), Bush culminated a career that included service as U.S. ambassador to the United Nations, chairman of the Republican National Committee, director of the Central Intelligence Agency, and vice president to Ronald Reagan.

Early Life

On June 12, 1924, George Herbert Walker Bush was born in Milton, Massachusetts, to Dorothy Walker Bush and Prescott Sheldon Bush. His father, who made a fortune as a Wall Street banker and eventually became the managing partner of the banking firm of Brown Brothers, Harriman and Company, also represented Connecticut as a Republican U.S. senator from 1952 to 1963. Bush's family lived in Greenwich, Connecticut, and he attended a private day school in the affluent New York City suburb before entering Phillips Academy, an exclusive preparatory school in Andover, Massachusetts. He excelled as a student and athlete at Phillips and was elected president of his senior class. After his graduation in 1942, Bush deferred his admission to Yale University and enlisted in the U.S. Navy, becoming its youngest pilot.

From 1943 to 1944, Bush was assigned as a bomber pilot to the USS *San Jacinto*. While he was flying a mission in September, 1944, his plane was hit by anti-aircraft fire. Forced to parachute into the Pacific, he was rescued several hours later by a U.S. submarine. His courageous service earned him the Distinguished Flying Cross and three Air Medals. In December, 1944, he was reassigned to a base in Virginia as a flight instructor and remained there until his discharge in September, 1945.

On January 6, 1945, shortly after his return to the United States, Bush married Barbara Pierce of Rye, New York, the daughter of a prominent magazine publisher. After the war ended, the young couple moved to New Haven, Connecticut, where Bush enrolled at Yale University. In 1948, after only three years of study, the economics major and varsity baseball captain was graduated Phi Beta Kappa. The new graduate then moved his fledgling family to Texas, where he worked in the oil industry as a salesman for Dresser Industries.

As a businessman, Bush was a success. In 1951, he and a colleague, John Overby, formed the Bush-Overby Oil Development Company. The business expanded into Zapata Petroleum Corporation, and by 1954, Bush was president of a Zapata subsidiary, Zapata Offshore, which developed offshore drilling equipment. Bush's family also grew. By 1959, he and Barbara had become the parents of four sons and two daughters. Unfortunately, their first daughter, Robin, died of leukemia in 1953.

George Bush *(Library of Congress)*

Life's Work

During his years in Texas, Bush became active in Republican politics. By 1964, he was party chairman in Harris County, and he took a leave of absence from the oil business to make a bid for a U.S. Senate seat. His opponent, Democrat Ralph Yarborough, was an ally of President Lyndon B. Johnson. Bush's bid, though unsuccessful, was impressive. In a year of overwhelming victory for the Democrats, he garnered a noteworthy 43.5 percent of the vote against a favored incumbent. He did not remain politically unsuccessful for long. In 1966, he was elected to the U.S. House of Representatives from the 7th District of Texas, the first Republican representative from the city of Houston. Bush quickly made his presence known in Washington. He was named to the influential House Ways and Means Committee, becoming the only freshman legislator to earn that honor in sixty years. Two years later, he ran unopposed for his seat in the House.

A staunch supporter of President Richard Nixon, Bush followed the president's advice and resigned his seat in Congress to run for the Senate in 1970. His opponent this time was Lloyd Bentsen, a conservative Democrat. Despite campaign support from both Nixon and Vice President Spiro Agnew and substantial financial contributions from the oil industry, Bush could not defeat Bentsen in Texas, historically a Democratic state.

Despite this setback, Bush continued his career in politics. Shortly after the election, Nixon appointed him to serve as the U.S. ambassador to the United Nations, where Bush learned the ground rules of foreign policy. Despite his lack of diplomatic experience, he performed well. In 1973, however, Nixon asked him to become chairman of the Republican National Committee, and he resigned his U.N. post.

As news of the Watergate scandal began to surface, Bush found his new appointment to be increasingly difficult. Initially, he was a resolute defender of the president; as evidence against the president mounted, however, he was forced to recognize Nixon's complicity in the affair. Thereafter, Bush tried to focus his attention as chairman on maintaining party strength in the face of Nixon's troubles. Finally, on August 7, 1974, concerned that Nixon's troubles would have negative repercussions on the Republican Party, Bush sent the president a letter asking for his resignation; Nixon announced his resignation the following day.

When Gerald Ford succeeded to the presidency, he rewarded Bush's loyalty to the Republican Party by allowing him his choice of several posts. Bush decided to move to Beijing as chief of the U.S. Liaison Office to the People's Republic of China. Given Nixon's renewal of U.S. relations with the communist country in 1972, his service there came at a crucial and delicate time. Again, he preformed admirably.

Bush continued in the China liaison position until December, 1975, when President Ford surprised him with a request to return to Washington to replace William Colby as head of the Central Intelligence Agency (CIA). The CIA's reputation had suffered severely in the face of revelations of its involvement in such illegal activities as assassination plots against foreign officials. Bush helped to restore the agency's credibility and morale, earning him bipartisan praise.

After Ford's loss to Jimmy Carter in the 1976 presidential election, Bush resigned his CIA post and returned to Houston, where he played an active role in several political campaigns. Frustrated with the Carter Administration, he announced his own presidential candidacy in May, 1979. Despite victories in the Iowa caucus and several primaries, including Massachusetts, Connecticut, and Pennsylvania, he lost the Republican nomination to Ronald Reagan.

At the Republican National Convention in July, 1980, Reagan initially approached former President Ford as a potential running mate. Ford, however, declined, and in a bid for party unity, Reagan asked Bush to join his ticket. Bush's extensive foreign-policy experience, more moderate stand on social issues, and relative youth all contributed to Reagan's electoral success. As in his previous positions, Bush proved to be a hard, loyal worker, and he earned the respect of many of his colleagues and constituents.

That work ethic dominated Bush's eight years as vice president, during which time his responsibilities focused primarily on foreign-policy issues. Building upon his diplomatic experience, he frequently traveled overseas to represent the White House. He also managed Reagan Administration involvement in worldwide efforts to halt both international terrorism and the drug trade. Toward the end of Reagan's second term, Bush again announced his intentions to seek the presidency.

Robert Dole, Senate Majority Leader from Kansas, offered Bush his stiffest competition in the 1988 primaries. Before the Republican convention, however, Bush had won enough delegates to secure his party's nomination. He and his running mate, Dan Quayle of Indiana, defeated Massachusetts governor Michael S. Dukakis and Texan Lloyd Bentsen, the Democratic presidential and vice presidential candidates, in an electoral landslide. Reagan campaigned vigorously for Bush, who promised to continue his predecessor's economic policies and to keep from raising taxes.

As president, Bush tackled several critical issues. Domestically, he faced the possible demise of the savings and loan system, continued the war against illegal drugs, signed a controversial deficit-reduction bill, and—despite his campaign pledge—agreed to increase taxes. In the international arena, his administration dealt with significant changes in Eastern Europe and the Soviet Union beginning with the 1989 fall of the Berlin Wall, long a symbol of Communist dominance. In meetings with Soviet president Mikhail Gorbachev, he negotiated START I and START II, historic arms-reduction treaties. Committed to a policy of international free trade, he spearheaded efforts that culminated in the eventual signing of the North American Free Trade Agreement (NAFTA).

Bush's greatest challenge came during the Persian Gulf War, which commanded his attention in the fall and winter of 1990-1991, following Iraq's invasion of Kuwait in August, 1990. When the Iraqi government refused to withdraw its troops in compliance with a United Nations-imposed deadline of January 15, 1991, a U.S.-led international coalition of troops launched a major offensive, Operation Desert Storm. The allied forces quickly succeeded in driving the Iraqis from Kuwait, and Bush's popularity soared.

During the next year, however, U.S. voters turned their attention to issues closer to home, primarily a sagging economy. By January, 1992, Bush's approval rating had plummeted, and his reelection, deemed a sure thing after the Gulf War, seemed in doubt. In the 1992 election, he was defeated by Governor Bill Clinton of Arkansas, whose campaign focused on such domestic issues as the economy and health care.

After leaving office, Bush and his wife returned to their adopted state of Texas. He continued his public service in many ways, including acting as a political adviser and serving on the board of the Episcopal Church Foundation.

Summary

Bush made his most significant contributions in the area of foreign affairs. From his early days as ambassador to the United Nations to his final days as president, he displayed an ability to grasp how the United States could most effectively relate to its fellow nations. In China, he helped to smooth the way for improved relations between the two countries. As vice president, Bush acted as an intermediary between other nations and Reagan, who was more skilled at home than abroad. As president, Bush's relationship with Soviet president Mikhail Gorbachev helped bring a peaceful end to the Cold War. His leadership in the Persian Gulf War helped to establish the importance of the United States in a post-Cold War world and to demonstrate the effectiveness of international cooperation in collective security measures.

Bush's domestic achievements are harder to assess. Many of his contemporaries point to the anemic state of the American economy at the end of his presidency and to his inability to gain a second term as evidence of his domestic failures. Nevertheless, several laws adopted during his tenure—especially the North American Free Trade Agreement, the Americans with Disabilities Act, and the Clean Air Act—had significant and widely lauded effects on domestic policy.

Bibliography

Beschloss, Michael R., and Strobe Talbott. *At the Highest Levels: The Inside Story of the End of the Cold War.* Boston: Little, Brown, 1993. Focuses on the roles Bush and Gorbachev played in ending the Cold War. An inside look at the intricacies of foreign-policy maneuvers.

Bush, George, with Victor Gold. *Looking Forward: An Autobiography.* New York: Doubleday, 1987. Released to coincide with the beginning of Bush's 1988 campaign, this autobiography provides insight into Bush's perceptions of himself and his quest for the presidency.

Campbell, Colin, and Bert A. Rockman, eds. *The Bush Presidency: First Appraisals.* Chatham, N.J.: Chatham House, 1991. Though written only halfway through Bush's term in office, this compilation of essays provides a solid assessment of various aspects of his work, from his leadership style to his choice of cabinet members.

Duffy, Michael, and Dan Goodgame. *Marching in Place: The Status Quo Presidency of George Bush.* New York: Simon & Schuster, 1992. A compelling, well-documented assessment of Bush's leadership style. Written by two *Time* magazine White House correspondents.

King, Nicholas. *George Bush: A Biography*. New York: Dodd, 1980. A straightforward account of Bush's life up to the time of his selection as Reagan's running mate.

Mervin, David. *George Bush and the Guardianship Presidency*. New York: St. Martin's, 1996. Mervin defines and judges Bush as a guardian president, a conservator of the status quo rather than an advocate of change. Extensive bibliography.

Whicker, Marcia Lynn, James Pfiffner, and Raymond Moore. *The Presidency and the Persian Gulf War*. Westport, Conn.: Praeger, 1993. A collection of well-written, thought-provoking essays that assess Bush's role in the Gulf War.

Woodward, Bob. *The Commanders*. New York: Simon & Schuster, 1991. Woodward examines Bush as commander-in-chief in this study of U.S. military policy just prior to the Gulf War. While the book has been popular, some analysts have questioned Woodward's scholarship.

Jane Marie Smith

JANE BYRNE

Born: May 24, 1934; Chicago, Illinois

Active in Democratic politics since 1960 and in Chicago city administration since 1964, Jane Byrne was the first woman to be elected mayor of Chicago.

Early Life

Jane Byrne was born Jane Margaret Burke on May 24, 1934, when her family resided at 6503 N. Claremont in Chicago. Her parents, William and Katharine (Nolan) Burke, had married in 1929; despite the Depression, their modest circumstances soon improved, and they moved their "lace curtain Irish" household to Sauganash, a fashionable neighborhood on Chicago's Northwest side. The warm, bright, ambitious son of a blacksmith, Bill Burke worked his way up from clerk to vice president of Inland Steel. In 1940, he formed Gordon-Burke Steel and later became the Steel Warehousemen Association's national president. Burke was a successful member of the "North Side Irish" elite.

"Janie" was the second of six children. Their mother, Katharine Nolan Burke, was strong-willed and well-read; she reared them by strict principles, within an insular Roman Catholic family structure. Janie attended Queen of All Saints Parish grammar school and all-girl St. Scholastica high school, graduating in 1951; she was an exemplary, serious student, though shy. At St. Mary-of-the-Woods College in Terre Haute, Indiana, she majored in biology and premedical studies, but grew homesick.

Transferring to all-female Barat College of the Sacred Heart, in wealthy north suburban Lake Forest, Jane Burke fit in well. She had impressive Catholic social credentials: Jane's uncle, the Right Reverend Monsignor Edward M. Burke, was the Chancellor of Chicago's Archdiocese; uncle Joseph Burke was also a priest. Jane had traveled with her uncle Ed to Rome in 1950, enjoying an audience with Pope Pius XII. She debuted at Samuel Cardinal Stritch's Presentation Ball of 1955.

Notably studious, shy, and ambitious, Jane made weekend treks to Notre Dame, where "Barat girls" hunted upwardly mobile Catholic husbands. During her junior year, Jane fell in love with William P. Byrne, a Naval ROTC student. They were graduated in 1955; Byrne was commissioned a Marine Corps officer, and from 1955 to 1956, Jane taught fourth grade at St. Juliana Grade School in Chicago. Rejecting a medical career, Jane Burke married Bill Byrne on New Year's Eve, 1956, satisfying 1950's social expectations.

The Byrnes were posted to Florida, Texas, and North Carolina. Jane delivered their daughter, Katharine Crane Byrne, in Chicago on December 31, 1957. Shortly before his scheduled discharge, Bill Byrne was killed on the foggy night of May 30, 1959, when his plane crashed at Glenview Naval Air Station. Jane Byrne was a widow at age twenty-five, with a seventeen-month-old daughter. This tragedy rerouted the course of Margaret Jane Burke Byrne's life: she would not follow her beloved mother's domestic footsteps.

Life's Work
Jane Burke Byrne assuaged her grief by joining her sister Carol on John F. Kennedy's 1960 presidential campaign. As a secretary for Margaret Zuehlke, executive director of Illinois Citizens for Kennedy, Byrne made important contacts with local and national Democratic Party supporters. After Kennedy was elected by a historically close margin—put over the top by Daley's Chicago machine—Jane Byrne attended education classes, received her master's degree from the University of Illinois at Chicago, and again taught grade school. A 1964 encounter with Chicago Mayor Richard J. Daley nudged Byrne back into politics.

Daley told Byrne to do political work in Sauganash, the city's Thirty-ninth Ward. As a reward for paying these political dues, Daley promised to secure a patronage position for Byrne. In the summer of 1964, Jane Byrne was hired at Head Start, controlled by the Chicago Commission on Urban Opportunity (CCUO), an agency created by Lyndon Johnson's Economic Opportunity Act. Byrne soon left Head Start for a personnel slot in the CCUO itself. She also continued her work on behalf of the city's Democratic machine, in part, organizing socials.

In March of 1968, Daley appointed Byrne to serve as commissioner of the small Chicago Department of Consumer Sales, Weights, and Measures. Some commentators believed her to be unqualified; she seemed Daley's "token woman." Commissioner Byrne controlled city inspection and regulation of consumer affairs, such as retail unit pricing, retail advertising, and toy safety. Byrne immediately leveled gender-based pay differentials among inspectors and began eliminating department corruption. She enforced fair inspection of retailers in poor neighborhoods, where grocery price gouging ran rampant; she pushed through a landmark ordinance banning phosphates in detergents. In 1973, her department prompted the Federal Trade Commission to undertake an antitrust investigation of Checker and Yellow Cabs, divisions of one company which controlled 80 percent of Chicago taxis. Consumer rights activist Ralph Nader applauded Byrne's efforts.

Byrne rode the consumerism wave of the 1970's to public visibility. As a relatively "clean" commissioner within the corrupt machine, her political clout rose. After the 1972 national convention, Mayor Daley made Byrne the new Illinois member of the Democratic National Committee, where she chaired the powerful Resolutions Committee. Daley appointed Byrne cochair of the Cook County Democratic Central Committee in January of 1975, clearly signalling Byrne's ascendance in the machine hierarchy.

Richard J. Daley died in December, 1976. Despite her status as a Daley protégé, Jane Byrne was maneuvered aside by male members of Chicago's Democratic political machine. Michael Bilandic became interim mayor; George Dunne replaced Byrne as cochair of the County Committee. Byrne, however, was still head of a second-class cog, the Democratic Women of Cook County and Chicago, and she remained in office as commissioner of the Department of Consumer Sales, Weights, and Measures. Oversight of the city's public vehicle licenses had been transferred to Byrne's department under Daley; when Bilandic sponsored a questionable cab fare increase in November of 1977, Byrne blew the whistle. The post-Daley machine cut Byrne off: her dismissal exploded into a media spectacle.

The public appreciated "Fighting Jane" Byrne's gutsy demeanor, and her speaking engagements established grass-roots support for a mayoral run. On St. Patrick's Day in 1978, Byrne married Chicago journalist Jay McMullen. Shortly thereafter, Byrne announced her candidacy for the office of mayor. Byrne's shoestring campaign used constant personal contact with the voters to advantage. Byrne preached "change" and reform, criticized "business as usual" in City Hall, and forged a multicultural voter coalition. Luck helped, since the frigid winter of 1979 burdened Chicago with catastrophic, record snowfalls. Bilandic's administration failed miserably at snow removal, and Byrne lambasted Bilandic and his machine for incompetence. Byrne won the February primary after a record turnout; she won the general election on April 3, 1979, with a startling 82 percent of the vote.

Jane Byrne was sworn in as mayor of the city of Chicago on April 15, 1979, the first female mayor of any major American city. Mayor Byrne faced grave problems. She had promised to improve Chicago's neighborhoods and aging infrastructure; she learned "the city that works" was verging on bankruptcy as 1970's inflation peaked in 1980. A transit strike loomed; Byrne had promised all city workers union contracts. The Democratic machine remained in place and was only semicooperative; State's Attorney Richard M. Daley (son of the late mayor) soon targeted Byrne's administration with investigations. Byrne's aggressive public persona both aided and hindered her progress.

Chicago Transit Authority workers went on strike in December of 1979, exposing Byrne's lack of a contingency plan, but shortly returned to work after succumbing to pressure from business interests. Chicago's end-of-year deficit of $102 million denied Byrne an easy solution to a $101 million shortfall in the public school system budget. The State of Illinois split bailout costs with the city, but in January of 1980, the teachers went out on strike. Byrne played a major role in the final settlement of the education crisis, but the city faced greater difficulties when it confronted what one historian has called a "strike-a-month schedule." Politically conservative firefighters struck in February of 1980, endangering the public safety during midwinter, and public opinion helped Byrne propel the firefighters back to work without a contract. The media often criticized Byrne for indecision and an acidic style during these three major strikes in her first mayoral year, yet she settled them by displaying a remarkable "sense of fiscal responsibility," according to Holli.

Byrne balanced the city budget every full year of her term (1980-1982); an unanticipated $15 million deficit occurred in 1983, when she left office at midyear. The balanced budgets were accomplished by adopting unpopular austerity measures, such as initiating city worker lay-offs, and some tax increases. To her credit, Byrne had not juggled the books or raided earmarked funds as previous administrations had. The city's bond ratings dropped, then improved. Byrne even launched some major development initiatives, such as 1981 revitalization plans for the city's North Loop district, a transit extension to and major renovation plan for O'Hare International Airport, an extension of the Chicago Transit Authority's rail service on the city's southwest side, and basic infrastructure improvements. She continued to support ChicagoFest, begun by Michael Bilandic, while initiating Taste of Chicago and various neighborhood festivals.

Byrne believed in public drama and spectacle, gaining popular approval. Her battles with the Chicago media were legendary. Byrne's political postures could flip-flop dizzyingly: She apparently offered Jimmy Carter her support at a 1980 election fund-raiser, but announced support of Edward Kennedy two weeks later. Political drama sometimes backfired. In 1981, Byrne's two-week tenancy in Cabrini-Green, a Chicago housing project suffering protracted gang violence, was widely praised for boldness and widely ridiculed as "grandstanding." She increased police, maintenance, and education provisions in public housing, with only short-term consequences. She also increased, then cut minority hiring. One study noted that 47 percent of employees hired between 1980 and 1981 were black in a city with a black population at 40 percent; 28 percent of new hires in 1982 were black. Byrne seemed racist defending her white Chicago Housing Authority (CHA) head against a 1982 federal agency power grab, realigning the CHA board's racial balance with controversial white appointees.

Poor ethnic relations hindered Byrne's reelection bid. The 1983 Democratic primary pitted Byrne against African American Congressman Harold Washington and white State's Attorney Richard M. Daley; the contest was racially polarized. Incumbent Byrne was a woman, with a mixed record, with limited (white) machine support and flagging minority support. Harold Washington won the Democratic primary with 36 percent of the vote; Byrne received 34 percent, and Daley netted 30 percent. Byrne withdrew her brief write-in candidacy; Washington won the bitterly fought general election.

Twice more, Jane Byrne ran unsuccessfully for mayor. She and Washington squared off in the March, 1987, Democratic primary, in which Washington polled a scant majority of the record turnout. After his election, Washington attempted to slate Byrne for clerk of the circuit court, but the machine refused. Byrne challenged Richard M. Daley in the February, 1991, Democratic primary, but came in a distant third.

Since that time, Jane Byrne has served as a political commentator; in 1992, she published her autobiography, *My Chicago*.

Summary

Jane Byrne's political career was startling in its contradictions. A privileged child, she became a civil servant. A machine functionary, she ran a "clean" city department. A 1979 mayoral long shot, she became the first woman to hold that office, yet she failed to support the Equal Rights Amendment. A coalition-builder, she became a divisive figure in City Hall despite her various administrative achievements. In the final analysis, although her credentials as an Irish-Catholic Democrat were impeccable, she could not maintain the power for which Richard J. Daley groomed her.

Because Jane Byrne was a woman, she faced constant opposition from male Democrats and the press. Her inability to present a stable, competent public image—regardless of actual performance quality—led to her rapid political downfall. One survey rating six recent Chicago mayors ranked Byrne fifth overall, but third for "accomplishments." Her most visible legacies are the Chicago Transit Authority and infrastructure projects as well as the summer festivals; her handling of "hard" issues— major strikes, budgeting, race relations—may acquire future cachet, but her later "perennial candidacy" seriously tarnished her reputation.

Bibliography

Byrne, Jane. *My Chicago*. New York: W. W. Norton, 1992. A sometimes self-serving, but readable, anecdotal autobiography that encompasses the history of Chicago, Byrne's genealogy, and her entire political career, especially her association with Richard J. Daley and her own term as mayor. Its Chicago-centered bibliography is wide-ranging.

FitzGerald, Kathleen Whalen. *Brass: Jane Byrne and the Pursuit of Power*. Chicago: Contemporary Books, 1981. Relying heavily on personal interviews of Byrne's friends and family, this extremely sympathetic biography is notable mainly for its germane explication of Byrne's Catholic, "lace curtain" Irish background and worldview.

Gove, Samuel K., and Louis H. Masotti, eds. *After Daley: Chicago Politics in Transition*. Urbana: University of Illinois Press, 1982. Essays by

Samuel Gove and Milton Rakove in this academic collection address Jane Byrne's mayoralty, complementing other essays addressing Chicago concerns. Rakove's explicit analysis is interesting, though undocumented.

Granger, Bill, and Lori Granger. *Fighting Jane: Mayor Jane Byrne and the Chicago Machine*. New York: Dial Press, 1980. This critical, occasionally hostile, biased account coauthored by a well-known, reactionary Chicago newspaper columnist details the Byrne mayoralty through 1980, incorporating Byrne's biography.

Green, Paul M., and Melvin G. Holli, eds. *The Mayors: The Chicago Political Tradition*. Carbondale: Southern Illinois University Press, 1987. Holli's essay analyzing Byrne's mayoral administration offers an astute, concise account of major events and objectively assesses its positive and negative outcomes; his expert survey rating recent mayors provides perspective.

Rivlin, Gary. *Fire on the Prairie: Chicago's Harold Washington and the Politics of Race*. New York: Henry Holt, 1992. In explaining how Harold Washington, Chicago's first black mayor, succeeded Byrne, Rivlin lends significant perspective on Byrne's tenure and on her unsuccessful campaigns after 1983, particularly emphasizing minority communities and racial problems.

Penelope J. Engelbrecht

JOHN C. CALHOUN

Born: March 18, 1782; Abbeville District, South Carolina
Died: March 31, 1850; Washington, D.C.

In addition to wielding great influence in national politics for four decades, Calhoun wrote incisively on the problem of protecting minority rights against majority rule in a democracy.

Early Life

John C. Calhoun was born on March 18, 1782. His birthplace was a settlement on the Savannah River in South Carolina, near the modern Abbeville. Of Scotch-Irish ancestry, Calhoun's forebears had made their way from Pennsylvania to Bath County, Virginia, then had been forced to migrate to South Carolina by the turmoil of the French and Indian War (1754-1760). The Up Country—as the western part of South Carolina is called—was a wild, untamed region, as evidenced by the murder of Calhoun's grandmother by marauding Cherokees in 1760. Calhoun's father, Patrick, was the youngest of four brothers who tenaciously carved out lives in the wilderness surrounding "Calhoun's Settlement." Patrick's first wife having died, he married Martha Caldwell, with whom he produced a daughter and four sons; the next-to-youngest child was named John Caldwell, after one of Martha's brothers.

Calhoun spent his youth on the family farm working in the fields with his father's slaves. Patrick's death in 1796 left John with a future seemingly bound by the needs of the farm and responsibilities to his family. Yet upon the urging of an older brother, he enrolled in Yale College in 1802 and was graduated with honors in 1804.

After Yale, Calhoun studied law at Tapping Reeve's Litchfield (Connecticut) Academy. During the two-year regimen at Litchfield, he developed habits in logic and discipline that would be his trademark in later years. Yet he also discovered that the prospect of being an attorney bored him. A stint in Henry De Saussure's Charleston law office and, shortly thereafter, his opening a successful practice of his own near Abbeville did not enliven his interest. He soon left the profession to become a prosperous planter and to follow his consuming interest in politics.

This career change was made possible by his marriage, in 1811, to his second cousin, Floride Bonneau Calhoun. The marriage brought Calhoun property which, when added to his, allowed him financial independence. Although Floride was ten years his junior, they were quite happy, and the marriage produced nine children. Calhoun would eventually establish residence at a plantation he built near his birthplace. He named it "Fort Hill" because the site once had been a garrison against Indian attack.

By the time of his marriage, Calhoun had developed those traits that would distinguish him for the remainder of his life. Physically imposing, standing over six feet tall, lanky, and with a rather hawklike face, he was craggily handsome. As the years wore away at him, ceaseless

John C. Calhoun *(National Portrait Gallery, Smithsonian Institution)*

labor and care combined with checkered health to render the stern countenance fixed in the minds of students by the photograph taken by Matthew Brady around 1848. In it, Calhoun, nearing sixty, sits with a face that is lined, hollow, and unsmiling, yet lit by an arresting and wild stare. Perhaps this face was merely a mirror of his lifelong personality. Even as a boy, he was overly serious, and he seems to have always conducted relationships outside his family with the same cold logic he applied to his political theories. Anything but outgoing, Calhoun commanded respect but seldom inspired affection. Associates sometimes referred to him as the "cast iron man," describing a man who, while not unfriendly, nevertheless remained ever aloof and hence, on a personal level, essentially alone and friendless.

Life's Work

Calhoun entered state politics in 1807 and, after one term in the South Carolina legislature, won election to the United States House of Representatives in 1810. There he joined the ranks of the War Hawks, that group of influential congressmen (Speaker of the House Henry Clay was the most conspicuous of their number) who were intent upon war with Great Britain to protect American maritime rights.

During the War of 1812, Calhoun steadfastly supported all measures to bolster the nation's failing defenses. When the Treaty of Ghent ended the war in 1814, he remained convinced that it was only a truce before the renewal of the conflict. Beginning in 1816, he urged the adoption of a national program to prepare for another wave of British aggression. He supported a protective tariff, a national bank, an improved transportation system through federally financed internal improvements, and a large standing army. His nationalism won for him both praise and a place in James Monroe's cabinet as secretary of war in 1817. Seeking to correct the many flaws made apparent by the poor showing of American forces in the recent war with Britain, Calhoun initiated numerous improvements for the army. These included the establishment of new departments, especially those of commissary, quartermaster, and surgeon general. Well suited to the administrative demands of the War Department, he filled the post during Monroe's two terms with a flair for innovative management.

Calhoun adroitly remained aloof from the angry political turmoil that marked the end of the Era of Good Feelings and the beginning of the formation of a new national party system. Elected to the vice presidency in 1824 and 1828, he thus served in the administrations of both John Quincy Adams and Andrew Jackson, despite the bitter feud between the two. At the end of the 1820's, it appeared that he would succeed Andrew Jackson as president with Jackson's blessing, but the nullification controversy in South Carolina irrevocably estranged them and nearly ruined Calhoun's political career.

In spite of his earlier advocacy of the protective tariff, he became convinced that steadily increasing its duties financially victimized Southern agriculturalists for the benefit of Northern industrialists. When he wrote "South Carolina Exposition and Protest" in 1828, which stated his theory of Nullification, it marked a significant turning point in his political career. Because he still hoped to attain the presidency, he kept secret his authorship of the doctrine. By turns, however, he was rapidly transformed from an American nationalist into a Southern sectionalist. Elaborating upon Thomas Jefferson's ideas in the Kentucky Resolutions of 1798, Calhoun declared that a state could nullify a federal law it deemed unconstitutional or harmful to its interests by refusing to enforce the statute within its borders. Essentially then, Nullification was a device whereby a minority could protect itself against the harmful will of the majority.

When South Carolina attempted to apply his theory by nullifying the Tariff of 1832, it brought the nation to the brink of civil war. Dismissing Nullification as illegal, Jackson threatened to invade South Carolina to enforce federal law, and when it was revealed that Calhoun was the doctrine's father, Jackson branded him a subversive. In disgrace with the Administration, Calhoun resigned the vice presidency, his national reputation in shambles. Yet the governor of South Carolina promptly appointed him to the Senate, and there he worked feverishly with Henry Clay to draft a compromise tariff that helped to diminish the immediate crisis.

After the Nullification controversy, Calhoun dropped all vestiges of his earlier nationalism and became the champion of Southern planter interests in particular and Southern rights in general. In the process, he earned the admiration of many Southerners, and in South Carolina he came to exert virtually total control over a political system which only occasionally was not a reflection of his will. His towering reputation and talent made him a fixture in the Senate, wherein he increasingly focused his intellectual and political energies on combatting what he perceived as Northern assaults upon the Southern way of life. Even his brief absence from the Senate—to serve as John Tyler's secretary of state from 1844 to 1845—was marked by his sectionalism: He successfully managed the annexation of Texas into the Union as a slave state.

As a strident antislavery movement grew in the North, Calhoun countered that slavery was a positive good. He opposed the Mexican War (which most of his Southern colleagues supported) because he feared that Northerners would try to exclude slavery from Western territories gained in the conflict. When his fears proved true, he was ultimately persuaded that Northern restriction of slavery in the territories was a preliminary step toward the thorough abolition of the institution in the South as well. The result, he thought, would be economic and social chaos, avoidable only by the South's secession from the Union.

His apprehension over both abolitionism and secession compelled him in his final months to attempt the unification of the South into an implacable front threatening secession. By so menacing the Union he hoped to frighten the North into concessions on the slavery question. Therein lay the safety of the South and the Union as well. His plan was unsuccessful, and as the nation reeled ominously toward disruption under the compounded sectional crises of 1850, he appeared before the Senate on March 4, 1850, almost for the last time. So ill that a colleague had to read his speech, Calhoun sat glowering from his chair as the chamber and crowded galleries heard his dire prediction that Northern agitation over the slavery issue would inevitably destroy the Union. His warning, unhappily prophetic, went unheeded. As the nation strained toward yet another compromise, his shattered health forced him to his deathbed. He died on March 31, 1850, in his Washington quarters. His last words were "The South . . . the poor South."

Summary

John C. Calhoun ranks as one of the most innovative political theorists in American history. Beginning with his complex arguments to justify Nullification, he ever afterward sought legal and logical means whereby to protect minority rights against the overriding and insensible will of the majority. His fears over the diminishing influence of the South in national councils drove him, in 1843, to begin drafting proposals for significant innovations in American constitutional government. The notion of the concurrent majority became central to his thesis in both *A Disquisition on Government* (1851) and *A Discourse on the Constitution of the United States* (1851).

In these works, Calhoun declared that the nation was composed of not only sections and states but also communities, each of these last possessing a unique character and interests different from the rest. The problem lay in the fact that any one community might be significantly smaller in relation to the others. The great danger in a democracy thoroughly wedded to majority rule, he insisted, was that a combination of larger communities could unjustly impose its will on any such minority through sheer force of numbers, ignoring the rights and privileges of the injured community. The resulting tyranny of the majority would be the very antithesis of the American ideal of government.

In order to avoid this result, he proposed that each unique community, regardless of its size, be given an equal voice in matters affecting the whole nation. A majority obtained under this arrangement would not reflect merely numerical strength, but would assure a general concurrence from all sectors of the society. In short, a concurrent majority would protect the rights of any minority. To reinforce the method further, he proposed instituting a dual presidency, one executive from each major section, each to have a veto on national measures.

Neither *A Discourse on the Constitution of the United States* nor *A Disquisition on Government* was completed when he died—indeed, his involvement in the sectional controversy of 1850 and his labors on these manuscripts combined to destroy his health—but they were published posthumously in 1851. They were lauded at the time by many Southerners and scorned by many Northerners. Calhoun's theories were complicated and made more so by the occasionally obscure prose of the former work. The latter work was often simply misunderstood. As the nation stumbled toward the disruption he had predicted, and after it had suffered the terrible Civil War, he was dismissed as both an ugly prophet of secession and a major cause of the catastrophe that followed.

Undoubtedly, before the Civil War he influenced in some degree the thinking of virtually every Southerner and, it might be argued, a significant number of Northerners. Yet subsequent scholarship has been unable to reach a consensus about Calhoun and the real meaning of the theories he produced. Cited as a major contributor to the outbreak of the Civil War, he also has been praised for tirelessly searching for ways to avoid it. Branded as little more than a sophisticated opportunist, always seeking his own advancement, he also has been eulogized as a careful statesman, aloof from the ordinary concerns of office and election. Labeled a stultifying obstructionist of the majority will, he also has been hailed as an innovative protector of minority rights.

In spite of the diversity of interpretation, one certainty emerges. For all of his imagination and mental agility, Calhoun never escaped the boundaries of his time and place. He bent his considerable talents to protecting and even extending the institution of slavery, a mockery of the ideals of liberty and, even in his time, disgraced by the considered judgment of mankind. Possessed of boundless vision, he yet remained blind to the fundamental evil of slavery and thus was at once a great man and a tragic figure.

Bibliography

Bartlett, Irving H. *John C. Calhoun: A Biography*. New York: W. W. Norton & Co., 1993.

Calhoun, John C. *The Papers of John C. Calhoun*. Edited by Frank M. Merriwether, Edwin W. Hemphill, and Clyde N. Wilson. 16 vols. Columbia: University of South Carolina Press, 1959-1985. An ambitious project consisting of Calhoun's papers from 1801 to 1843, with skillful editorial comment integrated throughout.

Capers, Gerald M. *John C. Calhoun, Opportunist: A Reappraisal*. Gainesville: University of Florida Press, 1960. A revisionist biography which argues that self-interest was the primary motive for all of Calhoun's actions. Marred by a polemical tone, but valuable as a counterweight to uncritical biographers.

Coit, Margaret L. *John C. Calhoun: An American Portrait*. Boston: Houghton Mifflin Co., 1950. Pulitzer Prize-winning biography that offers an extraordinarily favorable view of its subject. Coit lauds the agrarian ideal and praises Calhoun as its defender who resisted the evils of an industrial society. The most humanized depiction of Calhoun, but frequently overly sympathetic.

_____, ed. *John C. Calhoun*. Englewood Cliffs, N.J.: Prentice-Hall, 1970. A brief compilation consisting of selections from Calhoun's writings, contemporary observations about him, and scholarly interpretations regarding his political theories. A good introductory survey of the diversity of modern scholarly opinion concerning those theories.

Freehling, William. *Prelude to Civil War: The Nullification Controversy in South Carolina, 1816-1836*. New York: Harper and Row, Publishers, 1965. An excellent work on the great crisis which marked Calhoun's shift from nationalism to sectionalism. Includes a good description of his reluctant participation in the event and provides a penetrating analysis of the real significance of Nullification.

Hamilton, Holman. *Prologue to Conflict: The Crisis and Compromise of 1850*. Lexington: University Press of Kentucky, 1964. An indispensable study of the complex problems afflicting the nation at the time of Calhoun's death. His significant part in the drama is competently portrayed and explained.

Lindsey, David. *Andrew Jackson and John C. Calhoun*. Woodbury, N.Y.: Barron's Educational Series, 1973. Dual biography of these major figures that is surprisingly thorough, given its brevity. Offers a good introduction to Jackson and Calhoun and is marked by measured judgments supported by broad research.

Spain, August O. *The Political Theory of John C. Calhoun*. New York: Bookman's Associates, 1951. A learned and well-researched exposition of the origin, development, and maturation of Calhoun's theories on government, but flawed by Spain's defense of Calhoun's racial attitudes.

Wiltse, Charles M. *John C. Calhoun, Nationalist, 1782-1828*. Indianapolis: Bobbs-Merrill Co., 1944.

_____. *John C. Calhoun, Nullifier, 1829-1839*. Indianapolis: Bobbs-Merrill Co., 1949.

_____. *John C. Calhoun, Sectionalist, 1839-1850*. Indianapolis: Bobbs-Merrill Co., 1951. Grounded in decades of research and loaded with a wealth of detail, these three works (this and the two previous entries) comprise an almost definitive biography. Especially good in placing Calhoun in perspective with the social, economic, and political forces of the early nineteenth century, but somewhat imbalanced by an overly sympathetic view of Calhoun and his ideas while hypercritical of his adversaries.

David S. Heidler

JIMMY CARTER

Born: October 1, 1924; Plains, Georgia

President Carter was a conservative in some policies and a liberal in others. On the one hand, he attacked government bureaucracy, moved away from détente with the Soviet Union, and increased military spending; on the other, he supported racial equality, took seriously the problems of underdeveloped countries, and pressured repressive regimes to respect human rights.

Early Life

James Earl Carter, Jr., thirty-ninth President of the United States, was born on October 1, 1924, in Plains, Georgia, a town of 550 in Sumter County. Jimmy, as he liked to be called, was the first child of James Earl Carter, Sr., an up-and-coming farmer and rural businessman, and Lillian Gordy Carter, a registered nurse. Along with his sisters Gloria and Ruth and his brother William (Billy), he grew up on the family farm three miles from Plains. After being graduated from Plains High School in 1941, he briefly attended Georgia Southwestern College and Georgia Institute of Technology. Carter was appointed to the United States Naval Academy in 1943 and was graduated three years later, standing fifty-ninth in a class of 820. On the seventh of July, 1946, he married Rosalynn Smith, a friend of his sister Gloria. They had four children: John William (Jack), James Earl III (Chip), Jeffrey (Jeff), and Amy.

After two years' work on battleships, Carter transferred to the Navy submarine service in 1948 and then to the nuclear submarine program in 1951. Subsequently he served on the precommission crew of the nuclear submarine *Seawolf* and rose to the rank of lieutenant commander. Following his father's death in 1953, Carter returned to Plains, took charge of the family businesses, and quickly became a local leader. Between 1955 and 1962, he chaired the Sumter County Board of Education. In 1962, he was elected to the Georgia Senate. During two terms, he advocated governmental efficiency, regional planning, and better schools. In 1966, Carter lost the Democratic nomination for governor but ran a strong third in a field of six.

Carter's defeat produced a mild depression that led in turn to an important though undramatic religious experience. He had been

133

Jimmy Carter *(Library of Congress)*

reared a Baptist, conducted Bible classes in the Navy, and taught Sunday school at the Plains Baptist Church. Following his primary loss, however, Carter began to feel insufficiently devout. Guided by his sister, evangelist Ruth Carter Stapleton, he was "born again" and vowed to live a more godly life.

This religious conversion caused no basic change in his personality. On the contrary, Carter's determination to be a better Christian fitted into his long-standing habit of placing high demands on himself. He worked systematically, sometimes taking special courses to improve his memory, reading speed, and knowledge of art, music, and Spanish. He disciplined his body as well as his mind. A cross-country runner at Annapolis, he jogged in middle age to keep fit. In his late forties, Carter stood five feet, ten inches tall and weighed a trim 160 pounds. His stern commander in the nuclear submarine program, Admiral Hyman Rick- over, reinforced his perfectionism. Carter set high standards for his family and subordinates. Anyone who fell short risked "the look," as Carter's staff called a piercing stare from his hazel eyes.

Nor did spiritual rebirth dampen Carter's political ambition. Be- tween 1967 and 1970, he both visited Northern cities as a missionary and prepared for his next gubernatorial campaign. In 1970, he defeated former Governor Carl Sanders in the Democratic primary and easily won the governorship.

Life's Work

Governor Carter's inaugural address in January, 1971, attracted national attention when he declared that the "time for racial discrimination is over." Although Carter sometimes courted segregationist voters, he had remained personally moderate on civil rights issues. Now moving in a more liberal direction, he appointed blacks to state office and displayed a portrait of Martin Luther King, Jr., in the executive mansion. As governor, Carter worked hardest to streamline state agencies, but discrediting prejudice as a political issue was his greatest accomplishment. In 1972, he was mentioned as a dark-horse contender for the Democratic vice-presidential nomination. Yet, ineligible, for reelection and more conservative than leading Democrats, he was not a major figure in party or national affairs.

Four years later, Carter used his image as an outsider to win the presidency of a nation unsettled by the Vietnam War, the Watergate scandal, the cultural upheaval of the late 1960's, and the energy crisis of the early 1970's. Carter's book, *Why Not the Best?* (1975), announced the central theme of his campaign: government with effective leadership could be open, compassionate, and competent. Furthermore, claiming a governor's managerial skill, a nuclear engineer's technological expertise, and a born-again farmer's sound morality, Carter presented himself as uniquely qualified to lead. In addition, he blamed President Gerald R. Ford for high unemployment and Machiavellian foreign policy. Despite the wide appeal of these themes, Carter probably would have lost the Democratic nomination if liberal rivals had coalesced against him, and might have lost the general election if the economy had not been afflicted with rising unemployment and inflation. Carter beat Ford by 1.7 million votes.

Although Carter won a narrow victory, the country greeted the start of his term with enthusiasm. By the end of 1977, however, his legislative program had bogged down in Congress and, according to polls, fewer than half of all Americans approved of his leadership. With some justification, Carter attributed these problems to prejudice against a rural Southerner in the White House, but other factors were more

135

significant. While continuing to think of himself as an outsider, the president presented a legislative agenda that would have taxed the skill of an old Washington hand. Moreover, impatient with loose ends, Carter offered what he liked to call "comprehensive" programs. In 1977, he backed bills to reorganize the civil service, restructure the welfare system, lift regulations on major industries, create two new cabinet departments, and end price controls on natural gas. Furthermore, Carter and his aides initially underestimated the need to cultivate powerful senators and House representatives. More important than these considerations of style, temperament, and tactics, was Carter's ideological position to the right of most congressional Democrats. Unmoved by his rhetoric of efficiency, they resented his disinclination to promote national health insurance, full employment, and comparable liberal measures.

Conflicting aspirations, great expectations, and tactical errors also marked Carter's first efforts in international affairs. The president's chief foreign policy advisers symbolized his (as well as the country's) ambivalence about the Soviet Union: Secretary of State Cyrus Vance wanted to continue détente while National Security Council Chairman Zbigniew Brzezinski took a tough anti-Communist line. Giving mixed signals himself in 1977, Carter both decided against building a new intercontinental bomber and reneged on campaign promises to reduce military spending, while both repudiating the "inordinate fear of Communism" and condemning Soviet suppression of freedom. This criticism of the Soviets may have hindered progress on a strategic arms limitation treaty to succeed the limited accord (SALT I) signed by President Richard M. Nixon. A more decisive factor was Carter's presentation of a typically comprehensive disarmament plan. Suspicious Soviet officials rejected it, accusing the United States of reopening issues seemingly settled with President Ford.

From the outset, President Carter showed unprecedented concern about human rights abroad. Regimes sanctioning harassment, imprisonment, or murder of dissenters risked White House censure and loss of American aid. Realpolitik, congressional pressure, and bureaucratic maneuvering rendered Carter's human rights policy less "absolute" than he had promised in his inaugural address. Nevertheless, there were notable successes. Carter's intervention saved lives in Argentina, Brazil, Chile, and other nations ruled by military juntas.

His ambassador to the United Nations, Andrew Young, a black, cultivated Third World delegates, and, in April, 1978, Carter became the first president to visit Africa. Also in April, 1978, he secured Senate ratification of treaties that would end American control of the Panama Canal in 1999. Carter's human rights campaign and empathy for the Third World, however, were less popular at home than abroad. By late 1977, Republican and Democratic cold warriors charged that his soft and self-righteous policies damaged American interests.

Despite growing criticism from both the Left and the Right, Carter secured impressive victories between mid-1978 and mid-1979. Congress revised the civil service system, eased regulations on airlines, and enacted decontrol of natural gas prices. After grueling negotiations at Camp David, Maryland, Carter persuaded Egyptian President Anwar Sadat and Israeli Prime Minister Menachem Begin to accept a "Framework for Peace in the Middle East." In December, 1978, he established full diplomatic relations with the People's Republic of China. At the Vienna summit conference in June, 1979, Carter and Soviet President Leonid Brezhnev finally signed a strategic arms limitation treaty (SALT II). Yet none of Carter's successes was unmixed. Liberals complained that decontrol of natural gas prices enriched big business. Conservatives condemned the recognition of China and viewed SALT II as a needless concession to the Soviets. Perhaps most disappointing to Carter, though he brokered an Egyptian-Israeli peace treaty in March, 1979, the Camp David accords inspired no other Middle East settlements.

During the summer of 1979, Carter faced a faltering economy, oil shortages, and an angry nation. "Stagflation," the combination of rising unemployment and inflation, reappeared after two years in remission. Furthermore, when a revolution that deposed the Shah of Iran in January, 1978, also disrupted Iranian oil exports, the Organization of Petroleum Exporting Countries (OPEC) limited production and doubled prices. As American motorists clamored for scarce gasoline, Carter's bills promoting energy conservation and synthetic fuels stalled in Congress. On July 15, 1979, Carter attempted to rally the country against what he called a "crisis of the American spirit." This speech temporarily improved his standing in the polls and on Capitol Hill. Carter's subsequent decision, however, to remove several cabinet secretaries and fight inflation instead of unemployment cut short this resurgence. By the early fall, Senator Edward M. Kennedy had decided to contest the president's renomination.

In October, 1979, Carter made the most important decision of his presidency, allowing the exiled Shah of Iran to enter the United States for medical treatment. On November 4, Iranian revolutionaries seized the United States embassy in Tehran; fifty-two of the original sixty-six Americans stationed there (fourteen were released after a few weeks) remained captive for 444 days. The Middle East situation deteriorated further when Soviet forces invaded Afghanistan in December. Carter responded by withdrawing SALT II from Senate consideration, halting grain sales to the Soviet Union, urging a boycott of the Olympic Games in Moscow, and asking for a large increase in military spending. According to the Carter Doctrine announced in January, 1980, attempts by outside forces to control the Persian Gulf would be "repelled by any means necessary, including military force." The president's rhetoric masked relative American weakness in the region. Indeed, a military mission to rescue the hostages failed in April when American helicopters collided far from Tehran.

Although Carter turned back Kennedy's challenge to win renomination, his inability to free the hostages combined with the faltering economy cost him the presidency. On November 4, 1980, Republican nominee Ronald Reagan defeated Carter by 8.4 million votes. During his last months in office, Carter, now a convinced cold warrior, stopped aid to the leftist Sandinista government in Nicaragua. Negotiations to free the hostages remained his chief concern. They were released minutes after Ronald Reagan took office on January 20, 1981, and former President Carter flew to greet them at an American base in Germany.

Carter resettled in Plains but secular and religious interests often pulled him away from home. He represented the United States at Anwar Sadat's funeral in Cairo, received accolades in Latin America for his human rights efforts, and joined a church group repairing slum housing in New York City. Although his memoir *Keeping Faith* (1982) dealt primarily with foreign affairs, Carter also criticized Washington insiders who had opposed his domestic program. *The Blood of Abraham* (1985), his well-informed study of the Arab-Israeli conflict, rebuked President Reagan for failing to pursue the peace process begun at Camp David. By and large, however, Carter avoided public attacks on his successor.

Summary

Jimmy Carter was a more significant—and much better—president than his overwhelming defeat in 1980 suggests. Ironically, part of his significance lay in legitimating themes, such as the need to shrink the federal government, that Ronald Reagan used against him during the campaign. Similarly, by lifting regulations on major industries, moving away from détente, and increasing military spending, Carter initiated policies later continued by Reagan. Notwithstanding these unintended contributions to American conservativism, Carter's most important accomplishments derived from his liberal side. In the White House, as in the Georgia state house, Carter, a white Southern supporter of racial equality, discredited race prejudice as a political issue. His presidential appointments included many women and Hispanics as well as blacks. In foreign policy, Carter encouraged Egyptian-Israeli peace by accepting an evenhanded approach to the Middle East, paid respectful attention to underdeveloped countries, and placed human rights on the international agenda.

Bibliography

Anderson, Patrick. *Electing Jimmy Carter: The Campaign of 1976*. Baton Rouge: Louisiana State University Press, 1994.

Califano, Joseph A., Jr. *Governing America: An Insider's Report from the White House and the Cabinet*. New York: Simon and Schuster, 1981. A critical retrospective by the liberal secretary of health, education, and welfare whom Carter fired in 1979. Califano presents the president as an incompetent conservative but credits him with a good record on minority recruitment.

Campagna, Anthony S. *Economic Policy in the Carter Administration*. Westport, Conn.: Greenwood Press, 1995.

Carroll, Peter. *It Seemed Like Nothing Happened: The Tragedy and Promise of America in the 1970's*. New York: Holt, Rinehart and Winston, 1982. A lively history of the decade, especially perceptive on cultural trends and the social development of minorities. Places Carter in context and views him as a conservative Democrat.

Carter, Jimmy. *The Blood of Abraham*. Boston: Houghton Mifflin Co., 1985. Carter brings together a detailed knowledge of the Bible, recent Middle Eastern politics, and his own experiences in the region. Cautiously hopeful about the possibilities of peace, he offers sensible policy recommendations.

_____. *Keeping Faith: Memoirs of a President*. New York: Bantam Books, 1982. This defensive memoir shows Carter and liberal Democrats talking past each other. Contains comprehensive accounts of the Camp David negotiations and the Iran hostage crisis.

_____. *Why Not the Best?* New York: Bantam Books, 1976. This combination memoir and campaign tract contains Carter's fullest account of his childhood, naval service, and governorship. Especially useful for understanding his evolving position on Civil Rights.

Carter, Rosalynn. *First Lady from Plains*. Boston: Houghton Mifflin Co., 1984. A much more candid book than either of Jimmy Carter's memoirs. Although Mrs. Carter discusses her own experiences as a mental health reformer, the book is most valuable for the portrait of her husband.

Dumbrell, John. *The Carter Presidency: A Re-evaluation*. 2d ed. New York: Manchester University Press, 1995.

Glad, Betty. *Jimmy Carter: In Search of the Great White House*. New York: W. W. Norton and Co., 1980. One of the best biographies of a sitting president. Glad presents the most detailed scholarly interpretation of Carter's youth, early career, religious beliefs, and 1976 campaign strategy. Relatively little on the presidency.

Lynn, Laurence E., Jr., and David deF. Whitman. *The President as Policymaker: Jimmy Carter and Welfare Reform*. Philadelphia: Temple University Press, 1981. This thorough account of Carter's unsuccessful attempt to restructure the welfare system effectively uses interviews with cabinet members, senators, representatives, and civil servants. Reveals Carter's strengths and weaknesses as a policymaker along with the institutional constraints he encountered.

Mazlish, Bruce, and Edwin Diamond. *Jimmy Carter: A Character Portrait*. New York: Simon and Schuster, 1979. A subtle psychobiography by an intellectual historian and media critic. Especially good on Carter's religious beliefs, family relationships, and rhetorical exaggerations.

Smith, Gaddis. *Morality, Reason, and Power: American Diplomacy During the Carter Years*. New York: Hill and Wang, 1985. The best analysis of Carter's foreign policy. Smith places the Administration in broad historical context, applauds his human rights record, and regrets his abandonment of détente.

Leo P. Ribuffo

SALMON P. CHASE

Born: January 13, 1808; Cornish, New Hampshire
Died: May 7, 1873; New York, New York

As an attorney, politician, and constitutional theorist, Chase contributed to the abolition of slavery. During the 1850's, he served as a United States senator and as governor of Ohio, and he participated in the formation of the Republican Party. He was later appointed secretary of the treasury and was Chief Justice of the Supreme Court.

Early Life

Salmon P. Chase was born in Cornish, New Hampshire, in 1808. His father, Ithamar Chase, whose family had come to America during the 1640's, was a farmer who held minor local offices and occasionally served in the state legislature. His mother, Janette Ralston, was the daughter of Scottish immigrants who became prominent landowners in Keene, New Hampshire. Ithamar died when the younger Chase was eight, so the boy spent his youth living with various friends and relatives, including his uncle, Philander Chase, the bishop of the Episcopal Church in Ohio. In 1821, Chase entered Cincinnati College, where his uncle Philander was president. Philander's influence on his nephew was profound. For the rest of his life, Chase would be extremely pious. His later commitment to the abolition of slavery would be as much religious as political. By 1823, Chase had returned to New Hampshire, where he briefly taught school before entering Dartmouth College. In 1826 he was graduated eighth in his class, a member of Phi Beta Kappa. Chase then moved to Washington, D.C., where he taught school before beginning law studies under William Wirt in 1827. In December, 1829, he was admitted to the bar.

In 1830, the athletic, tall, vigorous, and ambitious Chase settled in Cincinnati, where he practiced law and took an active role in civic affairs. Between 1831 and 1833, he published historical essays in *The North American Review*, anonymous editorials in Ohio newspapers, and a three-volume, comprehensive compilation of Ohio's laws, *The Statutes of Ohio* (1833-1835). Chase was neither brilliant nor eloquent in court, but he was hardworking, careful, and scholarly. These traits brought him a comfortable and growing commercial practice which, by 1835, included such clients as the Bank of the United States and the Lafayette Bank of Ohio. By 1845, his firm of Chase and Ball earned an estimated ten thousand dollars a year—an extraordinarily large sum for the era. In 1834, Chase married his first wife, who died in 1835. Two other marriages (in 1839 and 1846) would also end with the death of his wives. Of his six daughters only two, Katherine Chase Sprauge and Jeanette Chase Hoyt, survived to adulthood.

Salmon P. Chase *(William F. Cogswell, collection of the Supreme Court of the United States)*

Life's Work

Chase's national career had four phases: abolitionist lawyer; United States senator and governor of Ohio; secretary of the treasury; and Chief Justice of the United States.

From 1830 to 1849, Chase lived in Cincinnati, where his law firm flourished. In addition to this profitable practice, Chase offered free legal services to abolitionists, fugitive slaves, and free blacks. In 1836, mobs destroyed the office of Cincinnati's antislavery newspaper, the *Philanthropist*, and threatened the life of its editor, James G. Birney. Also threatened was Chase's brother-in-law, Dr. Isaac Colby. Through this incident, Chase became an attorney for the antislavery cause. Chase was initially attracted to the abolitionist movement because he abhorred the mob violence and disrespect for law directed against it. He evolved into a passionate and articulate supporter of the cause. In 1836, he won a damage suit against members of the mob, recovering some money for Birney to rebuild the office of the *Philanthropist*. A year later, Chase unsuccessfully defended the freedom of a fugitive slave, Matilda, who had been harbored by Birney. Birney was then convicted for helping Matilda, but Chase won a reversal on appeal.

By 1841, Chase was a leading antislavery attorney in Ohio. Chase rejected the anticonstitutionalism of William Lloyd Garrison and instead developed a constitutional theory consistent with opposition to slavery. In 1843 and 1848, he was the chief author of the platform of the national Free Soil Party. Besides his Free Soil political activities, Chase defended numerous fugitive slaves and their white and black allies. In the 1840's, Chase corresponded with antislavery lawyers throughout the Midwest, convincing them to take cases that he had no time to handle and advising them on legal strategies. Chase lost his most famous fugitive slave case, *Jones v. Van Zandt* (1847), but his printed Supreme Court brief, titled "Reclamation of Fugitives from Service," added to his growing national reputation as the "attorney general for fugitive slaves."

In 1849, a small group of Free Soilers held the balance of power in the Ohio legislature. Guided in part by Chase, these political abolitionists secured two victories: They negotiated the repeal of most of Ohio's racially restrictive "black code," and they secured the election of Chase to the United States Senate.

In the Senate, Chase failed in his attempt to create a "Free Democracy" made up of antislavery Democrats such as himself. Effectively separated from all parties, he remained one of the most uncompromising Senate opponents of slavery, constantly challenging Southerners and their Northern allies. As a politician, Chase was somewhat ponderous, pompous, and self-righteous. While he was not a great debater, his carefully written speeches read well on the stump and in the Senate. In 1850, Chase was one of the leading opponents of the Fugitive Slave Law and other proslavery aspects of the Compromise of that year. While in the Senate, Chase continued to develop his antislavery constitutional analysis, arguing that the Fifth Amendment made slavery unconstitutional wherever the federal government had jurisdiction. This led to his concept of "freedom national, slavery sectional," which became a rallying cry for the Republican Party, especially after the Dred Scott decision (1857). Chase also laid out the theoretical basis for the Republican Party's slogan of 1856: Free Soil, Free Labor, Free Speech, Free Men. In 1854, Chase emerged as a leader of the opposition to the Kansas-Nebraska Act and in the process once again tried to organize a party of "Independent Democrats." No "Independent Democracy" emerged in 1854, but by 1855 a broader coalition of Free Soilers, Northern Democrats, and Whigs had united into an "Anti-Nebraska Party," which soon became the Republican Party. Chase was instrumental in the founding of this new political organization in Ohio. In 1855, he became one of the first Republican governors in the nation by defeating candidates from both the Whig and Democratic parties. In 1857, he was reelected governor of Ohio.

As governor, Chase helped create the Republican Party in Ohio and the nation. In part because of his cold personality, however, he was unable to unify the state party behind his own presidential ambitions; in both 1856 and 1860, he was unsuccessful in gaining the Republican nomination for that office. While governor, Chase opposed the extradition of fugitive slaves but was unable to prevent the removal of the slave Margaret Garner, who killed her own daughter to prevent the child's return to slavery. After the rescue of an alleged fugitive slave near Oberlin, however, Chase gave support to the rescuers and appeared willing to confront federal authorities. In another case, Chase prevented the extradition of a free black accused of helping slaves to escape from Kentucky. This ultimately led to the Supreme Court decision in *Kentucky v. Dennison* (1861), in which Chief Justice Roger B.

Taney chastised Ohio for its antislavery activities but refused actually to order the return of the accused fugitive. Throughout his governorship, Chase tried to walk a fine line between actual defiance of federal law and the Constitution, and his thoroughgoing opposition to slavery and the Fugitive Slave Law. When not sparring with the federal government, Governor Chase directed his energies to reorganizing the Ohio militia, which would ultimately be a major asset to the Union during the Civil War.

In 1860, Governor Chase failed to obtain the Republican presidential nomination. He was, however, elected to the United States Senate in the fall of that year. During the secession crisis, he served as a "peace commissioner" from Ohio, where he opposed any extension of slavery into the territories but also disclaimed any intention of interfering with slavery where it already existed. In March, he had barely taken his seat in the Senate when President Lincoln appointed him secretary of the treasury.

In his new office, Chase faced the formidable task of financing the Civil War. With the aid of financier Jay Cooke, Chase was able to market government bonds, thus providing a constant flow of capital into the national treasury. Chase's initiatives led to the establishment of a national banking system in 1863 with a system of currency backed by federal bonds and securities. Because the Treasury Department was also responsible for confiscated and abandoned property from the Confederacy, Chase was able to take an active role in the dismantling of slavery.

Chase, the most radical abolitionist in Lincoln's original cabinet, used his office to chip away at slavery in the period before the Emancipation Proclamation (1862). He supported generals who used their power to undermine or destroy the institution, as long as they did not overtly go beyond administration policy. Under Chase's protégé, Edward L. Pierce, the first steps toward educating ex-slaves for life as free men and women took place in 1862 on the sea islands of South Carolina. Chase encouraged dedicated abolitionists to run this "rehearsal for reconstruction." In the Cabinet, Chase argued for an early end to slavery itself. Chase strongly supported the Emancipation Proclamation, even though he believed that it did not go far enough. Chase's personal piety led him to convince Lincoln to ask for the "gracious favor of Almighty God" at the end of the proclamation.

Throughout his tenure as secretary of the treasury, Chase's relationship with Lincoln was strained. He had serious policy disagreements with Lincoln, especially on such issues as emancipation and black rights. Chase was far ahead of his president on these matters. In addition, Chase wanted Lincoln's job: Chase had his eye on the White House in 1856 and 1860. He thought that after a single term Lincoln would step aside, and he could step forward. Chase's feuding with Secretary of State William H. Seward and his persistent campaigning for the Republican presidential nomination in 1864 made it increasingly difficult for him to remain in the Cabinet. In June, 1864, a conflict over the appointment of a subordinate led Chase to offer his resignation. This was the fourth or fifth time he had done so. Much to his surprise, Lincoln accepted the resignation and Chase was out of the Cabinet.

In spite of his disagreements with Lincoln, Chase ultimately campaigned actively for the Republican ticket throughout the fall of 1864. After his reelection, Lincoln appointed Chase to replace the late Roger B. Taney as Chief Justice of the United States. Chase was a logical choice. He had been an eminent attorney and had developed the most coherent antislavery legal-constitutional arguments of the antebellum period. He was sympathetic to emancipation and the other war policies of the Lincoln Administration.

Rather than marking a fitting end to his lifetime of public service, however, Chase's years in the Supreme Court were an anticlimax if not an embarrassment. Chase joined a Court that was deeply divided between antislavery Lincoln appointees and proslavery holdovers from the prewar years. During Reconstruction, the court was asked to decide on questions which were at the heart of the political crisis of the period. The Court's answer, and Chase's leadership, were mixed.

Chase presided over the impeachment of Andrew Johnson with fairness and skill. He earned the respect of most of the Senate, and of much of the nation. This might have been the capstone of his career. Chase still had his eye on the presidency, however, and he used his newfound prestige to campaign for the office. Chase's hunger for the White House led him to repudiate his previous support for black suffrage, in hopes of getting the Democratic nomination. He failed in this effort and in the process lost support from moderates as well as former abolitionists.

When he appointed Chase, Lincoln told a friend "we wish for a Chief Justice who will sustain what has been done in regard to emancipation and the legal tenders." Had Lincoln lived, he would have been disappointed by Chase on the latter issue. In *Hepburn v. Griswold* (1870) and in the Legal Tender cases (1871), Chase voted to void the financial system that he had set up as the secretary of the treasury. The chief justice was severely criticized for this.

On black rights, Chase's record was more consistent. Despite his willingness to oppose black suffrage in order to gain the presidential nomination in 1868, Chase was a genuine supporter of black rights. In the Slaughterhouse cases (1873), Chase vigorously dissented, arguing that the majority opinion undermined the rights of the freedmen. In other Reconstruction decisions, Chase generally supported Congress over the president or the states. The one major exception was the loyalty oaths, which Chase opposed from the bench. In his most important Reconstruction decision, *Texas v. White* (1868), Chase upheld the basic theory of Congressional Reconstruction in an opinion that was sensitive to the political realities of the era. Chase also upheld the power of Congress to limit Supreme Court jurisdiction in the postwar South in *Ex parte McCardle* (1868). In *Ex parte Milligan* (1866), however, he denied the right of the executive branch to abolish civilian courts in those states which remained within the Union.

Summary

Few men in American history have held so many important governmental positions. Chase's contributions to the antislavery movement and the Republican Party were critical. His defense of fugitive slaves and abolitionists was unmatched by other lawyers of his age; his development of a coherent antislavery constitutional theory helped pave the way for Lincoln's victory in 1860 and the ultimate abolition of slavery. As secretary of the treasury, Chase was a valuable and hardworking member of Lincoln's cabinet. Besides organizing the financing of the war effort, Chase helped develop Reconstruction policy. In the early years of the war, he also helped Lincoln manage the War Department, which was being incompetently and corruptly run by Secretary of War Simon Cameron.

As chief justice, Chase was a disappointment. He was unable to assert the authority and leadership that he had displayed in his other public positions. His opinions were never as sharp as his prewar speeches had been. Moreover, his positions, so clear and consistent in the antebellum period, were sometimes vague on the bench. His grasping for the presidency reflected poorly on him and on the office he held. Nevertheless, Chase guided the Supreme Court through the impeachment crisis with dignity. He also avoided running afoul of Congress at a time when that branch might have seriously damaged the Supreme Court, had Chase and his brethren opposed Congressional Reconstruction policies. Similarly, Chase left the bench on a high note, vigorously asserting the rights of the freedmen in the Slaughterhouse cases, at a time when a majority of the Supreme Court and the nation were rejecting any commitment to racial equality.

Bibliography

Blue, Frederick J. *Salmon P. Chase: A Life in Politics.* Kent, Ohio: Kent State University Press, 1987.

Chase, Salmon Portland. *Inside Lincoln's Cabinet: The Civil War Diaries of Salmon P. Chase.* Edited by David H. Donald. New York: Longmans, Green and Co., 1954. Chase kept a detailed diary while in the cabinet. This carefully edited edition offers great insight into Chase and his role in the cabinet. Part of the diary is also available, along with many Chase letters, in volume 2 of the *Annual Report of the American Historical Association for the Year 1902,* published by the United States Government Printing Office in 1903.

Foner, Eric. *Free Soil, Free Labor, Free Men: The Ideology of the Republican Party Before the Civil War.* New York: Oxford University Press, 1970. Contains an important chapter on Chase's constitutional theory and its relationship to Republican ideology. Throughout this book, Chase is a major figure.

Hart, Albert Bushnell. *Salmon Portland Chase.* Boston: Houghton Mifflin Co., 1899. Although dated, this volume remains the best available biography of Chase. The book is relatively weak on his judicial career, but it is an excellent introduction to his abolitionist efforts and political career.

Hyman, Harold M., and William M. Wiecek. *Equal Justice Under Law: Constitutional Development, 1835-1875.* New York: Harper and Row, 1982. Covers the developments in constitutional and legal thought during Chase's career.

Kutler, Stanley I. *Judicial Power and Reconstruction Politics*. Chicago: University of Chicago Press, 1968. Best short introduction to the problems of the Supreme Court under Chase.

Niven, John. *Salmon P. Chase: A Biography*. New York: Oxford University Press, 1995.

Schuckers, Jacob W. *The Life and Public Services of Salmon Portland Chase*. New York: Da Capo Press, 1970. Written by one of Chase's protégés (and originally published in 1874), this book presents an overly heroic portrait of its subject but is nevertheless useful, particularly for the many Chase letters and speeches that it reprints.

Warden, Robert. *An Account of the Private Life and Public Services of Salmon Portland Chase*. Cincinnati, Ohio: Wilstach, Baldwin, and Co., 1874. Much like the Schuckers biography, this volume is useful but uncritical.

Wiecek, William M. *The Sources of Antislavery Constitutionalism in America, 1760-1848*. Ithaca, N.Y.: Cornell University Press, 1977. Places Chase's antislavery theories and legal arguments in the context of other abolitionist constitutional theorists.

Paul Finkelman

HENRY CLAY

Born: April 12, 1777; Hanover County, Virginia
Died: June 29, 1852; Washington, D.C.

Clay was a dominant figure in American politics during the first half of the nineteenth century. His American System and his efforts to bring compromise in the controversy over slavery helped ease the growing tensions within the Union.

Early Life

Henry Clay was born April 12, 1777, on a farm near Richmond. His parents, the Reverend John Clay, a Baptist minister, and Elizabeth Hudson Clay, were of English descent and reasonably prosperous, though certainly not wealthy. His father died when Henry was four, but his mother was remarried within a year to Captain Henry Watkins, who maintained the family's financial status. Henry received a few years of schooling and developed remarkable penmanship, a skill which served him well when his stepfather moved the family in 1792. Only fifteen, Clay stayed in Richmond to work for the Clerk of the High Court of Chancery. In 1793, Clay was hired by the famous lawyer George Wythe as a part-time secretary. Almost seventy, Wythe was a leader of Virginia's bar and had enjoyed a distinguished career as teacher of law and classics. Under Wythe's tutelage, Clay studied the law and, a few years later, left his clerk's position to study under Robert Brooke, former governor and later attorney general of Virginia. In November, 1797, Clay passed his bar examination.

Like other ambitious Virginians, the young attorney moved to Kentucky, where confusion over land claims created a lawyer's paradise. At twenty, Clay was over six feet tall, thin, and walked with a shambling gait. His face, capable of creating considerable impact with a change of expression, was capped by hair so light as to be almost prematurely white. His eyes were small, gray, and piercing, his nose prominent, and from his large mouth issued his most valuable asset: his voice. Coupled with an emotional temperament, this voice, suited for an actor, made him a formidable opponent in frontier courts, where persuasion was frequently more important than legal knowledge.

The stage for Clay's legal theatrics was Lexington, Kentucky, a village on its way to becoming the "Athens of the West." Though appearing in frail health, Clay demonstrated his skill in local debates and was admitted to the Kentucky bar on March 20, 1798. Before a successful legal career made him a local legend, the budding jurist married Lucretia Hart, daughter of the influential merchant Thomas Hart. The marriage not only connected Clay with an important local family but also provided him with a patient, loving wife, who bore him eleven children. By 1800, Henry Clay was a member of Lexington's establishment.

Life's Work

Clay's debut as a radical Jeffersonian came when he spoke for a liberalization of the state's constitution and made speeches attacking the Alien and Sedition acts. He supported Jefferson in 1800 and, in 1803, won election to the Kentucky legislature. There he demonstrated his talent as a parliamentary tactician and also flirted with disaster by becoming counsel for Aaron Burr, who was charged with an alleged conspiracy to invade Mexico. Unaware of the extent of Burr's activities, Clay successfully defended Burr in Kentucky's courts, but later, as the import of Burr's schemes became apparent, Clay repudiated his dangerous client.

While acting as counsel for Burr, Clay was selected to fill an unexpired term in the United States Senate. Apparently no one paid any attention to the fact that he was a few months short of the required age. This brief performance in Washington, D.C., began a lifelong crusade for a national program based on internal improvements at federal expense and a protective tariff. Such measures were joined by an expansionistic, anti-British foreign policy. Clay's jingoism increased when he moved to the House of Representatives and became its Speaker. There, along with other "war hawks," Clay helped push the nation into the War of 1812. When the struggle did not bring victory, Clay found himself a member of the American delegation sent to Ghent, Belgium, to negotiate an end to the war he had helped to create. In spite of the negative reaction of John Quincy Adams, head of the delegation, who objected to Clay's Western habits of drinking, swearing, and gambling, the Kentuckian proved an able diplomat.

In the postwar years, Clay became a chief proponent of American nationalism and envisioned a truly united country tied together by bonds of economic interest as well as a common ideology. The government's role in his American System was to promote harmony through economic development. Key to his system was a new national bank. Suspicious of the first Bank of the United States, Clay had helped to block its recharter in 1811, but financial confusion during the war convinced him that a centralized financial system was imperative. From this time until the end of of his career, Clay's name would be associated with the idea of a national bank.

His legislative success made it seem that Clay's elevation to the White House was only a matter of time. His successful solution to the slavery controversy further encouraged his supporters. In 1819, Missouri applied for admission as a slave state. Hostility on both sides of the question threatened to divide the Union. Though a slave owner himself, Clay had moral reservations about slavery and supported gradual emancipation coupled with colonization. In fact, Clay had been a founder of the American Colonization Society in 1816. In his mind, however, the abolition of slavery was of less importance than the preservation of the Union. In the House, he helped frame the famous Missouri Compromise, which brought in Maine as a free state to balance Missouri and divided the rest of the Louisiana Territory. Though many politicians were involved, the compromise was seen as Clay's handiwork.

Clay's popularity did not immediately convert into political success. Clay was unhappy with the Monroe Administration. The president selected a New Englander, John Quincy Adams, as secretary of state, a post that Clay had expected. Sectional harmony had been purchased at the cost of alienating Kentucky's "Hotspur." Clay frequently criticized the Administration's lack of support for the Latin American revolutions, a stand which made him popular in South America. His persistence was rewarded with Monroe's famous declaration in 1823, but from Clay's perspective it was too little, too late. Most important, however, his quibbling with the Monroe Administration obscured a serious threat to his political future: Jacksonian democracy.

Since 1800, the nation had been dominated by Jefferson's party, but, in 1824, four prominent leaders, Clay, Andrew Jackson, William H. Crawford, and John Quincy Adams, entered the contest for president.

Almost everyone underestimated the military hero, Jackson. When the final votes were in, no candidate had a majority, but Jackson won a plurality. Shocked and disappointed, Clay came in fourth and was thus eliminated from consideration by the House. When Clay announced his support for Adams, which in effect made Adams president, Jackson was furious. Suspicions of underhanded dealing seemed confirmed when Clay was appointed secretary of state. This supposedly "corrupt bargain" provided a rallying cry for Jacksonians in the next election. While there is no evidence of prior arrangement, Jackson's complaint reveals an important difference between him and his rivals. Adams, Crawford, and Clay were all part of the leadership in Washington. Jackson, while a national military hero, had never been part of the Washington establishment. There was simply not enough room at the top, and Jackson became a lightning rod attracting those in politics and society who felt left out. Moreover, Democrats, taking advantage of extended suffrage, directed their appeal toward the common man even though Jackson and his allies were hardly common men.

Clay's new role in foreign affairs turned out be of little political value. The real drama was taking place internally, where followers of Jackson made a wreck of Adams' administration. The president was no match for the new kind of politician. Adams' style of leadership suited an earlier age; politics now stressed personality. Cold, aloof, and even arrogant, the president introduced a program designed to improve his constituents. Jacksonians were content to direct their appeal to the lowest common denominator. In 1828, Jackson's presidential victory changed American politics forever.

With Jackson and his minions ensconced in the White House, the anti-Jacksonian opposition began to fall apart. By mid-1829, however, Clay's Kentucky estate had become the center of another presidential campaign, and, in late 1831, its master once again returned to the Senate and was quickly nominated for president by a national Republican convention. The ensuing struggle revolved around the second Bank of the United States. Motivated by partisan concerns, the bank's supporters pushed for recharter before it was necessary. Clay believed that the effort would place Jackson in an untenable position. He was wrong. Jackson reacted quickly by vetoing the recharter bill and destroying the bank by removing government deposits. Jackson's policies did cause defections among his supporters, but his enemies mis-

calculated the impact on the electorate. As ignorant of banking practices as their president, voters sympathized with Jackson's struggle,
and the result was a smashing defeat of Clay's presidential aspirations.

There was no time for recriminations. As dust from the election
settled, a South Carolina convention passed an Ordinance of Nullification against the tariffs of 1828 and 1832. The power to act rested with
the president. Supposedly in favor of states' rights and less than enthusiastic about a tariff, Jackson, as usual, surprised everyone. Standing
firmly for national supremacy, he asked Congress to pass the so-called
Force Bill, granting the executive special authority in the crisis. Congress began to scramble for a compromise that would avert a military
confrontation between South Carolina and the federal government. At
center stage was Henry Clay. His compromise tariff gave South Carolina an excuse to back down without losing face. Once again, Clay had
been instrumental in saving the Union.

In Jackson's second term, a new opposition party was created by a
single idea: hatred of Andrew Jackson. It reached into British history
for a name signifying resistance to tyranny: Whig. Its program was
dominated by Clay's American System coupled with a bias against
executive power, but it also adopted attitudes toward political opportunism pioneered by Jacksonians. To Clay's disappointment, the new
party was too fragmented to unite around a single candidate in 1836.
Hoping to throw the election into the House, the Whigs selected three
sectional candidates to face Jackson's successor, Martin Van Buren. The
strategy failed; Van Buren won. Whig frustration vanished when, a few
months into the new administration, the country was rocked by an
economic depression. Clay, secure in the Senate, was in an excellent
position for the election of 1840, but his fellow Whigs were unsure.
With his legions of enemies, Clay's name could unite Jacksonians as
nothing else could. As a result, the party's convention turned away
from its real leader and chose William Henry Harrison. Inwardly
furious, Clay publicly supported the Harrison ticket.

The Whigs won, at last, by turning the tables on their enemies.
Harrison was a military hero, and the campaign which elected him
avoided serious political discussion. Still, most Whigs viewed the victory as a chance to reverse the tide in favor of Clay's American System.
They soon realized that they were mistaken. Harrison's death a few
months after inauguration brought to the White House a man who did

not share Whig ideals. John Tyler had been nominated for vice president to ensure the loyalty of Southern Whigs. When Congress passed the Whig legislative agenda, Tyler promptly vetoed the most significant measure, a bill creating a national bank. The result was chaos. Most of the Cabinet resigned, and Tyler governed without party backing.

Tyler's defection left Clay the unchallenged leader of his party, and the presidency, in 1844, seemed his. Once again, however, fate intervened. Pressure for annexation of Texas had been growing. Clay, like other established leaders, feared Texas would rekindle the slavery controversy. Though generally an expansionist, he came out against annexation, expecting that a similar stand by the likely Democratic nominee, Van Buren, would remove the touchy question. After Clay's nomination, the Democrats repudiated Van Buren and nominated the ardent annexationist James K. Polk of Tennessee. As the campaign progressed, Texas captured the public imagination, and Polk's narrow victory was probably the bitterest defeat of Clay's career.

In such circumstances most men would have welcomed retirement, but Clay's unquenchable love of political combat made it impossible. Moreover, the country needed him. As feared, Texas brought with it the Mexican War and reopened debate over slavery. Clay hoped for the Whig presidential nomination in 1848, but for the last time his party betrayed him. Concerned about his age and poor health, the Whigs nominated another military hero, Zachary Taylor.

Bitter but unbowed, Clay played one last role on the American political stage. Unsophisticated in politics, newly elected President Taylor only exacerbated the conflict over slavery. When California applied for admission as a free state with the Administration's blessing, the country once again faced disunion. As always, the Senator from Kentucky stood in the way of a complete rupture within the Union. In spite of frail health, he framed a series of measures that became the famous Compromise of 1850. Working in the brutally hot Washington, D.C., summer until his health broke, Clay turned over the leadership of the compromisers to a younger colleague, Stephen Douglas of Illinois, and watched from the sidelines as Douglas pushed through the final legislation. This desperate attempt at sectional peace had only a brief life, but Henry Clay did not live to see it collapse. He died in Washington, D.C., the scene of so many of his triumphs, on June 29, 1852, two years before his last compromise unraveled.

Summary

Throughout his long career, Clay's programs and personality were always controversial. To supporters, he was the best that American politics had to offer, and they often regarded him with near adulation. To enemies, he represented America at its worst, and they hated him with unbridled passion. Like most politicians, some of his positions changed with time and circumstance, but one element remained consistent—his vision of national purpose. Clay saw his country as the hope of mankind. He genuinely believed the republican system to be superior and looked forward to its spread. In a sense, his American System was designed to further this aim by making America stronger. The Union could continue to exist, Clay believed, only if the states would work for mutual benefit. The cement which would glue the nation together was a cooperative economic system managed by the common government.

Clay's vision was a short-run failure. During his own time, the American System was submerged under the rising tide of Jacksonian democracy and the new style of politics it spawned. Only eight years after Clay's death the country he loved was embroiled in the civil war that his many compromises had sought to avert. Like so many of his generation, Clay had been unable to face the moral dilemma created by slavery, which could not be compromised away. In the long run, however, Clay's vision was a success. The country that emerged from the Civil War was much closer to Clay's America than to Jackson's.

Bibliography

Baxter, Maurice G. *Henry Clay and the American System*. Lexington: University Press of Kentucky, 1995.

Eaton, Clement. *Henry Clay and the Art of American Politics*. Boston: Little, Brown and Co., 1957. A concise biographical treatment in "The Library of American Biography," edited by Oscar Handlin. Concentrating on Clay's political career, it follows the evolution of Clay from an advocate of Western interests to a true nationalist.

Howe, Daniel Walker. *The Political Culture of American Whigs*. Chicago: University of Chicago Press, 1979. A thoughtful analysis of Whig ideology. Clay is a central figure, and the book contains valuable insights into the source of Whiggery.

Mayo, Benard. *Henry Clay: Spokesman of the New West*. Boston:

Houghton Mifflin Co., 1937. The classic, scholarly biography of Clay. A colorful, well-written account which deals with Clay's private as well as public life. The treatment of Clay's early life in Kentucky is particularly valuable.

Poage, George Rawlings. *Henry Clay and the Whig Party*. Chapel Hill: University of North Carolina Press, 1936. A biographical treatment which concentrates on Clay's role in the founding and development of the Whig Party. The work is well documented but somewhat dated.

Remini, Robert Vincent. *Henry Clay: Statesman for the Union*. New York: W. W. Norton, 1991.

Sargent, Epes. *The Life and Public Services of Henry Clay Down to 1848*. Buffalo, N.Y.: Derby, Orton, and Mulligan, 1853. Completed soon after Clay's death as a memorial to the leader of American Whiggery. Biased and dated, but still an excellent example of the pro-Clay biographies written during his era.

Van Deusen, Glyndon G. *The Life of Henry Clay*. Boston: Little, Brown and Co., 1937. A somewhat critical biography of Clay. Well researched and written, the study provides balance when compared with the usual attitude of Clay's biographers.

David Warren Bowen

GROVER CLEVELAND

Born: March 18, 1837; Caldwell, New Jersey
Died: June 24, 1908; Princeton, New Jersey

Cleveland, who was both the twenty-second and the twenty-fourth president of the United States, brought great strength of character and inestimable political courage to the United States during years of political turmoil and economic crisis.

Early Life

Steven Grover Cleveland was the fifth of nine children born to Richard Falley and Ann Neal Cleveland. His father, a graduate of Yale University, was a minister who moved his growing family from Caldwell, New Jersey, to Fayetteville, New York (where Grover spent most of his youth), Clinton, New York, and thence to Holland Patent, New York. The Cleveland family, staunchly middle-class, was influenced by their Puritan heritage, their Presbyterian faith, and their belief in hard work. Young Grover had few intellectual, cultural, or academic interests, preferring instead the outdoor life and fishing. When his father died in 1853, Grover found it necessary to work and help support his family. After teaching for one year as an assistant at the New York Institute for the Blind, he decided that his fortune and future lay to the West.

Cleveland followed the westward path, however, no further than the booming town of Buffalo, New York. There, Cleveland worked for and lived with his uncle, Lewis P. Allen, a wealthy cattle farmer, helping to keep the record books for the farm. After a year, he decided to read law and joined the office of Henry W. Rogers, Dennis Bowen, and Sherman Rogers as a clerk. By 1856, young Cleveland was completely self-supporting. In that year, also, he determined to join the Democratic Party—not a typical choice but one which reflected the party affiliation of the law office in which he worked and his own opinion that the Republican presidential nominee, John C. Frémont, was too radical. Cleveland began to work for the Democratic Party, attending meetings and working in the wards. At the age of twenty-five, he was elected ward supervisor and the same year served a brief appointment as assistant district attorney.

Grover Cleveland *(Library of Congress)*

Cleveland's years in Buffalo served as preparation for his meteoric rise to national fame. There he astounded his colleagues with his capacity for long hours, attention to tedious detail, powers of concentration, and phenomenal physical energy. He showed little flair or imagination or awareness of either a cultural world or a world much beyond the boundaries of Buffalo. Cleveland, a bachelor, associated in his spare time with the other young men of the town, hunting, fishing, and enjoying an occasional beer in the local saloons. He was a large, round-faced man, with sandy hair and brilliant blue eyes. His girth led his nieces and nephews to call him "Uncle Jumbo"; his size represented considerable strength, however, rather than excess fat.

Cleveland was a staunch Unionist, a war Democratic, but when the Civil War broke out, he felt no particular inclination to fight. He provided the major support for his mother and two sisters, and, when drafted in 1863, he hired a substitute soldier, as permitted by law. In 1870, Cleveland was elected sheriff of Erie County, a position attractive in part because of the regular income it provided. While sheriff, Cleveland himself pulled the lever to hang two convicts, believing that it was wrong to require of others that which he was not willing to do himself. This incident provided further evidence of the absolute integrity which was an integral part of Cleveland's character. After one term as sheriff, Cleveland resumed his practice of law.

For the next ten years, Cleveland was a diligent and respected member of the bar in the expanding city of Buffalo (its population grew from 42,000 in 1850 to 155,000 in 1880). He was a contented plodder, satisfied with his place in the world and admired for his common sense. With its larger size, however, Buffalo government and politics became more corrupt, and when the Republicans nominated a "ring" candidate for mayor in 1881, the Democrats looked for an honest alternative. Attracted to Cleveland by his integrity (though, as a political novice, he was not the party's first choice), the Democrats persuaded him to run. At the age of forty-four, Cleveland was sworn in as mayor of Buffalo in 1882. His attacks on corruption and his courage in defying political bosses quickly gained for him a statewide reputation.

Life's Work
Luck played a part in Cleveland's career. The New York Democratic Party was badly divided over the power of Tammany Hall. The same moral outrage of the people who had elected Cleveland mayor of Buffalo made him an attractive candidate for governor of New York. Once again, the Republicans nominated a machine politician and the Democrats looked for a reformer. The big, bluff man from Buffalo caught the party's attention, was nominated, and in 1882 was elected governor of New York. Cleveland's administration was notable for its honesty, openness, strong values, good appointments, and courage in quarreling with John Kelly, the leader of Tammany Hall.

Once again, luck played a role in Cleveland's career, for the national Democratic Party was seeking a reformer, especially after the Republicans nominated James G. Blaine, a politician tainted with corruption since the Ulysses S. Grant Administration, for President of the United States. The opposition of Tammany Hall to Cleveland's nomination merely endeared his candidacy to other Democrats across the country, and in 1884 he received the Democratic nomination for president. As in his races for mayor and for governor, the major issue was corruption, and Cleveland's strength was his unquestioned honesty and integrity.

The campaign of 1884, however, soon collapsed into mudslinging. Blaine was increasingly identified with corruption in government, while the Republicans countercharged that Cleveland had fathered an illegitimate child. In reaction to the rhyme "Ma! Ma! Where's my pa? Gone to the White House, Ha! Ha! Ha!" Cleveland responded only, "Tell the truth." The truth appeared to be that Cleveland had acted honorably in a relationship with Mrs. Maria Halprin, and his courage and honesty once again impressed itself upon his countrymen. Cleveland made only four speeches during the campaign, while Blaine traveled more widely. A turning point came in the closing days of the campaign, when the Reverend Mr. Samuel D. Burchard, who accompanied Blaine, charged that the Democrats were the party of "Rum, Romanism, and Rebellion." This influenced a heavy turnout among the Irish Catholic voters of New York City, and by a narrow margin Cleveland became America's first Democratic president since 1856.

Cleveland was admirably suited to the needs of the United States in 1885. He headed a government which endeavored to correct the abuses of the past and establish honesty and efficiency in the administration of government. Cleveland appointed an excellent cabinet, including the Southern wing of the party once again. The major issues of his first administration were civil service reform, the role of silver currency, and a reduction of the tariff. He successfully expanded the Civil Service Act and moved toward a more professional government bureaucracy. In connection with the many patronage bills which flowed through Congress, Cleveland vetoed more than three hundred measures in his first administration (compared to 132 vetoes by the previous twenty-one presidents). He opposed the free-silver faction in the party, supporting instead a sound money policy based on gold. He was forced to retreat on the tariff issue in the face of Congressional opposition.

His administration was also noteworthy for the passage of the Dawes Act, which encouraged the Americanization of the Indians.

Additionally, the Interstate Commerce Act was adopted under and signed by Cleveland. There was a greater awareness of labor unrest as well, provoked by the Haymarket Square Riot in Chicago in 1886, which left several persons dead and reawakened a fear of organized labor. For the public, however, the most memorable part of Cleveland's first administration was his marriage in 1886 to Miss Frances Folsom, the twenty-two-year-old daughter of his former law partner (Cleveland was the first president to be married in a White House ceremony). The public was delighted with the romance, and, indeed, the marriage was a remarkably happy one.

As the election of 1888 approached, the Republicans began to gather funds and support to regain control of the national government. To oppose Cleveland, they nominated Benjamin Harrison, who vigorously campaigned against Cleveland and especially against tariff reform. Cleveland once again won a majority of the popular vote, but this time he narrowly lost the electoral vote to Harrison. Cleveland took his family to New York City, where he resumed the practice of law and where his first child (known to the country as "Baby Ruth") was born.

As discontent with the extravagant policies of Harrison grew, the Democrats turned once again to Cleveland in 1892. Again opposed by the New York Tammany Hall machine, Cleveland nevertheless was nominated on the first ballot. With his usual courage, he endorsed the gold standard in the face of strong party support for free silver. He was reelected president and returned to Washington (where his daughter Esther became the first child born in the White House) on the eve of the great Panic of 1893. Once again, the country needed a man of courage and honesty and was fortunate to have the leadership of Cleveland—who possessed these qualities in great abundance, along with a certain stubbornness and a lack of vision.

Before attending to the economic problems of the nation, Cleveland had to attend to a problem of his own—a malignant growth was discovered in the roof of his mouth. Fearing that public knowledge of his illness would fuel the panic, Cleveland chose to undergo a secret operation on board a borrowed yacht. The operation was successful, and not for twenty-five years did the full truth of that cruise emerge. Meanwhile, the debate over free silver was spurred on by the economic crisis. Cleveland continued to stand firm for a solid currency. He called a successful special session of Congress to repeal the Sherman Silver Purchase Act, which Cleveland believed contributed to the continuing economic decline. Unable to obtain adequate tariff reform, Cleveland continued nevertheless to protest the high tariff as also contributing to the Panic.

In an effort to avert the constant drain of gold from the United States Treasury, Cleveland agreed to a sale of government bonds handled by J. P. Morgan. Although a financial success, this apparent "sell-out" to the interests of big business hurt Cleveland and his party, already badly divided over the question of free silver. Similarly, his action in sending federal troops to help put down the Pullman workers' strike (1894) and his hostility to the unemployed workers who marched to Washington, D.C., as Coxey's Army, convinced the working-class supporters of the Democratic Party that Cleveland had abandoned them in favor of the rich.

In the area of foreign policy, Cleveland opposed imperialism, refusing to bring the treaty for Hawaiian annexation before the Senate. He maintained strict neutrality in the Cuban revolt, though encouraging Spain to moderate her treatment of the Cuban people. In the border dispute between British Guiana and Venezuela, Cleveland encouraged arbitration. He supported the Monroe Doctrine and appeared ready to risk war with Great Britain if a peaceful settlement was not reached. Once again, Cleveland acted strongly and courageously and won both the respect of and stronger ties with Great Britain as a result.

Silver continued to be the simplistic, single answer for those in and out of the Democratic Party who sought relief from the Panic. As the election of 1896 approached, it was clear that Cleveland had lost much of his party's support. Once again, Cleveland stood with courage for his principles and against free silver; this time, courage without compromise proved fatal. Although he had no desire for a third term, the Democratic convention repudiated him thoroughly in their platform. With William Jennings Bryan as their candidate and free silver as their issue, the Democrats' repudiation was silently returned by Cleveland, who found his private sympathy with the Republicans in the election. He was satisfied with the election of William McKinley, though it must have hurt to notice that Bryan, in losing, received almost a million votes more than Cleveland had received in his 1892 victory.

After the inauguration of McKinley, Cleveland and his family planned to retire to private life. Because of the children, Cleveland and his wife preferred an area less crowded than New York City and chose to settle in Princeton, New Jersey. There, Cleveland mellowed and enjoyed to the fullest his children and his community. He became deeply involved in the life of Princeton University, where he received an honorary degree and in 1901 was named a trustee. There, the eldest of his five children (his daughter Ruth) died in 1904, leaving a great void in her father's life. There also Cleveland knew, liked, and quarreled with the next Democrat to be elected president, Woodrow Wilson. There, also, Cleveland died, in June, 1908.

Summary

Grover Cleveland was admirably suited to his time. His disciplined life made him more comfortable as a supporter of the status quo than as a reformer, and his courage and conscience made him strong in actions he believed best for the interests of the United States. It was Cleveland's misfortune sometimes to be wrong in his judgment of what was best; the rigid strength of character which held him firm before the winds of pressure from special interests held him equally firm against compromise when it would, perhaps, have been wise. Nevertheless, Cleveland brought conscience, courage, and honesty to the White House at a time when those qualities had often been lacking. He provided an image—backed up by reality—of the integrity and leadership which America needed. He worked long hours, bringing his legal intellect to the consideration of all sides of a problem before making a rational decision about the wisest course to follow. Once that decision was made, he did not depart from it.

Though Cleveland was wildly unpopular in 1896, especially among the Bryan faction of Democrats, it was always his position and never his character which came under attack. In later years, he emerged with much greater popularity, and Americans, Democrats and Republicans alike, honored him for his courage and his honesty. The nation had come to realize the value of his leadership and to believe that the economic stability which had eventually prevailed would not have been possible without his strong opposition to free silver. Cleveland was a good man in an age in which goodness was not often cherished. The verse of James Russell Lowell perhaps best memorializes his contribution to America:

We, who look on with critic eyes
Exempt from action's crucial test,
Human ourselves, at least are wise
In honoring one who did his best.

Bibliography

Cleveland, Grover. *Letters of Grover Cleveland: 1850-1908*. Edited by Allan Nevins. Boston: Houghton Mifflin Co., 1933. Reprint. New York: De Capo Press, 1970. Useful for insight into Cleveland's mind and the reasons for his decisions. Includes some delightful letters of a more personal nature as well.

_____. *Presidential Problems*. New York: Century Co., 1904. Writings of the president after leaving office. Clear and comprehensive but not particularly insightful, which is generally true of the many books and articles Cleveland wrote in his retirement.

Ford, Henry Jones. *The Cleveland Era: A Chronicle of the New Order in Politics*. New Haven, Conn.: Yale University Press, 1919. One of a series of books on American history. Concise, without much interpretation.

Hollingsworth, Joseph Rogers. *The Whirligig of Politics: The Democracy of Cleveland and Bryan*. Chicago: University of Chicago Press, 1963. Excellent coverage of political events from 1892 to 1904. A readable account, especially helpful on the antagonisms within the Democratic Party and the silver issue. Strong analysis of the election of 1896.

Merrill, Horace Samuel. *Bourbon Leader*. Boston: Little, Brown, and Co., 1957. Excellent analysis, again largely political, of Cleveland and the Democratic Party both nationally and in New York.

Nevins, Allan: *Grover Cleveland: A Study in Courage*. New York: Dodd, Mead and Co., 1966. Indispensable Pulitzer Prize-winning biography. The definitive study of Cleveland and his political career, covering all the details as well as offering a broad analysis of Cleveland's career. Wonderfully readable style.

Welch, Richard E., Jr. *The Presidencies of Grover Cleveland*. Lawrence: University Press of Kansas, 1988.

Carlanna L. Hendrick

BILL CLINTON

Born: August 19, 1946; Hope, Arkansas

A five-term governor of Arkansas who was especially successful in improving education in his state, Clinton was elected the forty-second president of the United States in 1992; in 1996, he became the first Democratic president since Franklin Delano Roosevelt to win election to two full terms.

Early Life

William Jefferson Blythe IV was born in the rural town of Hope, Arkansas, on August 19, 1946, three months after the death of his father in an automobile accident. Later, as a teenager, he changed his surname to that of his stepfather, Roger Clinton. He began to be popularly known as Bill Clinton at the start of his political career.

As an infant, Clinton was reared primarily by his grandparents and a nanny. His mother, although devoted to him, frequently had to be away. When he was seven, his family moved to Hot Springs, Arkansas, where he received his elementary and high-school education.

He distinguished himself in both his classwork and extracurricular activities, and his outgoing and congenial nature made him popular. He was elected president of his junior class and became a National Merit Scholarship semifinalist; he also played saxophone in his own band. As a senior, he was selected to participate in the Boys' Nation program in Washington, D.C. At the White House, he met his idol, President John F. Kennedy; for the young Clinton, the encounter was a momentous event that would help to determine his political dreams and ambitions.

Despite his academic and social successes, however, his home life was often fraught with instability and tension. Clinton's stepfather was an alcoholic who physically abused his wife; on some occasions, the young man had to intervene to protect his mother. He also helped to care for his younger half brother, Roger Clinton, Jr.

In 1964, Bill Clinton enrolled at Georgetown University, a Jesuit institution in Washington, D.C. He majored in international studies, and he was elected class president during his first two years there. (Although he was brought up as a Southern Baptist, Clinton had significant experience of Catholic education; his primary education began in a parochial school.) While at Georgetown, he worked in the office of Arkansas senator J. William Fulbright, who became his political mentor.

Upon his graduation in 1968, Clinton went to England to study at Oxford University, having received the distinction of a Rhodes Scholarship. At the time, the United States was embroiled in the Vietnam War, and Clinton was eligible for the military draft. Although the number he received in the draft's lottery system was high enough to ensure that he would not be called into military service, some of his political opponents would later point to his time abroad as an instance of "draft dodging."

After returning to the United States, Clinton in 1970 began studies at Yale University Law School. There he met Hillary Diane Rodham, a fellow student whom he married in 1975. After receiving his law degree in 1973, he returned to his home state, where he accepted a position teaching law at the University of Arkansas in Fayetteville.

Life's Work

In the 1970's, Clinton began his professional political career. His first efforts, though, were less than auspicious. In 1972, he managed the Texas campaign of Democratic presidential nominee George McGovern, who was badly defeated; in 1974, Clinton himself campaigned unsuccessfully for an Arkansas congressional seat. In 1976, however, his political career gathered momentum: He managed the Arkansas campaign of victorious Democratic presidential candidate Jimmy Carter, and he was himself elected the state's attorney general.

Clinton proved popular as attorney general, and he was credited with helping to hold down utility and phone-service rates. In 1978, at the age of only thirty-two, he was elected to a two-year term as governor of Arkansas; however, he alienated key supporters by raising taxes to fund a highway-improvement project and by challenging major business interests. Moreover, he was identified with the Carter Administration, which became particularly unpopular in Arkansas for relocating Cuban refugees in the state. When he ran for reelection in 1980, he was defeated.

Shocked by his defeat, Clinton and his staff perceived that he needed to modify his image as a youthful radical. He decided to reassess what issues he should address and how to pursue them. During this difficult period, he was consoled by the birth of his only child, a daughter, Chelsea. He regained the governorship in 1982, and he was reelected in 1984, 1986 (at which point a four-year term was established), and 1990. He made improving the quality of education a major theme of his administration, and he cultivated a less radical image.

Bill Clinton *(Library of Congress)*

The education issue brought him wide support, particularly from business interests that needed an educated workforce to improve their competitiveness as the South experienced an economic resurgence. Clinton lobbied for increased teacher qualifications and pay, more rigorous administrative standards, and more demanding attendance and testing requirements for students. Financing for these efforts came from increases in the state sales tax.

Clinton was soon dubbed the "education governor," and his national stature began to rise. He became chair of the National Governors Association at the end of 1986. At the 1988 Democratic National Convention in Atlanta, he gave the nominating speech for the party's presidential candidate, Michael Dukakis. In 1990, he chaired the Democratic Leadership Council, an organization of moderate and conservative Democrats. As a "New Democrat" reassessing the role of big government and emphasizing the role of the private sector, Clinton positioned himself to run for the presidency in 1992.

He began his bid to unseat Republican incumbent George Bush at the end of 1991. During the primaries, while he was competing for the Democratic nomination against numerous rivals, his campaign almost collapsed under allegations that he had been having an extramarital affair. Similar allegations had troubled him earlier during his tenure as governor.

With the support of his wife, he overcame these difficulties and triumphed at the Democratic National Convention in New York City in July, 1992. In his campaign, he emphasized the human consequences of the recession and unemployment that were plaguing the nation and against which Bush seemed ineffective. He also emphasized the need for national health insurance and called for the federal government to balance the federal budget by increasing taxes in the higher income brackets and by reducing defense spending.

Clinton was elected the forty-second president of the United States on November 3, 1992. He received only 43 percent of the popular vote; Bush received 38 percent, and an independent candidate, the mercurial billionaire H. Ross Perot, received 19 percent. Clinton garnered 370 votes in the electoral college to Bush's 168, Perot obtaining none. Clinton's running mate was Tennessee senator Al Gore, Jr., a fellow Southerner and valuable adviser with whom Clinton established an exceptional rapport.

Sworn in on January 20, 1993, Bill Clinton was the first Democrat elected president in twelve years. He was also the first president to be born after World War II and the first since Herbert Hoover not to have had the experience of military service. In addition, he was the first president to be inaugurated during the post-Cold War period, in a world without the Soviet empire.

Clinton made addressing domestic issues his top priority. The Clinton Administration's most difficult task was to find ways to support essential government programs, trim or eliminate others, and balance the federal budget, which had accumulated an enormous deficit during the Reagan-Bush years (1981-1993). To staff his administration, Clinton assembled a team that emphasized representation of minorities and women.

During his first two years in office, he had the advantage of working with a Democratic Congress, and he was successful in several areas of legislation, somewhat satisfying both liberal and conservative agendas. He obtained passage of a budget that included both higher taxes on the wealthy and cuts in federal programs. Landmark anticrime legislation was passed that included a ban on certain assault weapons and increased the number of police. He also lobbied successfully for passage of family-leave legislation. On the world economic stage, he was successful in obtaining tariff reductions through the North American Free Trade Agreement (NAFTA) and the Uruguay Round of the General Agreement on Tariffs and Trade (GATT). He also appointed two Supreme Court justices whom he hoped would restore a more moderate balance to the Court, which had become increasingly conservative after a series of Republican appointments.

In foreign relations, his administration's goals were principally economic in nature, rather than political or military. This emphasis represented a major shift in American foreign policy and vividly reflected the consequences of the post-Cold War period. Nevertheless, the Clinton Administration dealt forcefully and immediately with renewed threats of Iraqi aggression against its neighbors. In Haiti, the U.S. forces restored civilian government; Clinton also sent peacekeeping forces into the tinderbox of the Balkans. A peacekeeping expedition to war-torn Somalia, however, was widely viewed as a fiasco. The administration also supported the emergence of market economies and democracy in the newly independent states of Eastern Europe and gave important backing to Russian president Boris Yeltsin. In the Middle East, the administration worked steadily for peace between Palestinians and Israelis.

On the domestic front, however, Clinton failed to obtain congressional approval of his prime legislative objective, national health-care reform, a project headed by his wife. He was also forced to compromise with the military establishment over efforts to end discrimination against gays in the armed forces.

Moreover, the Clinton Administration became the focal point for a number of highly charged moral, ethical, and legal issues that received continuous attention from the media and from political opponents. These issues included allegations of the improper dismissal of personnel from the White House travel office; charges against the president of sexual harassment; and questions about possible criminal involvement by the Clintons in Whitewater, a failed Arkansas land-development deal from more than a decade earlier. The Whitewater affair touched off an ongoing, wide-ranging independent counsel investigation that, though inconclusive, caused the Clintons substantial personal and political embarrassment.

Clinton's first-term troubles helped contribute to one of the most dramatic political reversals in U.S. history in the 1994 congressional elections. The Republicans obtained majorities in the House and Senate for the first time since the Dwight D. Eisenhower Administration, reversing decades of Democratic congressional dominance. This was a blow as stunning to Clinton as that which he had suffered when he was defeated in his first bid for reelection as governor of Arkansas.

The 1994 reversal produced a similar reaction, as Clinton resolved to accommodate the conservative center on issues of reducing government size and cost. At the beginning of 1995, it seemed as if his presidency might become paralyzed by the powerful Republican Congress led by the new House Speaker, Newt Gingrich.

The Republicans, however, lost popular support as wrangling over the federal budget resulted in the shutting down of federal government operations at the end of 1995 and the beginning of 1996. Clinton's popularity rose as he stood firm against proposed drastic reductions in Medicare and Medicaid funding. His support was further solidified in midyear when, to the dismay of liberals, he vowed "to end welfare as we've known it" and signed legislation terminating many federal subsidies for the poor. Throughout his first term, he presided over a period of peace and relative prosperity, the recession abating and unemployment steadily diminishing.

He was well positioned for the 1996 presidential race. No Democrat challenged him in the primaries, and he was overwhelmingly nominated at the party's August convention in Chicago. Clinton and Gore campaigned on a well-articulated platform of support for education, the environment, and Medicare, emphasizing that these would be the means of "building a bridge to the twenty-first century." His Republican opponent, Senator Bob Dole, did not articulate as extensive a program. In what was once again a three-way race, with Perot entering the campaign as the candidate of the new Reform Party, Clinton was reelected. He obtained 49 percent of the popular vote; Dole received 41 percent and Perot 8 percent. In the electoral college, Clinton obtained 379 votes to 159 for Dole; Perot again received none. The Republican majority was also returned to Congress.

Bill Clinton was inaugurated for a second term on January 20, 1997. He thus became the first Democratic president since Franklin Delano Roosevelt to be inaugurated for two full terms.

Summary

As a centrist and "New Democrat," Clinton positioned himself cautiously to the left or right of issues as political circumstances demanded. He thereby helped to salvage many of the liberal Democratic policies first instituted in the New Deal. These historic policies—and, therefore, the Clinton presidency—were sorely challenged by leaner economic conditions, diminishing federal budgets, and a conservative political and ideological environment.

Clinton demonstrated foresight and effort in regard to public policy and practices. He also demonstrated leadership in such diverse areas as international trade, education, and the environment and became an effective advocate for the poor and the elderly as well as for women and minorities. He notably failed, however, in one of his principal objectives, the creation of a national health-care system. Furthermore, he compromised one of his party's major tenets, financial assistance for the poor, by consenting to drastic cuts in federal welfare programs. Occasional episodes of political clumsiness and recurring questions about his ethics and personal character clouded his government. Finally, ethical questions concerning "soft money" contributions to his second presidential compaign (an issue which in a larger context involved both the Democratic and Republican Parties) began to receive congressional and public scrutiny during his second term in office.

Throughout his political career, and in his life in general, Clinton has shown a clear tendency to lead through conciliation. As a boy and a young man, he worked to reconcile mother and stepfather, Protestant and Catholic traditions, upper and lower classes, and black and white in the Deep South. In dealing with political opponents, too, he has typically avoided confrontation. He also has developed policy in exceptionally substantive, thorough, and analytical terms, and conveyed it in an articulate manner. Like Thomas Jefferson, Abraham Lincoln, and John F. Kennedy before him—presidents he has deeply admired—he may prove to have been a president inadequately understood in his own time, yet out of office soberly respected for his foresight and diligence.

Bibliography

Allen, Charles F., and Jonathan Portis. *The Comeback Kid: The Life and Career of Bill Clinton*. New York: Carol Publishing Group, 1992. Issued on the eve of the 1992 presidential election, this book examines Clinton's previous elections and strategies for them. Emphasizes his political shrewdness, resolution, and resilience.

Carville, James, and Mary Matalin, with Peter Knobler. *All's Fair: Love, War, and Running for President*. Carville was a principal strategist for the Clinton presidential campaign in 1992; he is married to Matalin, a Republican political consultant and strategist for President Bush. This book contains their varied, not necessarily opposing, views on the 1992 campaign.

Clinton, Bill, and Al Gore, Jr. *Putting People First: How We Can All Change America*. New York: Times Books, 1992. Published during the 1992 presidential campaign. The authors explain their views on and strategies for dealing with issues such as arms control, children, education, the environment, health care, trade, and many other topics.

Drew, Elizabeth. *On the Edge: The Clinton Presidency*. New York: Simon & Schuster, 1994. A noted journalist's analysis of the early years of the Clinton presidency. Focuses on its unevenness and on questions about the president's character.

Maraniss, David. *First in His Class: A Biography of Bill Clinton*. New York: Simon & Schuster, 1995. Examines the complexity of Clinton's character in the context of the schools and social environment that molded him.

Oakley, Meredith L. *On the Make: The Rise of Bill Clinton*. New York: Regnery Publishing, 1994. An analysis of Bill and Hillary Clinton as an ambitious couple. Includes balanced and candid insights.

Renshon, Stanley A. *High Hopes: The Clinton Presidency and Politics of Ambition*. New York: New York University Press, 1996. Attempts a psychological analysis of Clinton, studying his presidency within the framework of his contradictions and accomplishments.

Stewart, James B. *Blood Sport: The President and His Adversaries*. New York: Simon & Schuster, 1996. A temperate, even compassionate, analysis of the Whitewater affair.

Will, George F. *The Leveling Wind: Politics, the Culture, and Other News, 1990-1994*. New York: Viking, 1994. An anthology of articles by a noted conservative columnist. Describes the sociopolitical context in which Clinton assumed the presidency.

Woodward, Bob. *The Agenda: Inside the Clinton White House*. New York: Simon & Schuster, 1994. Woodward rose to prominence as an investigative reporter during the Watergate scandal; here he examines the early years of the Clinton presidency, focusing on the conflicts and dilemmas of the president and his core advisers.

_____. *The Choice*. New York: Simon & Schuster, 1996. Analyzes the 1996 presidential campaign. Based on interviews and primary sources.

Edward A. Riedinger

DeWitt Clinton

Born: March 2, 1769; Little Britain, New York
Died: February 11, 1828; Albany, New York

Clinton controlled New York State for his faction of the Republican Party, advocating both social stability and an active role for government. He was an unsuccessful presidential candidate and fought the emerging power of Martin Van Buren. His best-known project is the Erie Canal, concrete and practical, like his approach to politics, and exemplifying a proper resolution of several types of problems in a growing nation.

Early Life

DeWitt Clinton was born in Little Britain, Ulster (later Orange) County, New York colony, on March 2, 1769. His ancestors, Englishmen who were transplanted to Ireland, had immigrated to America in 1729, settling in New York in 1731, where DeWitt's father, James, was born. James, married to Mary DeWitt, of Dutch ancestry, had been a major general in the Revolution; his brigade had received the British colors at Yorktown. DeWitt was educated at the grammar school of the Reverend Mr. John Moffat and then studied for two years at the Kingston Academy, the best in the state. Two years later, in 1786, having emphasized courses in natural philosophy and mathematics, he was graduated from Columbia College at the head of his class. After studying law with Samuel Jones, Jr., he was admitted to the bar in 1790 but did not often practice; his legal training aided him in land transactions and in his growing involvement in politics.

Clinton's uncle, George Clinton, was the first governor of New York and the creator of a powerful political machine; thus, Clinton was accustomed to a political environment. In the *New York Journal* in November, 1787, Clinton published a series of letters from "A Countryman," opposing ratification of the proposed constitution; he attended sessions of the New York ratifying convention at Poughkeepsie and wrote a report from the Anti-Federalist position. He became his uncle's private secretary and shortly thereafter also secretary of the board of regents and of the board of fortification. While early involved in politics, he did not engage in politicking at the lower levels of party workers; this fact may explain his inability to deal with the mechanics and compromises of factional and party maneuvering.

Clinton was an impressive man, six feet tall and often referred to as "Magnus Apollo." His high forehead, large square face and firm features, and dark eyes gave the impression of strength and determination. He married Maria Franklin, daughter of an important Quaker merchant, who brought him four thousand pounds and landed property, on February 13, 1796. They had ten children, of whom four sons and three daughters were still living when Maria Clinton died in 1818. At the time of his marriage, Clinton was not active in politics, as the Republicans had succumbed to the greater political strength of the Hamiltonians (Federalists); Governor George Clinton retired in 1795, and the Federalists elected John Jay to the office. Clinton would undoubtedly have become a scientist of note had not opportunity and environment joined to bring him back into politics. Defeated for the state assembly in 1796, he was elected in 1797, and in 1798 won a four-year term in the state senate.

In 1801, the assembly elected Clinton as one of the four senators who, with the governor, constituted the council of appointment. This body controlled nearly fifteen thousand civil and military appointments and was therefore deeply entwined with the complex politics of both state and nation, still in flux in the early constitutional period, and with a two-party system not yet fully developed. The policy and partisan balances of state and national governments were also still unclear, and the tensions between executives and legislatures stemming from Revolutionary politics were institutionalized in the new constitution and exacerbated when different parties controlled the two branches. With its large number of presidential electors, the state of New York was vital, under the influence of Aaron Burr, in the "Revolution of 1800," which brought the Republicans to national power. State politics, however, were characterized by factions among the Republicans; Burr did not attempt to control the state, and the influential Livingston family, politically neglected by the Federalists, gave its support to the popular Clinton group. Clinton emerged as the state's Republican political leader.

The relative powers of the governor and council had not been completely clarified in the 1777 constitution, and consequently a bitter argument developed, ending in an appointment stalemate. Clinton at this time was young, energetic, and ambitious; his integrity and self-confidence and his ability to attract political loyalty were major advantages, balancing his ineffectiveness in handling people and in developing compromises. He was not a political theorist, always preferring the concrete and the practical, but his ideas were clear concerning the proper approach of the victorious Republicans to the offices of government. Opposing the Federalists' exclusion of Republicans from office, Clinton maintained that Republicans must be appointed in order that appointive positions might correspond to the verdict of the elections. To accomplish this, it was necessary to remove Federalists from most if not all major offices and from a sufficient number of minor ones to equalize the parties. As a dominant council member, Clinton took the lead in removing most of the governor's power over appointments and in implementing the appointment of Republicans. Rather than being the origin of the "spoils system," as many historians have suggested, this policy was simply more active in accommodating the appointive positions rather closely to the elective ones under the new political conditions of a developing national two-party system (rather than the older one of personal and local factions within the state alone).

On February 19, 1802, Clinton was appointed to a vacant seat in the United States Senate. During the next two sessions, he opposed a Federalist proposal to seize New Orleans from Spain over the issue of the right of deposit and supported the proposed Twelfth Amendment. The Senate at this time tended to be overshadowed by the House, however, and Clinton's personal and party interests were in New York. Late in 1803, Clinton resigned from the Senate to accept appointment (from Governor George Clinton and the council) as mayor of New York City. This was an important office, and its fifteen-thousand-dollar annual income was also welcome to Clinton, whose finances were frequently in disorder.

Life's Work

For the remainder of his career, Clinton acted in the state, rather than in the national, political arena. From 1803 to 1815 (except for 1807-1808 and 1810-1811), he was mayor of New York. At the beginning of his political career, in the assembly, he had been concerned with sanitation laws, debt reform, abolition, and the encouragement of steam navigation and agriculture. As mayor, he organized the Public School Society and aided the New York Orphan Asylum and the New York Hospital. In 1806, he supported the removal of political disabilities from Roman Catholics. As required of a mayor, he attended fires, helped to calm mobs, and inspected markets and docks. With a $100,000 defense appropriation, he supervised construction of fortifications on Governor's Island and elsewhere in the city. He took a firm stand against British impressment and blockade attempts off New York City. He supported a plan for city development and presided in the mayor's court. During his tenure as mayor, he served also as state senator (1806-1811) and lieutenant governor (1811-1813).

Dominating New York politics, Clinton assured the nomination of Morgan Lewis as governor in 1804. Thereafter, the Burr wing lost power in the party and Clinton broke with the Livingstonians, succeeding in having his choice, Daniel D. Tompkins, elected governor. Although basically a Republican, Clinton not only often attracted the support of Federalists but also was frequently in opposition to the Virginia Dynasty and to New York's Tammany Society. The Tammany "Martling-Men" or "Bucktails" viewed him as a political heretic and a cunning dealer in political offices and influence.

Federalist leaders in 1812 strongly favored Clinton as a presidential candidate, and the New York Republican legislature nominated him; his position on the War of 1812 was, however, equivocal. Had he received Pennsylvania's twenty-five electoral votes, Clinton, rather than James Madison, would have been president. (Soon afterward, on December 22, 1812, Clinton's father died.) Following his defeat, Clinton turned his energies to the development of "Clintonianism," a political position rather than a party, opposed to party labels and organization, seeking a wide base of support in the state. Clintonian Republicans saw an intellectual and benevolent elite, opposing "Jacobinical" chance, factions, and mobs, urban vice, and crime; yet they considered governmental power as derived from the people as a whole and to be used to meet their needs. An urban politician, hoping to make New York a cultural center to rival Boston and Philadelphia, Clinton was sufficiently Jeffersonian to develop a strong rural bias in his programs; the canal project was designed to stimulate both commercial prosperity and a westward movement, thereby reducing poverty and violence and averting the development of an urban proletariat and demagoguery. Clinton was ambivalent about both urban centers and government itself; appealing to both Federalists and Republicans, operating outside the increasingly delimited national party boundaries, Clinton emphasized the work of private societies to accomplish the necessary expansion of knowledge and the provision of facilities for "the people" in general.

Clinton's involvement in voluntary societies was by no means merely a personal and private activity but was closely associated with his political life. He belonged to several dozen societies, was active in most, and held offices in many. He was a member of several agricultural societies, the New York Bible Society, the American Bible Society, foreign and domestic scientific societies (natural history, geology, biology), the American Antiquarian Society, the Western Museum Society, the American Academy of Arts and Sciences, the American Philosophical Society, the New York Military Society, the New York Historical Society, and the Education Society of the Presbyterian Church. He was a prominent Mason; in 1814, he was cofounder and president of the Literary and Philosophical Society, presenting a book-length paper on American natural history; in 1816, he was able to get one large building to gather all the cultural societies in New York under one roof. His defeat in 1812 reduced his political power; he lost renomination for lieutenant governor and in 1815 lost the mayoralty as well. Yet he was rebuilding his support: His brother-in-law, Ambrose Spencer, was influential in President James Monroe's administration, he continued to attract Federalist as well as Republican voters, and the canal project was very popular.

As early as 1810, Clinton had been one of the commissioners planning a state canal between the Hudson River and the Great Lakes. The War of 1812 delayed the project, but by 1816 Clinton was actively promoting it; he was on the commission responsible for planning the canals between the Hudson, Lake Erie, and Lake Champlain. When Governor Tompkins resigned in 1817 to become vice president, Clinton was nominated (by a state convention including both Federalists and Republicans) and won by a landslide over Tammany's Peter B. Porter. Thereafter, however, President Monroe directed the majority of the federal patronage in New York not to the Clintonians but to their minority opposition, Martin Van Buren's Tammany Bucktail faction. Monroe's encouragement of intraparty strife was intended to avert a successful bid by Clinton in the 1820 presidential election; Monroe also believed that Clinton's associates in Congress were intensifying the Missouri crisis in order to reorganize national parties along sectional lines, a development which he considered a threat to the nation. Although Clinton won the gubernatorial election in 1820, the New York Republican Party schism was permanent: The Bucktails controlled the legislature and therefore the state patronage as well (through the council of appointment). At this point, Clinton attacked Monroe for having interfered in the state election process, a states' rights stand which could evoke support from both parties. In order to affect the 1821 state constitutional convention, Clinton had to prove his charges, which he did by submitting bulky documents, in a green cover, to the assembly. His "Green Bag Message" set off a debate over the permissible extent of political activity on the part of federal officials.

The Administration's hostility having prevented him from consolidating his political position, Clinton decided not to seek a third gubernatorial term in 1822. Van Buren was therefore able to develop his control and establish the "Albany Regency," which controlled New York State politics for a long time thereafter. (Tammany Hall was to benefit also from the flood of Irish voters resulting from the constitutional amendment Clinton had supported, eliminating the property requirement for voting.) The regency's removal of Clinton from the canal commission in 1824 provoked a reaction which helped the "People's" party elect him governor in November of that year. It was therefore as the state's executive that he participated in the 1825 celebrations opening both the Erie and Champlain canals.

Clinton declined the post of minister to England offered to him by President John Quincy Adams. In 1827, an Ohio convention nominated him as a presidential candidate, but he would have had little chance: He had a states' rights stand, there was a strong Anti-Masonic movement, and the issues of patronage and party organization continued to alienate support from the Clintonian group. On February 11, 1828, Clinton died suddenly. He was survived by his second wife, Catharine Jones, daughter of a New York physician, whom he had married on May 8, 1819; the New York legislature voted to appropriate ten thousand dollars for his minor children, as Clinton had left debts. His chief association in the public mind was with one of his most cherished projects, the great Erie Canal.

Summary

DeWitt Clinton, at the outset of his political career, was associated with the great national political figures of the time, the young postrevolutionary leaders who were to dominate national politics until the Civil War. He was always to be involved in the complex and bitter partisanship of the early nineteenth century, pitting state, sectional, and national interests against one another, swirling in a confusion of intrastate and intraparty factions. In contrast to his political contemporaries such as James Monroe, John C. Calhoun, John Quincy Adams, Henry Clay, Martin Van Buren, and Andrew Jackson, Clinton's primary political service was to be in his state rather than at the national level. Yet as a dominant politician in New York State, Clinton was necessarily a factor in national politics, and he shared the presidential aspirations of his colleagues: The electoral votes of only one state kept him from the presidency in 1812, and he remained a real political threat to the Virginia Dynasty.

As a politician, Clinton was a figure of ambiguities and contradictions. His preferences and policies placed him from time to time in all the varying political denominations; an elitist with a power base in one state only, he could never have developed a party organization around his own national leadership. He was never able in the mechanics of politics, and his personality, reserved and cold, did not attract supporters. Despite these shortcomings, he was usually admired and respected for his governmental abilities and positive programs. He supported states' rights yet viewed government as the necessary agency for developing programs to ensure general prosperity, balance and order in society, economic expansion and opportunities. His version of an earlier "country ideology" led him to numerous local agricultural societies, to the Society for the Promotion of Agriculture, Arts, and Manufactures, and to the canal project. At the same time, he was concerned with urban problems, advocating, for example, the inexpensive Lancasterian educational system and supporting the establishment of Emma Willard's academy at Troy; from 1805 until his death, he was president of the New York Free School Society. His concept of the role of government frequently gained for him Federalist support, yet he had begun in politics as a Republican. Conflicts with the Virginia Dynasty and Tammany Hall meant that he could never control the Democratic Republican Party, despite his support of Jackson, yet to play a prominent part among the National Republicans, he would have had to cooperate with John Quincy Adams, whom he disliked. A patrician elite providing leadership for the independent yeomanry was an idea belonging more to the eighteenth century than to the nineteenth, but Clinton was somewhat ahead of his time in his concept of government as a meliorative agency in society.

Closely connected to Clinton's emphasis on learned and benevolent societies was his own work in the sciences. In the undifferentiated field of early nineteenth century science, professionals and amateurs studied and worked over a wide range. Contemporaries (including the eminent scientists David Hosack, Samuel Latham Mitchill, and Constantine S. Rafinesque) considered Clinton a great naturalist, and he was responsible for the discovery of a type of American indigenous wheat and of the archaeological remains of prehistoric Indian tribes in New York. No theorist, he nevertheless agreed with the intellectual radicals of the day in accepting the concept of biological extinction as opposed to the consensus view of a static "chain of being." He played a major role as a patron and promoter of science, primarily through the voluntary societies and whatever governmental aid he could provide, as in the establishment of the New York Institution for the Promotion of the Arts and Sciences.

Not a Renaissance man, not a scientific theorist, not the founder of a new political alliance, long a state governor but never president, Clinton enjoyed a fruitful career of public service. Less of a national figure in historical perspective than his fellow senators were to be, he has been less well-known than they, to later times. The Erie Canal, one of his favorite projects, has enjoyed greater publicity than the man who helped to develop it in the context of wide programs for public improvement. Although Clinton may have taken a narrower view of public policies than his contemporaries, he nevertheless worked to acquire political support for his programs from a wide range of intrastate interests and areas, a political condition which, if operating at the national level, might have helped avert the increasing political polarization obvious even before the Missouri crisis. Although he died at a relatively young age, he had probably already accomplished nearly all that would have been possible for him in the social and political conditions of his time.

Bibliography

Bobbé, Dorothie De Bear. *De Witt Clinton*. New York: Minton, Balch and Co., 1933. Reprint. Port Washington, N.Y.: I.J. Friedman, 1962. Written in the early 1930's, this is the only full-length biography since James Renwick's in the early 1840's. A rather uncritical admiration.

Fish, Carl Russell. *The Civil Service and the Patronage*. Cambridge, Mass.: Harvard University Press, 1904. Reprint. New York: Russell and Russell, 1963. A general history of the subject. A clear and concise summary, with references to Clinton.

Hanyan, Craig R. "De Witt Clinton and Partisanship: The Development of Clintonianism from 1811 to 1820." *New-York Historical Society Quarterly* 56, no. 2 (1972): 108-131. Clear analysis of the political developments and programs, and intraparty factionalism in the state. Based chiefly on primary sources.

Hanyan, Craig R., with Mary L. Hanyan. *De Witt Clinton and the Rise of the People's Men*. Buffalo: McGill-Queens University Press, 1996.

Harris, Jonathan. "De Witt Clinton as Naturalist." *New-York Historical Society Quarterly* 56, no. 4 (1972): 264-284. Examines Clinton as a scientist and concludes that his contributions were more as a promoter of science. Includes 1825 portrait of Clinton by George Catlin.

Hopkins, Vivian C. "The Empire State—DeWitt Clinton's Laboratory." *New-York Historical Society Quarterly* 59, no. 1 (1975): 6-44. Has higher opinion of Clinton as a scientist than in the Harris article.

McBain, Howard Lee. *De Witt Clinton and the Origin of the Spoils System in New York*. Columbia University Press, 1907. Reprint. New York: AMS Press, 1967. Volume 28, number 1 in "Studies in History, Economics and Public Law," edited by the faculty of political science at Columbia University. This book is based largely on previously unused primary documents. Insightful study of developing party politics in the early national period and Clinton's role.

Nadler, Solomon. "The Green Bag: James Monroe and the Fall of DeWitt Clinton." *New-York Historical Society Quarterly* 59, no. 3 (1975): 202-255. Good examination of national and state politics and issues of the 1810's and 1820's and Clinton's position.

Siry, Steven E. *De Witt Clinton and the American Political Economy: Sectionalism, Politics, and Republican Ideology, 1787-1828*. New York: P. Lang, 1990.

Marsha Kass Marks

CALVIN COOLIDGE

Born: July 4, 1872; Plymouth, Vermont
Died: January 5, 1933; Northampton, Massachusetts

Practicing the virtues most Americans seemed to honor in absentia, Calvin Coolidge served as president of the United States during the central years of that extraordinary decade, the 1920's.

Early Life

John Calvin Coolidge was born in Plymouth, Vermont, on July 4, 1872. His father, Colonel John Calvin Coolidge (the rank was an honorary one bestowed for service on the governor's staff), was a prominent local figure who had served several terms in the state legislature. His mother, the former Victoria Josephine Moor, died when young Calvin was twelve. It was a painful loss to the boy, and his memories of his mother were very precious to him. It was from her family that he inherited the dash of Indian blood which so charmed political pundits during his presidential years. His only sister, Abigail, who was three years younger than Calvin, died in her teens. Her death was another blow to the sensitive youth.

After a brief period spent teaching school, Coolidge entered Amherst College in 1891. There he joined the College Republican Club and, in his senior year, a social fraternity. He was one of three persons in his class chosen to speak at graduation. His was the task of presenting a humorous speech, which he completed with considerable wit and the approval of his class. In 1895, he moved to Northampton, Massachusetts, and began the study of law. At the age of twenty-five, he was admitted to the bar and settled into the quiet, sober, often dull, and always frugal life-style which he followed until his death.

Standing slightly over five feet eight inches tall, Coolidge was a slim, rather drab, and colorless figure. His once reddish hair became a sandy brown as he matured. With his broad forehead, cleft chin, and thin features, he lived up to the Washington description of him as one who was "weaned on a dill pickle." Well deserving the sobriquet "Silent Cal," Coolidge began his diligent climb through small-town politics. Always listening and working rather than talking—though he could speak effectively, with his dry, raspy voice and flat New England accent—Coolidge became a local Republican committeeman before he was thirty and not long thereafter was elected to the Republican State Committee. In addition, Coolidge served on the town council, was named vice president of a local savings bank, and, in 1900, was appointed city solicitor.

At the age of thirty-two, Coolidge courted and wed Grace Goodhue,

Calvin Coolidge *(Library of Congress)*

a teacher at the local school for the deaf and dumb. Her charm and vivacious personality were a perfect foil to his lack of, and disregard for, the social graces. Theirs was a happy and contented marriage, each understanding and accepting the foibles of the other. They had two sons, John and Calvin, Jr., who completed the family.

In 1906, Coolidge was elected to the Massachusetts House of Representatives, where the same qualities that had served him so well in Northampton led to his slow but steady rise to leadership. Coolidge was elected mayor of Northampton in 1910; in 1912, he was elected to the state Senate; and two years later, was chosen president of the state Senate. The next logical step was the office of lieutenant governor, to which he was elected in 1916, and in 1918, he was elected governor of Massachusetts.

Life's Work

Events conspired to make Governor Coolidge a national figure. The labor unrest which followed the end of World War I produced the Boston police strike in 1919. Though the strike was settled largely without the intervention of the governor, Coolidge captured the imagination of the country and the convictions of the time with a dramatic phrase in a telegram sent to American Federation of Labor president Samuel Gompers: "There is no right to strike against the public safety by anybody, anywhere, any time." This statement catapulted Coolidge into national prominence and made him the popular choice for vice president among the delegates to the Republican National Convention in 1920. Safely elected with President Warren G. Harding in the Republican return to "normalcy," Coolidge gave undistinguished service in an undistinguished office.

Calvin Coolidge had no part in the scandals which pervaded the Harding Administration. He remained untouched by the revelations of bribery and misuse of high office. When he succeeded to the presidency upon the death of Warren G. Harding in 1923, he seemed to represent the incorruptible side of a tarnished Republican coin. As if to symbolize his virtues, Coolidge, visiting his home in Vermont when he learned of Harding's death, was sworn in as president by his father (a notary public) in the light of a kerosene lamp. The rugged simplicity of the swearing in was in sharp contrast to the bright urban lights and fast-paced life that seemed more typical of the 1920's. Coolidge made no changes in Harding's cabinet. He came especially under the influence of Secretary of the Treasury Andrew W. Mellon, who represented the established wealth that was, to Coolidge, the result of success in America. Coolidge particularly identified his and the country's interests with the class represented by Mellon in his most often quoted statement that "the business of America is business."

Coolidge presided over a government largely retreating from the activism and reform of the Progressive Era and from the demands of victory in World War I. He was personally honest, loyal, and frugal—and he served as the keeper of America's conscience. While the nation indulged itself in an orgy of spendthrift frivolity, the silent approval of so austere a president seemed to make virtuous an otherwise hedonistic attitude toward life.

Coolidge was personally popular and was always an adroit politician, so it was with ease that he was nominated for president in his own right in 1924. These same factors, supported by an accelerating prosperity and aided by a seriously divided Democratic Party (whose nominating convention cast 103 ballots before deciding upon John W. Davis of West Virginia as their candidate), led to a Republican victory. The Coolidge years saw decreasing governmental activity and few legislative accomplishments. Coolidge vetoed one of the few major bills of the era, the McNary-Haugen bill, which was designed to bring stability to the farm market. He continued the traditional high tariff policy supported by the Republicans, and both his policy and his pronouncements encouraged the upward movement of the stock market that characterized his years as president.

Coolidge vigorously supported economy in the operation of the government. He believed that a reduction in government costs, while beneficial in its own right, would also make possible a reduction in taxes, particularly for the business classes. He mildly favored railroad consolidation in the interest of greater efficiency and was interested in a waterways project in the St. Lawrence area (though never the Mussel Shoals project proposed during his term, which formed the base of the future Tennessee Valley Authority). In spite of a growing reputation as "Silent Cal," Coolidge held frequent and often lengthy press conferences during his years as president.

In foreign policy, Coolidge, like his party, opposed American membership in the League of Nations. He did, however, unsuccessfully support American participation and membership in the World Court. In line with his respect for business, Coolidge staunchly demanded that European nations repay to the United States their debts from World War I. He supported efforts to work out a schedule of payments (tied to the payment of German reparations), and he believed that the payment of the valid debts was necessary to provide worldwide economic stability. He was also a strong advocate of the Kellogg-Briand Pact and its effort to promote peace by outlawing the use of war as a national policy.

Coolidge's personal popularity, combined with the continuing prosperity of the nation during his administration, made him seem a logical candidate for renomination in 1928. Therefore, it was a stunning surprise when, while on vacation in 1927, he informed reporters that "I do not choose to run for President in 1928." It was a statement on which he never elaborated and from which he never deviated. Many contemporaries believed that he wanted another full term but wanted to be drafted by his party. Others believed that the decision stemmed from a reluctance to violate the two-term tradition (since he had already served the remainder of Harding's term). For others, it seemed that the death of his youngest son in the White House had taken much of the joy from public life, and he seemed tired of holding office. Whatever the reason, the decision was never effectively challenged, and the Republicans turned to Secretary of Commerce Herbert Clark Hoover as their candidate in 1928.

Coolidge and his wife left the White House in the same quiet style which had always characterized their life. Coolidge refused many offers of employment, lest his name and former position be used to advertise a business. He and Grace returned to Northampton, where, for the first time in all of their years of marriage, Coolidge finally purchased a house. He kept busy writing his autobiography, as well as a number of magazine articles, and served on several committees. He died quietly and alone of a coronary thrombosis on January 5, 1933.

Summary

With the advent of the Great Depression in 1929, the Roaring Twenties, the Coolidge Era, came to an end. Coolidge was deeply concerned about the effect of the Depression, especially so for those whose losses were heavy. Yet he had always had a clear perception of credit as another form of debt and was, himself, largely untouched by the crash. Far more a Hamiltonian than a Jeffersonian in his philosophy of government, Coolidge supported the interests of property as necessary for the stability of the government. He believed that a healthy business environment was essential to the national well-being of the United States. Coolidge was personally frugal, always saving a part of his salary no matter how small, and he carried that same commitment to frugality with him into government.

Coolidge believed that government should not intrude in the daily lives of its citizens. It is one of the great ironies of American history that his years of inactivity at the head of the nation helped to pave the way for the enlarged role of government which the New Deal of President Franklin D. Roosevelt brought about in an effort to recover from the Depression.

The decade of the 1920's was unique in American history. Presiding over this boisterous era was an essentially shy little man; competent, respectable, cautious, loyal, and honest. These were qualities of character held in high regard by Americans even as they flouted them. Coolidge was always an intensely political person—a quality often overlooked as more flamboyant personalities strutted on center stage. He had a politician's sensitivity to the public's needs and wishes. He captured in himself those qualities Americans both desired and trusted—an island of stability and old-fashioned virtue in an ocean of new values.

Coolidge Prosperity was more than simply a campaign slogan. It was a very real perception of cause and effect, and much of Coolidge's popularity stemmed from that perception. Coolidge was an enormously popular president—popular more as a symbol than as an individual whose idiosyncrasies and foibles were well-known and well loved. He was precisely suited to the public temperament in the 1920's, and perhaps he could have succeeded in no other era. His personality and philosophy could not have provided effective leadership for either the surging reforms of the Progressive Era or the demands for an enlarged government under the New Deal. Rather, he provided a period of rest and retreat from government activity.

Calvin Coolidge was not a great president; neither was he a failure. He was a man unusually suited to an unusual time. More a symbol of an imagined past—in which simplicity, honesty, and frugality were cherished—than a reflection of the roaring rush of modernity that characterized the 1920's, Coolidge gave Americans what they wanted, though the lesson of history might suggest that he was not exactly what they needed.

Bibliography

Abels, Jules. *In The Time of Silent Cal.* New York: G. P. Putnam's Sons, 1969. Excellent brief survey of Coolidge, the man, and a useful analysis of the years in which he served the United States.

Allen, Frederick Lewis. *Only Yesterday.* New York: Harper and Row, Publishers, 1931. An indispensable contemporary account of the 1920's. Has little comment on Coolidge but is valuable for the insights and the immediacy of its portrayal of those times.

Booraem, Hendrik. *The Provincial: Calvin Coolidge and His World, 1885-1895.* Cranbury, N.J.: Associated University Presses, 1994.

Bradford, Gamaliel. *The Quick and the Dead.* Boston: Houghton Mifflin Co., 1931. With his usual wit and perspicacity, Bradford profiles Coolidge, as well as others, who marched more colorfully across the stage of American history.

Coolidge, Calvin. *The Autobiography of Calvin Coolidge.* New York: Cosmopolitan Book Corp., 1929. The length of this work certainly refutes the idea of an always "Silent Cal." It offers some insights into the mind and philosophy of this generally unknown president. Like most autobiographies, it must be read with caution and supplemented by other, more objective works.

Fuess, Claude Moore. *Calvin Coolidge: The Man from Vermont.* Boston: Little, Brown and Co., 1940. A lively, well-written account of a not-so-lively man. It is, however, very partisan toward Coolidge and needs to be balanced by other works.

Hicks, John D. *Republican Ascendancy, 1921-1933.* New York: Harper and Row, Publishers, 1960. An excellent book for background on the 1920's from a governmental and political perspective.

Hoover, Irvin Hood. *Forty-two Years in the White House.* Boston: Houghton Mifflin Co., 1934. The always lively account of life behind the scenes at the White House written by chief usher "The" Hoover. He did not particularly like Calvin Coolidge, and his comments provide a useful, though not always to be trusted, view of Coolidge's personal life.

McCoy, Donald R. *Calvin Coolidge, The Quiet President*. Lawrence: University Press of Kansas, 1988.

Murray, Robert K. *The Politics of Normalcy: Governmental Theory and Practice in the Harding-Coolidge Era*. New York: W. W. Norton and Co., 1973. Yet another excellent account of the 1920's, with an emphasis upon the part played by Coolidge. There are not many available biographies of Coolidge, and books such as this one on the 1920's are thus especially valuable to the student.

Thompson, Charles Willis. *Presidents I've Known and Two Near Presidents*. Freeport, N.Y.: Books for Library Press, 1956. Moderately useful personal view of Calvin Coolidge with less insight into his impact on his time.

White, William Allen. *A Puritan in Babylon: The Story of Calvin Coolidge*. New York: Macmillan, 1938. An excellent standard biography of Coolidge. White was well acquainted with Coolidge and admired him, so this book also should be balanced by a less admiring view. White's verbose style somewhat dates this book, but his talent and insight make it well worth reading.

Carlanna L. Hendrick

JEFFERSON DAVIS

Born: June 3, 1808; Christian County, Kentucky
Died: December 6, 1889; New Orleans, Louisiana

Davis served his country ably as senator and secretary of war; his commitment to the South led him to accept the presidency of the Confederacy and attempt to preserve Southern independence against bitter opposition and overwhelming odds. Reviled or idealized as a symbol of the Confederacy, Davis' consistency of principle and unflagging efforts balance out the fact that he was not well fitted for the demands of the times and the position.

Early Life

In the turbulent decades of the early 1700's, a son of Welsh immigrants moved his family from Philadelphia to the Georgia area; Evan Davis' son Samuel, as reward for his services as a Revolutionary guerrilla captain, was granted land near Augusta. He was chosen county clerk and in 1783 married Jane Cook. Continuing the family pattern, Samuel migrated often; in 1792 he moved to Kentucky, where his tenth and last child, Jefferson (Finis) Davis, was born at Fairview in Christian (later Todd) County, on June 3, 1808. By 1811, the family was living in Louisiana but later moved to Wilkinson County, Mississippi Territory. In these frontier areas, owners worked in the fields with their slaves; Samuel Davis was able to give only a single slave to each of his children when they married. His eldest son, however, Joseph Emory Davis, demonstrated in his life the "flush times" and upward mobility of the Lower South: He became a lawyer, the wealthy owner of a great plantation, and a "father" to his youngest brother.

In his youth, Jefferson Davis spent two years at the Roman Catholic St. Thomas' College in Kentucky and then attended local schools near home; in 1821, he studied classics at Transylvania University in Lexington, Kentucky. Just after his father's death, late in 1824, he entered West Point Military Academy. He was over six feet tall, slender, an active, high-spirited young man, with brown hair and deep-set gray-blue eyes, a high forehead and cheekbones, and an aquiline nose and square jaw. In 1828, twenty-third out of a class of thirty-three, he was graduated as a second lieutenant. For the next seven years he was on frontier duty at the dangerous and lonely posts in Wisconsin and Illinois, acquitting himself well and with initiative; in 1832, he briefly guarded the captive chief Black Hawk. In 1833, at Fort Crawford, Wisconsin, he met Sarah Knox Taylor, daughter of the commandant, Colonel Zachary Taylor; despite the latter's objections, they were married June 17, 1835, at her aunt's home in Kentucky.

Despite Davis' conviction of his aptitude for the military, he resigned his commission; Joseph gave the young couple an adjoining new plantation, Brierfield, and fourteen slaves on credit. As neither was acclimatized, they left for the Louisiana plantation of a Davis sister, but they both contracted malaria, and Knox Davis died on September 15, 1835. A grieving Davis, convalescing in Havana and New York, spent some time also in a senatorial boardinghouse in Washington, D.C., but soon returned to Brierfield. For the next eight years he led a solitary and reclusive life, reading extensively in literature, history, and the classics and associating primarily with his brother. During this period he developed the basic system of Brierfield, which was almost an ideal plantation: benevolent master, slaves trained and working according to their abilities and making many decisions concerning their labor and earnings, and Davis' personal slave James Pemberton as overseer with a practically free hand. During these years Davis developed his attachments, both theoretical and personal, to the soil, the South, and the new aristocratic society of the Lower South. His identification was completed and symbolized by his marriage on February 26, 1845, to Varina Anne Banks Howell; she was half his age, a black-haired beauty of Natchez high society, with a classical education and a vivacious temperament. Throughout her life, "Winnie" Davis was high-strung, demonstrative, and emotionally turbulent, a determined woman who fought fiercely for those she loved and who was not always either tactful or forgiving.

By this stage of his life, Davis' personality had been formed. Despite his military experience and life as a planter, he had never really had to fight for place and position; he was more of a theoretician than a realist. He was affectionate with family and friends, essentially humorless, coldly logical, with a deep-rooted egotism and a sense of his own merit; he was never able to believe that others' criticism or disagreement could be sincere or impersonal. Committed firmly to aristocracy and slavery, state sovereignty and states' rights (under the Constitution and within the American nation), always a Democrat, Davis moved into politics. In 1843, he lost an election for the state legislature to a well-known Whig; in 1844 he was a Polk elector. In 1845, he was elected to the United States House of Representatives.

Davis entered into marriage in February, 1845, and entered Congress in December; in June, 1846, on the outbreak of the Mexican War, he resigned from the House to become colonel of the volunteer mounted First Mississippi Rifles. He trained his regiment and equipped his men with the new percussion rifles, and under Major General Zachary Taylor it participated creditably in the victory at Monterrey. When, in the following February, General António Lopez de Santa Anna led fifteen thousand men across two hundred miles of desert to confront Taylor's five thousand at Buena Vista, Davis' Mississippi Rifles fought off a Mexican division in an action (the famous V-formation) that may have been decisive for the American victory. Davis led the regiment despite a wound in the foot that kept him on crutches for two years and in intermittent pain for the next decade. This episode gained for Davis a popular reputation as a military hero and reinforced his already ineradicable conviction of his own military capability.

After Buena Vista, with Taylor's influence waning and the regiment's enlistment expiring, Davis again resigned a military commission, and in December, 1847, was appointed to a vacancy in the Senate. An expansionist, he supported President Polk on the Mexican Cession, even suggesting American acquisition of Yucatan; although he acquiesced in extending the Missouri Compromise line to the Pacific, he asserted that there was no constitutional power to prohibit slave property in any territory. The complex politics associated with the Compromise of 1850 included several Southern groupings: Unionists, radical states' righters (in favor of immediate secession), Southern "nationalists" (or "cooperationists," anticipating possible later secession by the South as a whole). When his fellow Mississippi senator Henry S. Foote ran for governor on a Union ticket (a coalition of Whigs and some Democrats), Davis was persuaded to resign from the Senate (in September, 1851) and oppose him on the Democratic ticket; Davis lost by a thousand votes. Political defeat was offset by the birth of the Davis' first child, Samuel Emerson, on July 30, 1852.

Having aided in the campaign to elect Franklin Pierce, Davis was appointed secretary of war in March of 1853. Ironically, these four years were to be the most congenial and productive of his life. He was in good health and spirits; "Winnie" Davis was a charming and vivacious hostess and the Davis house was the social center of official Washington circles. There was a growing family: Although Samuel died on June 30, 1854, Margaret Howell (Maggie or Pollie) was born on February 25, 1855, and Jefferson, Jr., on January 16, 1857. As secretary of war, Davis supported the concept (developed by John C. Calhoun during his tenure of the office) of an expansible army; infantry units were issued the new percussion-cap muzzle-loading rifles and Minié balls; infantry tactics were made somewhat more flexible; West Point officers were encouraged to study in Europe and to develop military theory; and the regrettable system of army departments was strengthened. Davis urged the use of camels in the Southwest, but the experiment failed. Davis was unable to influence the Administration on the issues of the *Black Warrior* seizure and the Ostend Manifesto, but as a Southern expansionist he enthusiastically organized a research expedition to the Southwest to provide data which led to the Gadsden Purchase.

The end of Davis' term in the cabinet was soon followed by his election to the Senate; he took his seat in March, 1857. Another son, Joseph Evan, was born on April 18, 1859. Davis' time as senator would have been the peak and epilogue of his political career, had it not been prologue to suffering and defeat. Nearly fifty, he was gaunt and neurotic; he suffered from dyspepsia and neuralgia and lost the sight of his left eye. He was an effective orator, aided by the obvious intensity of his convictions, and he strongly supported the South's interests in the increasingly bitter sectional confrontations of the 1850's. Within the Democratic Party, he fought the popular sovereignty position of Stephen A. Douglas and worked to prevent the latter's nomination as Democratic candidate in 1860.

Abraham Lincoln's election and nonnegotiable stand against expansion of slavery into the territories convinced Davis of the necessity and inevitability of secession; on January 21, 1861, upon learning of Mississippi's secession, he resigned from the Senate. Like few others at the time, Davis expected war, probably anticipating a command position; he was indeed appointed major general of Mississippi's troops. The Montgomery convention, which established a provisional government, however, needed a president more acceptable to the moderates (or earlier "cooperationists") and early in February, 1861, elected Jefferson Davis.

Life's Work

Davis was elected president of the Confederate States of America, for the constitutional six-year term, on October 6, 1861; on December 16, William (Billy) Howell was born. Davis was inaugurated in the official Confederate capital of Richmond, Virginia, on February 22, 1862. On March 6, 1861, the Confederate Congress had authorized a hundred thousand volunteers for a twelve-month enlistment, but even after Fort Sumter, Davis did not move to ensure an adequate munitions supply or a financial base (for example, the use of cotton supplies to secure paper currency). The emphasis on protecting the capital at Richmond effectively divided the Eastern and Western Confederacy; Davis retained the system of military departments, their heads responsible directly to him, and therefore eliminated the possibility of unified strategy or well-coordinated action. His military strategy was only to defend, meeting Union forces wherever they might move. He failed to understand that the military situation, as well as the political situation, was a revolutionary one; he could not come to grips with the conditions and concepts of this first modern war. It is true that few at that time fully comprehended its implications; Lincoln, Ulysses S. Grant, and William Sherman were probably the only ones who realized its necessities.

Davis' long-standing quarrel with Joseph E. Johnston stemmed from the latter's failure to be ranked highest of the five Confederate full generals. Late in the war, Davis removed Johnston from command in Georgia at a critical point: General John Bell Hood's loss of Atlanta aided in Lincoln's reelection and continued Northern support of the war. Public and congressional opinion did not influence Davis: He refused to remove General Braxton Bragg despite that officer's ineffectiveness in battle, and when forced to remove Judah P. Benjamin as secretary of war, he "promoted" him to secretary of state. Davis spent too much time in battle areas; he neglected the West and refused to authorize the transfer of troops across the boundaries of military departments to areas where they were needed. Even after Antietam, he could not see that only a major offensive held any hope of victory and independence; instead, he insisted on scattering garrisons and attempting to hold every inch of territory. Robert E. Lee's offensive into Pennsylvania came too late and could not thereafter be repeated.

Close control of military policy overshadowed all other considerations in Davis' administration, although all policy in fact concerned the pursuit of the war. Davis' commitment to a "Southern nation" provoked opposition, from "fire-eaters" such as Robert Barnwell Rhett and William L. Yancey, states' righters such as Governors Joseph E. Brown of Georgia and Zebulon B. Vance of North Carolina, and Vice President Alexander H. Stephens. The influential *Richmond Examiner* and *Charleston Mercury* regularly opposed Davis' policies; his imperious approach and inability to handle the political situation gave rise to vague but frightening rumors that he was a despot who at any moment might take over the entire government and even use the army to control the people. The tension between sovereign states and an embryo national government in wartime can be seen in most of the controversial issues: general conscription was denounced as unconstitutional, attempts to suspend the writ of habeas corpus were deemed tyrannical. The "rich man's war and poor man's fight" continued with increasing military setbacks and declining supplies and morale.

During the last winter of the war, Davis remained strangely optimistic. He had always had strong faith; in May of 1862 he had joined St. Paul's (Episcopal) Church. Although devastated by the death of Joseph, who fell from a balcony on April 30, 1864, he was consoled by the birth of Varina Anne (Winnie) on June 27, 1864. He urged a draft of forty thousand slaves (to be freed after victory); he sent an agent to offer Great Britain an emancipation program in return for recognition and military alliance. Peace movements, projects to remove Emperor Maximilian from Mexico, the Hampton Roads conference: Davis would consider no compromising of Southern independence (just as Lincoln was committed absolutely to the Union). He seemed to believe that at the last moment the South might yet be saved, perhaps by one great battle led by General Lee and by himself that would sweep the Union armies from the field.

Having evacuated his family, Davis, along with several associates, left Richmond on April 3, 1865, still committed to continuing the war. News of Appomattox convinced the party to head southward; a cabinet meeting in Greensboro, North Carolina, agreed that General

Johnston should ask for terms. At Charlotte, twelve days later, the group recognized Confederate defeat and dispersed, Davis moving south into Georgia to rejoin his family and attempt to leave the country. On May 10, the Fourth Michigan Cavalry came upon them at Irwinville, Georgia; Davis' brief attempt to slip away in a hastily snatched-up rain cape belonging to his wife gave rise to the story that he had tried to disguise himself as a woman to evade capture.

For the next two years, Davis remained a state prisoner in a damp casemate cell in Fortress Monroe. He was once put forcibly in irons for five days, with a lamp burning continually and the guard marching regularly outside, without adequate clothing or books, and suffering from erysipelas. His fortitude, faith, and kindliness impressed the doctors assigned to him, and finally he was placed in more comfortable quarters in the fortress, his family (which had been kept in Savannah) permitted to join him and friends permitted to visit him. On May 4, 1867, he was arraigned on a charge of treason in the federal district court in Richmond and released on bail supplied by ten men, among them Horace Greeley and abolitionist Gerrit Smith. Thereafter, he and his family traveled at various times to Canada, Cuba, New Orleans, Vicksburg, and Davis Bend, as well as to Europe. He was never brought to trial, as the complex constitutional issues surrounding secession remained too controversial and politically incendiary (especially during the Reconstruction period) to be aired in connection with the former president of the defeated Confederacy. His case was dropped on December 5, 1868.

During the remaining years of his life, Davis experienced a series of business failures, several unprofitable European trips, and a gradual recovery of his health. Maggie became Mrs. J. Addison Hayes and settled in Memphis, but Billy died of diphtheria in 1872, and the remaining son, Jefferson, Jr., having failed at Virginia Military Institute, died of yellow fever in 1878. Davis was able to salvage only part of the value of his old plantation in 1878. A friend of Varina, the widowed Mrs. Sarah A. E. Dorsey, gave him a cottage in which to work, on her plantation "Beauvoir," near Biloxi, on the Mississippi Gulf coast. Varina was finally reconciled to this cooperation, and to Davis' inheritance of the estate in 1879, and aided him in his writing of the two-volume *Rise and Fall of the Confederate Government* (1881), primarily a justification of the constitutionality of secession. In the South, Davis was largely "rehabilitated," being often invited to make speeches and dedicate memorials (including one near his birthplace). His youngest, Winnie, the "Daughter of the Confederacy," was assailed for wishing to marry a New York lawyer, grandson of an abolitionist, and died in 1898 at thirty-three, still single and grieving.

Despite financial problems, Davis, as he had done previously, continued to support both Howell and Davis relatives and several poor children and to entertain a variety of visitors. In 1889, he fell ill with bronchitis in New Orleans, Louisiana, and died there on December 6; he was buried there but, on May 31, 1893, reinterred in Richmond. He had steadfastly refused to ask for a federal pardon, even in order to be elected senator from Mississippi, averring that he had committed no legal offense. On October 17, 1978, a unanimous joint resolution of Congress restored his citizenship.

The year after Davis' death, his widow wrote her two-volume *Memoir* (1890); living in New York, she kept his reputation alive, with the help of Joseph Pulitzer and the Confederate "expatriates" in the North. She died in New York on October 16, 1906, at the age of eighty, and was given a military funeral in Richmond.

Summary

Jefferson Davis was poorly suited for the task of political leadership of the Confederacy at its birth. He had a strong will and iron self-discipline, willing to drive himself relentlessly despite failing health and personal troubles, but he could neither deal effectively with political personalities nor catch the public imagination and gain popular support. In a revolutionary situation he was a conservative and a legalist. Satisfied as to the right of secession and the constitutional basis of state sovereignty, he regarded Northern opposition as motivated only by jealousy, greed, and aggression; yet committed to the ideal of the Southern nation, he could not tolerate independent action by state governments or opposition to policies (such as drafting slaves) that the Confederate government believed were necessary to the war effort. He shared with many the delusion that cotton was king and that economic pressures would lead quickly to European aid and victory; he therefore agreed to policies that resulted in the Confederacy's economic isolation. Free to act out his lifelong perception of himself as master strategist and commanding general, Davis kept tight control over all military aspects, never freeing even Lee from it completely, and refusing sound advice at crucial moments. Up to the end of the war, Davis never believed that defeat was possible; he thought that one more major campaign would turn the tide.

Davis' policy was passive-defensive; he always expected European aid even though he was informed of the actual situation. Politically naive, he apportioned cabinet appointments evenly among the states, thereby making bad choices and alienating the powerful radical secessionists. He dominated his cabinet, so that its able members could not act effectively, yet did not urge his cautious treasury secretary, C. G. Memminger, to be as financially audacious as necessary for real accomplishment. He himself frequently functioned as secretary of war, a position he would have preferred to the presidency or to any other except that of commanding general. He understood neither the proper role of the executive nor the exigencies of strategy, and in attempting to be both president and general, he failed to fulfill either function well.

A nationalist facing sovereign states, a logical theoretician dealing with volatile personalities and political realities, an egotist who could see only the goal but who could not believe that his political opponents also strove for ideals, a leader in revolutionary times who could not rally popular support for great sacrifices: Davis was more of a debit than a credit entry in the Confederacy's account. Yet his dedication was total and his efforts unrelenting, and in the aftermath of defeat, Davis enjoyed more popular admiration than at any other time in his life. He had been a great senator and a great secretary of war. He had never sought public office, but accepted it as a duty. He attracted intense loyalty and admiration as well as provoking bitter enmity, and with all his failings, it is impossible to imagine that any other man in the Confederacy could have done better in those circumstances. Surviving personal tragedies and the loss of an independent South, Davis died unshaken in his beliefs and conscious of his own rectitude and unswerving loyalties, in his own mind fully justified and fulfilled.

Bibliography
Davis, Jefferson. *Jefferson Davis: Private Letters, 1823-1889.* Edited by Hudson Strode. New York: Harcourt, Brace and World, 1966. Very effectively edited, providing practically a condensed biography. As with the three-volume biography, strongly biased, placing even

more emphasis than Strode's work on personalities.

Davis, Varina. *Jefferson Davis, Ex-President of the Confederate States of America: A Memoir by His Wife.* 2 vols. New York: Belford Co., 1890. A laudatory account, more than sixteen hundred pages; includes long quotations from Davis' speeches and correspondence as well as biographical information dictated by Davis shortly before his death and valuable information from participants in events. Apart from Davis' obvious bias, the book is detailed and usually reliable.

Davis, William C. *Jefferson Davis: The Man and His Hour.* New York: HarperPerennial, 1991.

Dodd, William Edward. *Jefferson Davis.* Philadelphia: G. W. Jacobs and Co., 1907. Reprint. New York: Russell and Russell, 1966. Written by a professor at Randolph-Macon College, the book reflects nineteenth century biases of time and place: contented slaves, good masters, Anglo-Saxon civilization. Dodd attempts to balance his own commitment to the United States with strong attachment to the rightness of Davis and the South on the constitutional issues and the "War Between the States."

Strode, Hudson. *Jefferson Davis: American Patriot, 1808-1861.* New York: Harcourt, Brace and Co., 1955.

_____. *Jefferson Davis: Confederate President.* New York: Harcourt, Brace and Co., 1959.

_____. *Jefferson Davis, Tragic Hero: The Last Twenty-five Years, 1864-1889.* New York: Harcourt, Brace and World, 1964. This detailed, three-volume biography by a professor of creative writing is the result of painstaking research, based on both secondary sources and primary documents including a thousand previously unavailable personal letters. Neither scholarly nor analytical; detailed narrative and quotations replace the historian's generalizations. Pro-Davis with a pro-Southern, secessionist bias; often reads more as special pleading than as careful interpretation.

Tate, Allen. *Jefferson Davis.* New York: G. P. Putnam's Sons, 1969. A very brief account by one of the Nashville "Agrarians." Emotional and often contradictory defense of Davis as representative of the stable agrarian Southern society facing the aggression of the new industrial North; simultaneously blames Davis for the Confederate defeat.

Warren, Robert Penn. *Jefferson Davis Gets His Citizenship Back.* Lexington: University Press of Kentucky, 1980. Very brief, almost a memoir of the author's boyhood in the early twentieth century South, by a master writer. Effective evocation of the war and the man.

Wiley, Bell Irvin. *Confederate Women.* Westport, Conn.: Greenwood Press, 1975. Relatively brief but informative work, based on primary sources. Excellent portrayal of the lives, ideas, and influence of Virginia Clay-Clopton, Mary Boykin Chesnut, and Varina Davis.

Woodworth, Steven E. *Jefferson Davis and His Generals: The Failure of Confederate Command in the West.* Lawrence: University Press of Kansas, 1990.

Marsha Kass Marks

ROBERT J. DOLE

Born: July 22, 1923; Russell, Kansas

A prominent Republican senator and presidential candidate, Dole was an effective legislator, mediator, and deal maker who supported legislation for civil rights, farm reform, aid for the disabled, Social Security, and a balanced federal budget.

Early Life

Robert Joseph (Bob) Dole was born on July 22, 1923, in a small house in Russell, Kansas, the second of four children. His father, Doran Dole, operated a cream-and-egg station, purchasing dairy products from local farmers and shipping the products by rail to larger markets. He later became manager of a grain elevator. Known for his commitment to work, Doran missed only one day on the job in forty years. From his father, young Bob learned some early political lessons by watching Doran conduct business with farmers and merchants.

Dole's mother, Bina, one of twelve children, grew up on a poor farm. A hardworking housewife, Bina demanded her two daughters and two sons be industrious. To help with expenses, she sold Singer sewing machines door to door. Both parents instilled in their children a sense of responsibility and a hard work ethic.

Although Doran and Bina worked extremely long hours, the Doles, like countless other Americans, endured the ravages of the Great Depression. The Dole children performed various duties to help their parents: All helped their mother keep house, while Bob and his brother did odd jobs such as milking cows, washing cars, and doing yard work to earn extra income.

At twelve, Bob became a soda jerk at Dawson's Drug Store, a central gathering place for Russell townspeople. He had developed a biting wit and got along well with the customers, readily exchanging jokes and stories. While working at the drugstore, Bob decided to become a physician; he was impressed with the dedication of doctors and the respect they received.

During high school, Bob was a member of the National Honor Society and participated in sports, lettering in track, football, and

Bob Dole *(Reuters/Rick T. Wilking/Archive Photos)*

basketball. His tenacious determination to excel drove him to establish a rigorous training regimen, jogging either early in the morning or after practice. Additionally, he and his brother lifted homemade weights.

After his high-school graduation in June, 1941, Dole enrolled at the University of Kansas with the intent of fulfilling his goal of becoming a doctor; he also intended to be the first in his family to obtain a college degree. World War II intervened, however, and he enlisted in the U.S. Army in December, 1942; he was called to duty on June 3, 1943. In 1944,

Dole was graduated from Fort Benning, Georgia, as a second lieutenant and was sent to Italy in December. As an officer, he cared for his men's welfare and gained their respect.

On April 14, 1945, platoon leader Dole and his men of the Tenth Mountain Division participated in Operation Craftsman, which had as its objective to push the Germans north of the Po Valley and to secure northern Italy. During the fierce fighting, the Tenth Mountain Division suffered tremendous casualties, one of whom was Dole, who led his men into battle. An exploding shell shattered his right shoulder, broke his collarbone, and penetrated a lung and vertebrae, paralyzing him from the neck down. After he lay immobile for nine hours, medics took him to a hospital, where no one believed he would survive. Relying on his Kansas roots and parents' teachings, Dole not only survived but overcame physical problems—including excruciating pain, numerous operations, and the loss of a kidney—that might well have defeated a lesser man. For his valor, Dole received the Purple Heart and the Bronze Star with Clusters.

Life's Work

A new phase in Dole's life began with his injury. Common sense dictated that he give up his dream of becoming a doctor; his withered right arm would not allow him to pursue such a career. Disabled, Dole compensated for his physical deficiencies by pursuing another course of action with characteristic intensity and tenacity. The injury that ended his hopes of a medical career became the impetus for him to reevaluate his life and establish a new objective, to study law. This decision would ultimately lead him to national prominence as a politician.

Dole returned to Russell in late 1946. In November, 1947, Dole met Phyllis Holden, an occupational therapist, at a dance for patients at Percy Jones Army Medical Center in Battle Creek, Michigan, where he was undergoing another operation. The two were married on June 12, 1948, in Concord, New Hampshire. Later that same year, the Doles moved to Tucson, Arizona, where Bob enrolled as a junior at the University of Arizona under the G.I. Bill.

He left after one year because of lingering health problems and his unhappiness with the law program at Arizona. He returned to Kansas and entered Washburn University in Topeka to pursue a career in law and to be close to medical laboratories that could treat his blood and lung problems. At Washburn, Dole began to flirt with the possibility of entering politics.

In 1950, Dole's political career began when Kansas Republicans recruited him to become a candidate for the Kansas House of Representatives because of his status as a war hero. Dole, whose parents were Democrats, accepted the Republican offer. At twenty-seven, Dole became the youngest member of the Kansas house. He compiled an exemplary record, voting on every key issue during the three-month legislative session. Even though he decided not to seek reelection, his appetite for politics had been whetted.

Dole was graduated magna cum laude from Washburn in 1952, and he passed the state bar exam and joined a law firm in Russell. In the same year, he ran successfully for the office of county attorney, a position to which he was reelected in 1954, 1956, and 1958. As county attorney, Dole displayed a cunning wit and sharp mind. His advocacy of juvenile code issues, concern for better treatment of neglected youth, and opposition to an oil-and-gas severance tax enhanced his reputation as an effective politician. During his years as county attorney, the Doles had a daughter, Robin, who campaigned with her father in 1960 when Dole ran for the U.S. House of Representatives.

President Dwight D. Eisenhower, another famous Kansas war hero, aided Dole in his successful campaign. Dole served eight years in the House, during which time he never missed a vote. He sat on the House Agriculture Committee and played a key role in exposing the illegal activities of Billy Sol Estes, a businessman involved in a major grain-elevator fraud. A staunch Republican conservative, Dole opposed President Lyndon B. Johnson's Great Society programs, but he supported the 1964 Civil Rights Bill and the 1965 Voting Rights Act.

In 1968, Dole was elected to the U.S. Senate, a seat he held until 1996. His first major address on the Senate floor called for increased aid to the disabled, an issue he continued to champion. He sat on the Senate Agriculture Committee, where he continued to support farm legislation. Dole became an ardent supporter of President Richard M. Nixon, whom he viewed as a fellow survivor. He supported Nixon's Vietnam War policies and campaigned unsuccessfully for the confirmation of two of Nixon's Supreme Court nominees.

In return for his loyalty, Nixon offered Dole the Republican National Committee chairmanship in 1971. In this capacity, Dole worked hard to ensure Nixon's reelection. As Dole's political prominence increased, however, his relationship with his wife disintegrated. Always a workaholic, Dole spent increasingly little time with Phyllis, resulting in their divorce in 1972. In that same year, Dole met his future wife, Elizabeth Hanford, who worked in the Office of Consumer Affairs.

Nixon was reelected in 1972. Two weeks after the election, however, Nixon asked for Dole's resignation as Republican National Committee chairman. Nixon had apparently lost faith in his loyal supporter, and he had even devised a scheme in which an unsuspecting Dole asked U.N. Ambassador George Bush to succeed him (Nixon had already approached Bush).

Many Kansas voters were uneasy about Dole's divorce. Moreover, in 1974, the Watergate scandal resulted in Nixon's resignation; although Dole had no role in the Watergate affair, his association with Nixon was politically damaging to him. Nevertheless, we won reelection to the Senate in 1974 by a small margin. Returning to Washington, Dole began courting Elizabeth, whom he married on December 6, 1975. The new Mrs. Dole was as ambitious, competitive, and career-oriented as her new husband. They were a "symbiotic and synergistic" couple who intrigued Americans. Their honeymoon, however, was abruptly interrupted by the sudden death of Dole's father.

In 1976, Gerald Ford, who had succeeded to the presidency in the wake of Nixon's resignation, selected Dole as his running mate for his own reelection effort. They began their campaign in Dole's hometown of Russell, Kansas; Dole worked relentlessly, traveling more than sixty thousand miles and visiting forty-four states during the campaign.

Ford and Dole agreed to televised debates with the Democratic nominee, Jimmy Carter, and his running mate, Walter Mondale. Dole debated Mondale on October 15, 1976, in Houston, Texas; in the opinion of most observers, Dole "lost" the debate by appearing insensitive, flippant, and arrogant. Dole's responses seemed to justify the derogatory appellation "hatchet man" his opponents often leveled at him. Dole later regretted his performance. Carter and Mondale won a narrow victory, and Dole suffered his first defeat in fifteen campaigns.

Returning to his Senate duties, Dole opposed the Panama Canal Treaty, introduced legislation to balance the federal budget, and teamed with Senator George McGovern, a Democrat, to cosponsor foodstamp reform and farm legislation. In 1980, Dole made an unsuccessful bid for the Republican nomination for president, which went to Ronald Reagan. Dole considered retiring from politics but decided instead to seek a third Senate term.

During the 1980's a new vigor seemed to possess Dole. In 1981, he became chairman of the powerful Senate Finance Committee. He supported passage of the Economic Recovery Tax Act of 1981, which cut individual income taxes and federal spending, and the Tax Equity and Fiscal Responsibility Act of 1982, which lowered the federal deficit. In 1983, Dole favored legislation establishing the birthday of Martin Luther King, Jr., as a national holiday. Also in 1983, he formed the Dole Foundation to promote employment of the disabled. Before the year ended, Dole experienced the loss of his mother.

Recognition of his power was confirmed when Dole became Senate Majority Leader in 1984 and 1994 and Senate Minority Leader in 1986 and 1992. He unsuccessfully sought the Republican nomination for President in 1988; in 1996, however, Dole became the Republican nominee and gave up his Senate seat to devote more time for the campaign. In a series of televised debates with incumbent President Bill Clinton, Dole proved more effective than he had in his 1976 debate with Mondale; however, his campaign never established much momentum, and he was soundly defeated in the November election.

Summary

Although he was often criticized as an unsmiling "hatchet man," Dole demonstrated his concern for the disabled, the poor, and powerless by supporting key legislation to ease their suffering. Moreover, he never forgot his roots, exhibiting the same concern in his support of agricultural reforms to help the nation's farmers. In addition, although he had long been notorious for his sardonic, strident attacks on his opponents and for a tendency to blame others for his political defeats, Dole refined his image after the 1996 election. His appearances on several popular television programs seemed to reflect a man who could joke about his defeat and who was able to use his acerbic wit against himself instead of others. In a television credit card commercial aired during the 1997 Super Bowl football game, Dole again poked fun at himself, further dispelling the notion that he was a bitter, sore loser. Dole donated $90,000 from the commercial to establish scholarships for disabled students at Russell High School and Emporia State University in Kansas.

Bob Dole never attained the highest office in the United States, but he served his country in war and in Washington as a congressman and senator for thirty-five years. In these roles, he had a major impact on American politics. Overcoming severe physical disabilities, including a 1991 bout with prostate cancer, to forge one of the most significant political careers of the latter twentieth century, Dole exhibited a relentless determination that inspired many others.

Bibliography

Dole, Bob, and Elizabeth Dole. *The Doles: Unlimited Partners*. New York: Simon & Schuster, 1988. A candid, thought-provoking autobiography of one of Washington's most powerful and successful couples, detailing both their private and public lives.

Hilton, Stanley G. *Bob Dole: American Political Phoenix*. Chicago: Contemporary Books, 1988. A counsel on Dole's Senate Judiciary Committee staff, Hilton critically details Dole's humble past and its impact on his political career.

_____. *Senator for Sale: An Unauthorized Biography of Senator Bob Dole*. New York: St. Martin's Press, 1995. As the subtitle suggests, this work conveys a chilling portrait of Dole, compares him with Nixon, and speculates what a Dole presidency would entail.

Wertime, Marcia. *Bob Dole: Politician*. Philadelphia: Chelsea House, 1997. A brief, lucid, and positive study of Dole's life, focusing on his triumphs in the face of his physical problems.

Williams, Donald. *Upstream Cloudburst: Russell, the War, and the Shaping of Bob Dole*. Wichita, Kans.: The Wichita Eagle and Beacon Publishing Company, 1996. A newspaper supplement that poetically and metaphorically details the impact Dole's upbringing and military service had on his political career. Includes a number of colorful personal observations and anecdotes by friends and family members.

Woodward, Bob. *The Choice*. New York: Simon & Schuster, 1996. A behind-the-scenes account of the personal and political relationship between Dole and Clinton as they prepared for the 1996 presidential election. The campaign roles of Elizabeth Dole and Hillary Clinton are also examined.

Sharon K. Wilson and Raymond Wilson

HELEN GAHAGAN DOUGLAS

Born: November 25, 1900; Boonton, New Jersey
Died: June 28, 1980; New York, New York

As a congresswoman from California and in her private life, Douglas was an outspoken advocate of civil liberties and opportunities for oppressed minorities.

Early Life

Mary Helen Gahagan (she was always called Helen) was born on November 25, 1900, in Boonton, New Jersey, where her parents briefly rented a home so that her father could supervise a construction project nearby. Her twin brothers had been born two years earlier, and a sister and brother would follow in 1902 and 1910. She grew up in Brooklyn, New York, in a comfortable household with strong-willed parents intent on imbuing their children with strong moral and educational ideals. Her father, Walter, was an engineer who founded his own construction company in 1899 and prospered from the outset. A graduate of the Massachusetts Institute of Technology, he read insatiably and filled the Gahagan house with shelves of books. Helen's mother Lillian had been reared on the Wisconsin frontier. She was a country schoolteacher before her marriage, and her beauty, optimistic outlook, and exquisite singing voice were inherited by her elder daughter.

Helen had the benefit of the accoutrements of affluence during her childhood. These included a summer home in Vermont, a family trip to Europe when she was twelve, accompanying her mother to the opera (which, ironically, Helen disliked intensely), and private schools. The first of these was the Berkeley School for Girls, which was located only a block from the Gahagans' home. It was at this school that her interest in acting blossomed under the direction of her drama teacher, Elizabeth Grimball. Her grades were mediocre in subjects unrelated to performing, but she studied intensely for a college preparatory school. She matriculated at Barnard College in New York in order to be close to the stage and her drama instructor.

She would spend only two years at Barnard College before her debut into the Broadway theatrical world. Her impressive performances in school productions and an Off-Broadway play led director William A. Brady, Jr., to cast her as the ingenue in *Dreams for Sale* in 1922. Over the extremely strong protests of her father, who insisted that she complete her education, Helen accepted.

She quickly became a star. Her generally favorable reviews led to contracts with Brady and other well-known producers and assured her a niche in the roster of leading ladies of the 1920's stage. Practically every new theatrical season brought a new role, and she toured the country in roles she established in New York. She was the subject of much press coverage, not only for her acting talent but also for her great beauty.

Gahagan's ambition to perform ultimately led in another direction. During the run of a New York play in 1926, she began to take vocal lessons from a Russian émigré, Madame Sophia Cehanovska. For the next several years, Gahagan would devote time, money, and trips to Europe to the pursuit of performing operatic roles with leading companies, a pursuit that was never as successful as her Broadway acting career.

Helen's performance in the 1930-1931 Broadway production of *Tonight or Never* was important for a number of reasons. The play was her only collaboration with the legendary David Belasco (he would die during its run), her father died during the same run, and she married her costar, Melvyn Douglas. By the end of 1931, she had moved from New York to the West Coast, where Melvyn began his career in motion pictures. Except for some brief performing engagements, Helen would not live in New York again until after her immersion in and forced withdrawal from another career of a very different type.

Life's Work

The first task for Helen Gahagan Douglas and her husband, upon reaching California, was to establish a new way of life in new surroundings. Melvyn had a studio contract with Metro-Goldwyn-Mayer (MGM), and Helen was busy with singing lessons and performances on the West Coast stage in both acting and singing roles. Although Helen would have the opportunity to read dozens of film scripts in search of suitable parts, her efforts to find strong roles or to receive reasonable financial offers were stymied. She appeared in only one picture, *She* (1935), a film later considered a "classic" for its overblown production and acting rather than for any positive contributions to the cinematic arts.

The hectic pace of life on the dramatic and sound stages for the couple soon led both to seek a respite. They accomplished this by traveling around the world in 1933. A few months after their return home, Helen gave birth to their first child, Peter. A daughter, Mary Helen, would follow five years later. Helen continued her theatrical performances and vocal training, and the family settled into a new home built on three acres in the hills above the Hollywood Bowl.

Two significant events contributed to Helen's involvement in political causes. The first involved her awakening to conditions in Germany and Austria during a concert tour there in 1937. She ultimately canceled several engagements on the tour after encountering anti-Semitism directed against the pianist who was traveling with her. Although she was not Jewish, her husband Melvyn was, so she regarded these sentiments as a personal affront.

Back in California, she became involved in Democratic Party campaign activities in 1938. Her husband had joined in the statewide gubernatorial and congressional campaign efforts; at first, she merely accompanied him to meetings. After becoming acquainted with social and economic conditions firsthand, however, she began to take the lead in organizing efforts to assist migrant workers. As a result of their activities on behalf of California Democrats, the Douglases were invited to visit President and Mrs. Franklin D. Roosevelt in the White House in 1939. Helen was greatly impressed by Eleanor Roosevelt, who became something of a political mentor and role model for the actress.

Helen's intelligence and capacity for hard work, as well as her friendship with Eleanor Roosevelt, led to her rapid rise within the leadership of the Democratic Party in California. In 1940, she was selected as the state's Democratic National Committeewoman. In that capacity, she attended the Party's national convention, where she was an enthusiastic supporter of a third term for FDR. Following Roosevelt's reelection, she was appointed vice-chair and head of the Women's Division for the California state Democratic party. Her efforts for Southern California Democratic candidates in 1942 contributed to party successes there in spite of Republican victories throughout the rest of the state.

Helen's high visibility in state Democratic politics made her a natural choice for the congressional race in the Fourteenth District in 1944, when popular Congressman Thomas Ford announced his retirement. Although she did not live in the largely working-class district in central Los Angeles, she campaigned thoroughly there and won the nomination in the May primary. Prior to the general election, she delivered a principal address before the Democratic convention in Chicago, in which she reviewed the accomplishments of the Roosevelt administrations. In the fall campaign, she followed the lead of Democrats nationally in identifying her programs with FDR and the New Deal, a strategy that produced a narrow victory. She became only the third woman elected to Congress from California and the first who did not take over her seat from a deceased husband.

In Washington, D.C., Helen adhered to the same formula that had produced political success in California. She maintained a grueling schedule, largely eschewed social events, and applied her keen mind to the process of absorbing all available information on issues pending before Congress. Her legislative interests lay in two areas, one involving foreign affairs, the other domestic. She secured an appointment to the House Foreign Affairs Committee, which is usually an unimportant body, since only the Senate ratifies treaties. Nevertheless, with negotiations under way for the postwar international organization that became the United Nations, Helen believed that the House as well as the Senate would play an integral role in the increased nationwide commitment to internationalism. Membership on the Foreign Affairs Committee would provide a forum for activities designed to ensure world peace. In domestic affairs, Douglas' natural inclinations were bolstered by the makeup of her congressional district. She lent support throughout the postwar period to legislation benefiting organized labor and African Americans and other minorities.

Through her diligence, her charismatic appeal, and her high visibility in the press, Douglas became a leading figure in California politics. Following her second reelection, in 1948, her congressional seat seemed to be secure; she and her supporters now looked to a greater challenge—the seat in the U.S. Senate held by the conservative Democrat Sheridan Downey. Following the incumbent's withdrawal from the 1950 primary, Helen won the nomination in spite of vicious attacks on her internationalist position as being procommunist.

The smear tactics begun in the Democratic primary intensified in the general election, when Helen faced Congressman Richard Nixon. In an election that has since become famous for the infamous dirty tricks of the Nixon campaign, Helen Gahagan Douglas was removed from public office. In her autobiography some thirty years later, she wryly remarked: "There's not much to say about the 1950 campaign except that a man ran for the Senate who wanted to get there, and didn't care how."

Helen's life after politics was spent partly in the public eye, since she continued to speak in favor of causes such as world peace. She campaigned for Democratic presidential candidates Lyndon Johnson in 1964 and George McGovern in 1972. During the last three decades before her death from cancer in 1980, she was certainly not forgotten, but neither was she occupying her accustomed place in the limelight.

Summary

In a number of respects, Helen Gahagan Douglas had an enviable life and a great deal of good fortune. She became a famous actress almost overnight, not only because of her talent but also because of her great beauty. Capitalizing on her acting fame, she became a force in politics through intelligence and hard work. Although her fame boosted her political career at the outset, it eventually became a liability to Douglas as a politician seriously intent on pursuing an important agenda. She constantly downplayed her glamour in order to be taken seriously.

She was able, in the end, to use the press attention focused on her in order to advance an international and domestic social program that was liberal, enlightened, and forward-looking. She did not hesitate to challenge bigotry, isolationism, and red-baiting. Although her public service was cut short because of a malicious campaign against her in 1950, she stood as a symbol for other intelligent, forthright, public-spirited women and men to emulate.

Bibliography

Douglas, Helen Gahagan. *The Eleanor Roosevelt We Remember*. New York: Hill & Wang, 1963. In her autobiography, Helen Douglas clearly indicated that Eleanor Roosevelt was a major influence in her decision to become a political activist. This book, a tribute to Roosevelt, contains photographs from a variety of sources and an admiring text by Douglas.

_____. *A Full Life*. Garden City, N.Y.: Doubleday, 1982. An engaging autobiography in which the author thoroughly discusses her family life, stage experiences, and involvement in political affairs.

Douglas, Melvyn, and Tom Arthur. *See You at the Movies: The Autobiography of Melvyn Douglas*. Lanham, Md.: University Press of America, 1986. A posthumously published autobiography that focuses on the author's acting career and includes occasional anecdotes about his wife's careers and their marriage.

Morris, Roger. *Richard Milhous Nixon: The Rise of an American Politician*. New York: Henry Holt, 1990. Includes the fullest description and analysis of the 1950 Senate campaign in California; it is especially valuable for establishing the context of California politics. Morris covers the Douglas and Nixon primary campaigns as well as the general election.

Scobie, Ingrid Winther. *Center Stage: Helen Gahagan Douglas, a Life*. New York: Oxford University Press, 1992. A thorough biography by a professional historian who conducted research in manuscript and oral history collections around the country. Scobie also met with and interviewed Helen and Melvyn Douglas.

Richard G. Frederick

STEPHEN A. DOUGLAS

Born: April 23, 1813; Brandon, Vermont
Died: June 3, 1861; Chicago, Illinois

Endowed with a vision of nationalism, Douglas worked to develop the United States internally and to preserve the Union.

Early Life

Born on April 23, 1813, in Brandon, Vermont, Stephen A. Douglas spent his early life in Vermont and western New York State. His father died when Douglas was only two months old, and he lived on a farm with his widowed mother until he was fifteen. At that point, he set off for Middlebury, Vermont, to see "what I could do for myself in the wide world among strangers." He apprenticed himself to a cabinetmaker, but a dispute developed and he returned home after eight months. His mother remarried in late 1830, moved with her new husband to his home in western New York near Canandaigua, and Douglas accompanied them.

His early schooling in Vermont had been of the sketchy common-school variety, but in New York he entered the Canandaigua Academy, where he boarded and studied. There, he began to read law as well as study the classics, until he left school on January 1, 1833, to devote himself to full-time legal study. Early interested in politics, and particularly that of Andrew Jackson, Douglas associated himself for six months with the law office of Walter and Levi Hubbell, prominent local Jacksonians. New York State requirements for admission to the bar being very stringent—four years of classical studies and three of legal—Douglas decided to move. He was a young man in a hurry, and in June, 1833 (at twenty years of age), he moved west to seek his fortune.

He went first to Cleveland, Ohio, before finally settling further west in Illinois. Douglas taught school briefly in Winchester, Illinois, and then decided to apply for his law certificate. Requirements for admission to the bar were far easier to satisfy on the frontier than they were in the settled East, and in March, 1834, Douglas was examined by Illinois Supreme Court Justice Samuel D. Lockwood and received his license to practice. At age twenty-one, he had a vocation as a licensed attorney and could pursue his real love, which was politics. Douglas was not physically imposing, standing only five feet, four inches, with a head too large for his body, but he possessed tremendous energy. He would later receive such nicknames as the "Little Giant" and "a steam engine in britches."

Douglas' rise up the political ladder was meteoric. In 1835, he was elected state's attorney for the Morgan (Illinois) Circuit, and his political career was launched. He held a series of elective and appointive offices at the state level and was elected to the United States House of Representatives for the first time in 1843, at age thirty. He held that position until he resigned in 1847, having been elected to the United States Senate, a post he held until his death in 1861 at age forty-eight.

Life's Work

Douglas' life work was clearly political in nature. He had a vision of America as a great nation, and he wanted to use the political system to make his dream of "an ocean bound republic" a reality. He was willing to do whatever was necessary to develop and expand the United States and to preserve what was sacred to him, the Union. He expended enormous amounts of energy on his dream of developing the West by working to organize the Western territories and by urging the construction of a transcontinental railroad to bind the nation together.

Two of the highlights of Douglas' career in the Senate involved the Compromise of 1850 and the Kansas-Nebraska Act of 1854. There is a certain irony in the fact that the former was thought to have saved the Union while the latter destroyed it. Upon the acquisition of a vast amount of territory in the Mexican War, the nation was on the verge of disunion in 1849-1850 over the question of whether slavery should be allowed to expand into the area of the Mexican concession. It was Douglas, taking over from an ailing Henry Clay, who put together the package which has come to be called the Compromise of 1850. That compromise, which required months of intense political maneuvering, included such items as California's entry into the Union as a free state, the organization of New Mexico and Utah as territories without restriction on slavery, a stronger fugitive slave law, the abolition of the slave trade in the District of Columbia, and the settlement of the Texas Bond issue. That this legislation was passed is a testimony to Douglas' ability to put together what appeared to be impossible voting coalitions.

With that compromise widely acclaimed as the "final settlement" of the nation's problems, Douglas sought but failed to get the Democratic nomination for the presidency in 1852. It went instead to Franklin Pierce, who defeated General Winfield Scott in the general election and who is regarded in retrospect as one of the weakest American presidents. Pierce, fearing Douglas' unconcealed political ambitions, excluded him from the inner circle of presidential power, and that exclusion compounded the great despair into which Douglas was plunged following the death of his first wife in January, 1853. His wife was the former Martha Martin of North Carolina, and her short life ended from the complications of childbirth. In an effort to overcome his grief, Douglas left the United States for a tour of Europe in the spring of 1853, and when he returned for the opening of the Thirty-third Congress that fall, he was out of touch with political developments in this country.

In the preceding session of Congress, Douglas' Senate Committee on Territories had reported a bill to organize Nebraska Territory with no mention of slavery. By the time he returned from Europe, the political dynamics had changed, and the pressure mounted to organize two territories and to include a section dealing directly with the slavery question. Kansas-Nebraska lay wholly within the area acquired by the Louisiana Purchase in 1803, where slavery had been forbidden by the Missouri Compromise of 1820. Convinced that it was crucial to the national interest to get these territories organized as quickly as possible, and firmly believing that the slavery question was a phony issue, Douglas rewrote his organization bill. The new version called for two territories, Kansas and Nebraska, and included a sentence which stated that the 36°30' section of the Missouri Compromise was inoperative as it had been "superseded by the principles of the legislation" passed in 1850, which had made no reference to slavery. Such a statement was consistent with Douglas' long-standing belief in popular sovereignty, the idea that the people of a given territory should determine for themselves the institutions they would establish.

When the bill passed after months of the most hostile infighting in the United States Congress, and the president signed it into law in May, 1854, a storm of protest swept over the United States the likes of which had not been seen before and has not been seen since. The Kansas-Nebraska Bill split the Democratic Party and occasioned the rise of the

Republican Party as the vehicle for antislavery sentiment. Douglas had misjudged the growing moral concern over slavery, and the nation was aflame; the flame would not be extinguished for more than a decade of controversy and bloody war. The situation was so critical as to make impossible an effective concentration by the government on other issues deserving of attention. The man who in 1850 and 1853 wanted to avoid the slavery issue and sought to consolidate and unify the United States became an instrument of its division.

His association with the Kansas-Nebraska Bill and his consistent failure to perceive the moral nature of the slavery question would haunt the rest of Douglas' abbreviated political career. It would frustrate his efforts to secure his party's nomination for the presidency in 1856 and would cost him dearly in the momentous election in 1860 which Abraham Lincoln won. In between, in 1858, Douglas defeated the Republican Lincoln for the United States Senate from Illinois, but that was a small victory in the overall scheme of national life.

Summary

If ever a man represented the best and the worst of his times, it was Stephen A. Douglas. He was born in 1813 as the nation moved into an intensely nationalistic period; he lived through the Jacksonian period with its turbulent trends toward democracy; he died just as his beloved Union came apart in the Civil War. Douglas was devoted to the concept of democracy, but it was a democracy limited to white adult males. Given his view (widely held at the time) that blacks were inferior beings, he saw no reason to be concerned about their civil rights—they simply had none. His political career was shaped by his love for the Union and by his desire to see the United States grow and expand, for he was truly a great nationalist. He thought in terms of the West and of the nation as a whole and did not constrict himself to a North-South view.

Douglas was, perhaps, the most talented politician of his generation, but his moral blindness, while understandable, was his tragic flaw. He alone among his contemporaries might have had the capacity and the vigor to deal with sectionalism and prevent the Civil War, but his fatal flaw kept him from the presidency. Once the war broke out, Douglas threw his support to his Republican rival Abraham Lincoln and in an attempt to rally northern Democrats to the cause of Union he said, "We must fight for our country and forget our differences."

Beset by a variety of infirmities at the age of forty-eight, Douglas hovered near death in early June, 1861. On June 3, 1861, with his beloved second wife Adele by his bed, he died. His last spoken words, passed through Adele as advice for his young sons, suggest Douglas' ultimate concern as a politician: "Tell them to obey the laws and support the Constitution of the United States."

Bibliography

Capers, Gerald M. *Stephen A. Douglas: Defender of the Union.* Boston: Little, Brown and Co., 1959. As the title suggests, this volume is generally pro-Douglas and forgives his moral blindness. It is fairly brief and is well written.

Hamilton, Holman. *Prologue to Conflict: The Crisis and Compromise of 1850.* New York: W W Norton and Co., 1966. A valuable work and one which was a pioneering effort in quantitative history. Hamilton uses statistics to analyze voting patterns and to clarify the way Douglas put the compromise together. The writing is excellent, as one might expect from a former newspaper man. Hamilton was the first historian to give Douglas the credit he deserved.

Johannsen, Robert W. *The Frontier, the Union, and Stephen A. Douglas.* Urbana: University of Illinois Press, 1989.

_____. *Stephen A. Douglas.* New York: Oxford University Press, 1973. This volume is the definitive work on Douglas. Johannsen is meticulous in his research, fair in his assessment, and thorough in his coverage.

Meyer, Daniel. *Stephen A. Douglas and the American Union.* Chicago: University of Chicago Library, 1994.

Nichols, Roy Frank. *The Democratic Machine: 1850-1854.* New York: Columbia University Press, 1923. While Nichols' book is dated, it is still worth reading. The author probably knew more about the politics of the 1850's than any single individual.

Potter, David M. *The Impending Crisis: 1848-1861.* New York: Harper and Row, Publishers, 1976. This major interpretation puts Douglas' political activity in the context of his times and provides many insights into his character.

Charles J. Bussey

FREDERICK DOUGLASS

Born: February, 1817?; Tuckahoe, Talbot County, Maryland
Died: February 20, 1895; Washington, D.C.

Douglass' lifelong concerns were with freedom and human rights for all people. He articulated these concerns most specifically for black Americans and women.

Early Life

Frederick Douglass was born a slave in Tuckahoe, Talbot County, Maryland, and originally was named Frederick Augustus Washington Bailey. He was of mixed African, white, and Indian ancestry, but other than that, he knew little of his family background or even his exact date of birth. Douglass believed that he was born in February, 1817, yet subsequent research indicates that he may have been born a year later in February, 1818. Douglass never knew his father or anything about him except that he was a white man, possibly his master. Douglass' mother was Harriet Bailey, the daughter of Betsey and Isaac Bailey. Frederick, his mother, and his grandparents were the property of a Captain Aaron Anthony.

In his early years, Frederick experienced many aspects of the institution of slavery. Anthony engaged in the practice of hiring out slaves, and Douglass' mother and her four sisters were among the slaves Anthony hired out to work off the plantation. Consequently, Douglass seldom saw his mother and never really knew her. The first seven years of his life were spent with his grandmother, Betsey Bailey, not because she was his grandmother but because as an elderly woman too old for field work she had been assigned the duty of caring for young children on the plantation.

The boy loved his grandmother very much, and it was extremely painful for him when, at the age of seven, he was forced by his master to move to his main residence, a twelve-mile separation from Betsey. It was there, at Anthony's main residence, that Douglass received his initiation into the realities of slavery. The years with his grandmother had been relatively carefree and filled with love. Soon, he began to witness and to experience personally the brutalities of slavery. In 1825, however, Douglass' personal situation temporarily improved when Anthony sent him to Baltimore as a companion for young Tommy Auld, a family friend. Douglass spent seven years with the Aulds as a houseboy and later as a laborer in the Baltimore shipyards. The death of Anthony caused Douglass to be transferred to the country as a field hand and to the ownership of Anthony's son-in-law. Early in 1834, his new owner hired him out to Edward Covey, a farmer who also acted as a professional slave-breaker. This began the most brutal period of Douglass' life as a slave.

After months of being whipped weekly, Douglass fought a two-hour battle with Covey that ended in a standoff, and the beatings stopped. Douglass' owner next hired him out to a milder planter, but Douglass' victory over Covey had sealed his determination to be free. In 1836, Douglass and five other slaves planned an escape but were

Frederick Douglass *(The Associated Publishers)*

detected. Douglass was jailed and expected to be sold out of state, but the Aulds reprieved him and brought him back to Baltimore, where he first served as an apprentice and then worked as a ship caulker. However improved Douglass'situation might be in Baltimore, it was still slavery, and he was determined to be a free man. On September 3, 1838, Douglass borrowed the legal papers and a suit of clothes of a free black sailor and boarded a train for New York.

In New York, he was joined by Anna Murray, a free black woman with whom he had fallen in love in Baltimore. Douglass and Anna were married in New York on September 15, 1838, and almost immediately moved further north to New Bedford, Massachusetts, where there were fewer slave catchers hunting fugitives such as Douglass. It was also to elude slave catchers that Douglass changed his last name. He had long abandoned his middle names of Augustus Washington; he now dropped the surname Bailey and became Frederick Douglass. The move and the name change proved to be far more than symbolic; unknown to Douglass, he was about to launch on his life's work in a direction he had never anticipated.

Life's Work

New Bedford was a shipping town, and Douglass had expected to work as a ship caulker; however, race prejudice prevented his working in the shipyards and he had to earn a living doing any manual labor available: sawing wood, shoveling coal, sweeping chimneys, and so on. Anna worked as a domestic when she was not caring for their growing family. Anna bore Douglass five children: Rosetta, Lewis, Charles, Frederick, Jr., and Annie. Unexpectedly, the abolition movement of the 1830's, 1840's, and 1850's changed both Douglass' immediate situation and his whole future.

Within a few months of his escape to the North, Douglass chanced on a copy of William Lloyd Garrison's abolitionist newspaper, *The Liberator*. *The Liberator* so moved Douglass that, in spite of his poverty, he became a subscriber. Then, on August 9, 1841, less than three years after his escape, Douglass and Garrison met. This and subsequent meetings led to Garrison offering Douglass an annual salary of $450 to lecture for the abolitionist movement. Douglass was so convinced that he would not succeed as a lecturer that he accepted only a three-month appointment. In fact, he had begun his life's work.

Scholars have debated whether Douglass' greatest accomplishments were as an orator or a writer; both his speaking and his writing stemmed from his involvement with the abolition movement, and both were to be his primary activities for the remainder of his life.

From the beginning, Douglass was a powerful, effective orator. He had a deep, powerful voice which could hold his audiences transfixed. Moreover, Douglass was an impressive figure of a man. He had a handsome face, bronze skin, a leonine head, a muscular body, and was more than six feet in height. He stood with dignity and spoke eloquently and distinctly. Indeed, his bearing and speech caused critics to charge that Douglass had never been a slave; he did not conform to the stereotypic view of a slave's demeanor and address. Even Douglass' allies in the abolition movement urged him to act more as the public expected. Douglass refused; instead, he wrote his autobiography to prove his identity and thus began his career as a writer. *Narrative of the Life of Frederick Douglass: An American Slave* (1845) remains his most famous and widely read book. It was an instant success. Yet in the narrative, Douglass had revealed his identity as Frederick Bailey, as well as the identity of his owners, making himself more vulnerable than ever to slave catchers. Anna was legally free, and because of her their children were free also, but Douglass was legally still a slave. To avoid capture, he went to England, where he remained for two years.

In England, Douglass was immensely successful as a lecturer and returned to the United States, in 1847, with enough money to purchase his freedom. By end of the year, he was legally a free man. Also in 1847, Douglass moved to Rochester, New York, and began publication of his own newspaper, *North Star*. While editing *North Star*, Douglass continued to lecture and to write. In 1855, he published an expanded autobiography, *My Bondage and My Freedom;* he also published numerous lectures, articles, and even a short story, "The Heroic Slave" in 1853. Much later in life, he published his third, and most complete, autobiography, *Life and Times of Frederick Douglass (1881).*

In all of his writings and speeches, Douglass' major concerns were civil rights and human freedom. As a person born in slavery, and as a black man living in a racially prejudiced society, Douglass' most immediate and direct concerns were to end slavery, racial prejudice, and discrimination. Yet he always insisted that there was little difference between one form of oppression and another. He proved the depth of his convictions in his championing of the women's rights movement at the same time he was immersed in his abolitionist activities. In fact, Douglass was the only man to participate actively in the Seneca Falls Convention which launched the women's rights movement in the United States in 1848. Moreover, his commitment was lasting; on the day of his death, in 1895, Douglass had returned only a few hours earlier from addressing a women's rights meeting in Washington, D.C.

By the 1850's, Douglass was active in politics. He also knew and counseled with John Brown and was sufficiently implicated in Brown's Harpers Ferry raid to leave the country temporarily after Brown's capture and arrest. From the beginning of the Civil War, Douglass urged President Abraham Lincoln not only to save the Union but also to use the war as the means to end slavery. Douglass also urged black men to volunteer and the president to accept them as soldiers in the Union armies. By the end of the Civil War, Douglass was the most prominent spokesman for black Americans in the country. With the end of the war and the advent of Reconstruction, Douglass' work seemed to have reached fruition. By 1875, with the passage of the Civil Rights Act of that year, not only had slavery been ended and the Constitution amended but also the laws of the land had guaranteed black Americans their freedom, their citizenship, and the same rights as all other citizens. Yet the victories were short-lived. The racism, both of North and of South, that had dominated the antebellum era triumphed again in the 1880's and 1890's. According to the Constitution, black Americans remained equal, but it was a paper equality. In fact, prejudice and discrimination became the order of the day across the whole United States.

For Douglass personally, the years following the Civil War contained a number of successes. He was financially solvent. He served in a number of governmental capacities: secretary of the Santo Domingo Commission, marshal and recorder of deeds in the District of Columbia, and United States minister to Haiti. For twenty-five years, he was a trustee on the board of Howard University. Nevertheless, these personal successes could not alleviate Douglass' bitter disappointment over the turn of public events, and he never ceased to fight. He continued to write, to lecture, and even began another newspaper, *New National Era.*

Summary

Frederick Douglass' career and his personal life were all the more remarkable when one considers the times in which he lived. His life was an example of the human will triumphing over adversity. Born into slavery, by law a piece of chattel, surrounded by poverty and illiteracy, he became one of America's greatest orators, an accomplished writer and editor, and for more than fifty years he was the most persistent and articulate voice in America speaking for civil rights, freedom, and human dignity regardless of race or sex. Douglass, more than any other individual, insisted that the ideals of the Declaration of Independence must be extended to all Americans.

Douglass' personal life reflected the principles for which he fought publicly. He always insisted that race should be irrelevant: Humanity was what mattered, not race, and not sex. In 1882, Anna Murray Douglass died after more than forty years of marriage to Frederick, and in 1884, Douglass married Helen Pitts, a white woman who had been his secretary. The marriage caused a storm of controversy and criticism from blacks, whites, and Douglass' own family. Yet for Douglass there was no issue: It was the irrelevance of race again. His own comment on the criticism was that he had married from his mother's people the first time and his father's, the second.

Douglass is most frequently thought of as a spokesman for black Americans and sometimes remembered as a champion of women's rights as well. Up to a point, this is accurate enough; Douglass was indeed a spokesman for black Americans and a champion of women's rights, because in his own lifetime these were among the most oppressed of America's people. Douglass' concern, however, was for all humanity, and his message, for all time.

Bibliography

Douglass, Frederick. *Frederick Douglass: The Narrative and Selected Writings.* Edited by Michael Meyer. New York: Vintage Books, 1984. In addition to being a readily accessible, complete edition of *Narrative of the Life of Frederick Douglass,* this book includes excerpts from Douglass' two later autobiographies and twenty selected writings by Douglass on various topics which are not easily obtainable.

_____. *Narrative of the Life of Frederick Douglass: An American Slave.* Boston: Anti-Slavery Office, 1845. Reprint. Garden City, N.Y.: Doubleday and Co., 1963. Originally published in 1845, the work covers Douglass' life up to that time; it was his first book and remains the most widely read of his three autobiographies.

_____. *My Bondage and My Freedom*. New York: Miller, Orton and Mulligan, 1855. Reprint. New York: Dover Publications, 1969. Originally published in 1855, this is the least read of Douglass' autobiographies.

_____. *Life and Times of Frederick Douglass*. Hartford, Conn.: Park Publishing Co., 1881. Reprint. New York: Citadel Press, 1984. First published in 1881 and reissued in 1892. The 1892 edition is the most commonly reproduced and the most complete of the three autobiographies.

Foner, Philip. *Frederick Douglass*. New York: Citadel Press, 1969. A thorough biography, unfortunately out of print, but available in libraries.

Factor, Robert L. *The Black Response to America: Men, Ideals, and Organization from Frederick Douglass to the NAACP*. Reading, Mass.: Addison-Wesley Publishing Co., 1970. Factor offers an interesting theoretical interpretation of Douglass as a black spokesman and informative comparison of Douglass with other black spokesmen and leaders.

Huggins, Nathan Irvin. *Slave and Citizen: The Life of Frederick Douglass*. Boston: Little, Brown and Co., 1980. Brief and readable, this is among the later publications on Douglass.

Meier, August. *Negro Thought in America: 1880-1915*. Ann Arbor: University of Michigan Press, 1963. Meier offers a good account of the varieties of thought among black Americans for the period covered and suggests an intriguing, plausible thesis regarding shifts of opinion in the black community. Although the era dealt with by Meier covers only the last fifteen years of Douglass' life, it is still worth reading the book for insight into Douglass and especially for any comparison or contrast of Douglass with later black spokesmen such as Booker T. Washington and W. E. B. Du Bois.

Quarles, Benjamin. *Frederick Douglass*. Washington, D.C.: Associated Publishers, 1948. Reprint. New York: Atheneum Publishers, 1976. Originally published in 1948, this is an easily available, thorough biography.

D. Harland Hagler

John Foster Dulles

Born: February 25, 1888; Washington, D.C.
Died: May 24, 1959; Washington, D.C.

As secretary of state from 1953 to 1959, a period marked by major crises in Asia and Europe, Dulles advocated a policy of firmly countering Soviet and Chinese Communist advances; in doing so, he enunciated a diplomatic doctrine that had great influence in the Cold War era.

Early Life

Born in his parents' home in Washington, D.C., on February 25, 1888, John Foster Dulles was the first son of Allen Macy Dulles, a Presbyterian minister of modest means, and Edith Foster Dulles, who came from a family of prominent business and political figures. The boy's given names were taken from his maternal grandfather, John Watson Foster, an experienced diplomat who became secretary of state under President Benjamin Harrison. Another son and three daughters were later born to the Dulles family, two of whom, Allen and Eleanor, later became well-known for government work and authorship. When the family moved to upstate New York, young Dulles was educated in local schools, including Watertown High School; he read widely in literary classics but was also a budding outdoorsman, spending his summers fishing and sailing. In 1903, with his mother and his sister Margaret, Dulles spent some time in Lausanne, Switzerland, where he acquired a knowledge of French; the following year, at the age of sixteen, he entered Princeton University.

He performed creditably in his schoolwork; an important interlude came in 1907, when, at the invitation of John Watson Foster, who was then a special counsel to the Chinese delegation, Dulles served as a general secretary to the Second Hague Peace Conference. He returned to Princeton and was graduated second in the class of 1908. His bachelor's thesis earned for him a fellowship to support a year's study at the Sorbonne in Paris; he took courses in international law and, at this point, evidently decided upon a legal career instead of entering the ministry. Dulles spent two years at the law school of George Washington University, in Washington, D.C. He had great powers of concentration and a remarkably retentive memory; seemingly with slight effort he was able to complete his coursework a year early, in 1911.

Dulles returned to his father's home, and while he was there, he renewed his acquaintanceship with Janet Avery, who had visited Paris while he was at the Sorbonne. When he took his bar examination, Dulles, working rapidly, answered many of the questions and then left early; he caught a train to meet Janet for a canoeing date. It was there that he proposed marriage to her. He learned later that he had been admitted to the practice of law. With the assistance of John Watson Foster, Dulles obtained a clerk's position at the reputable and established firm of Sullivan and Cromwell in New York. In 1912, Dulles and Janet Avery were married; for many years he was to value her companionship and advice and to find her supportive during troubled periods of his career. During the six years that followed, two sons and one daughter were born to them.

John Foster Dulles *(AP/Wide World Photos)*

Life's Work

With his knowledge of international law, Dulles was given several Latin American assignments; early in 1917, he was entrusted with a mission to Central America involving the defense of the Panama Canal. During World War I, he received a commission in the Army General Staff and served with the War Trade Board in Washington; he was rejected for combat duty because of his poor eyesight. Later, with his maternal uncle, Secretary of State Robert Lansing, he accompanied the American delegation to the Paris Peace Conference of 1919. As chief counsel on reparations and other financial matters, Dulles vigorously opposed the Allies' demands on Germany. His warning that burdensome reparations would produce further instability and international turmoil went unheeded. Upon his return to private practice, Dulles took on a number of international cases; on several occasions, he was called back to Washington to assist in the government's negotiation of foreign loans.

Dulles was a burly, strongly built man with a somewhat ponderous, deliberate manner. He had broad oval features, a wide mouth, and a blunt, protruding nose. His strong, heavy jaw, heavy eyebrows, and penetrating blue eyes behind wire-rimmed glasses gave an impression of firm determination. Even in his impromptu speeches, Dulles spoke incisively and in a well-organized manner, but his voice was often described as flat, and he had a tendency to slur some consonants.

As his professional career developed, Dulles, as a Presbyterian elder, remained active in church work. In 1940, he became chairman of the Commission on a Just and Durable Peace, an organization created under the auspices of the Federal Council of Churches. He acted as well as an adviser to Thomas E. Dewey when the Republican governor of New York ran for president in 1944. Dulles' experience in foreign policy was also appreciated by the Democratic Administration in power; he was made a State Department adviser to the San Francisco Conference of 1945, which led to the foundation of the United Nations. He served on several other diplomatic assignments; he also entered politics again when, in 1949, he was appointed to the seat of a retiring senator from New York. He lost the ensuing by-election, and then was called back to the State Department. In one of the major achievements of his career, Dulles, in 1951, concluded negotiations which, while circumventing the Soviet Union and Communist China, led to a formal peace treaty with Japan and widened the United States' security arrangements in the Pacific.

In 1952, Dulles served as an adviser to Dwight D. Eisenhower in his campaign for the presidency; his own views were expressed in articles calling for "a policy of boldness" and the "rollback" of Soviet power in Europe. In a press interview, Dulles stated his belief that the United States should "go to the brink of war" to reverse Communist advances, and the phrase "brinkmanship" was widely used to describe his views on foreign policy. Upon Eisenhower's victory in the election, Dulles was made secretary of state; forthwith he concerned himself with negotiations to end three years of conflict in Korea. Dulles issued veiled warnings about the bombing of Chinese airfields and the use of nuclear weapons shortly before an armistice was concluded, in July, 1953. Another crisis loomed in Indochina, where Communist guerrillas in Vietnam threatened to displace French forces who were fighting to preserve their colonial outposts. Although he was unable to obtain support elsewhere for a proposed American military intervention, Dulles exerted his influence to limit Communist gains in territory during the negotiation of the Geneva Accords of 1954. France then granted independence to Laos and Cambodia and accepted the partition of Vietnam between Communist and non-Communist factions.

Dulles urged the United States' allies to improve their military preparations and enunciated a doctrine of "massive retaliation," with nuclear weapons, as a means of deterring Soviet ventures. When European leaders could not agree on the creation of a multinational army, he announced his approval for the formation of a West German army, to be used in conjunction with the Atlantic alliance. In May, 1955, Dulles took part in the negotiations by which the United States, Britain, France, and the Soviet Union ended their occupation of Austria and guaranteed that country's independent, neutral status; some of the secretary's admirers maintained that his insistence on a rapid resolution of this issue forced the Soviet representatives to make concessions otherwise not forthcoming. During the summer and autumn of 1955, allied leaders met their Soviet counterparts at summit conferences held in Geneva; disarmament and European security problems were discussed there. During the meetings, Dulles was decidedly more wary of Soviet officials than were the other Western participants.

Problems of a different order arose in the Middle East, where Dulles promoted regional defense organizations to counteract Soviet ambitions. In 1955, Egypt began to buy military equipment from the Soviet bloc; the next year, Dulles rejected Egypt's request for financial assistance in building the Aswan Dam. President Gamal Abdul Nasser of Egypt retaliated by nationalizing the Suez Canal Company. Britain and France, which depended upon oil supplies from the Middle East, argued for international sanctions against Egypt and attempted to obtain Dulles' support against Nasser. In October, 1956, Israel launched a surprise invasion of the Sinai peninsula, and British and French forces occupied the Suez Canal zone. There was profound dismay in London and Paris when Dulles openly condemned the attack and urged the invading powers to withdraw. Although the crisis subsided, the Atlantic alliance had undergone serious strain.

Another crisis broke out within days of the Suez war: An insurrection in Hungary led to a massive invasion of that country by Soviet armored forces. In spite of Dulles' proclaimed policy of the "liberation" of Eastern Europe, President Eisenhower was compelled to acknowledge that the United States was in no position to challenge the Soviet Union's domination of small nations within its orbit.

More vigorous responses were possible elsewhere. To combat political instability in the Middle East, where it was feared that Nasserist or pro-Soviet influence was spreading, marines were sent to Lebanon in July, 1958. An acute crisis arose when Communist China began shelling islands situated between Formosa and the mainland; the American Seventh Fleet was then stationed in the Formosa Straits, and Dulles bluntly warned against any further hostile actions. European concerns arose once again in the last crisis of Dulles' life. In November, 1958, Soviet premier Nikita Khrushchev demanded a change in the status of Berlin. On behalf of his government, Dulles insisted that American forces would remain in the divided city.

Dulles had recurrently been troubled with ill health, which he tolerated with remarkable courage and good humor. During the Suez crisis of 1956, he had been hospitalized for treatment of a cancerous colon; this condition hampered him during later years, and eventually further operations were necessary. In February, 1959, he was treated for a hernia; the cancer also was found to have spread. Dulles later offered his resignation as secretary of state, which was accepted on April 15.

After a gallant struggle with his illness, he succumbed finally on May 24, 1959, at the Walter Reed Hospital in Washington, D.C.

Summary

During his tenure as secretary of state, Dulles was alternately regarded as a defender of free nations or a threat to peace; he explained his policy as the calculation of means short of war by which Communist powers might be constrained to yield. His diplomatic style was forthright and audacious. Many of his statements were couched in moral and religious summons to combat Communist encroachments around the world. On the other hand, his participation was important for the conclusion of major international agreements, such as the Korean armistice and the Austrian State Treaty. Summit meetings with Soviet leaders went ahead. Dulles warned of difficult and prolonged periods of international rivalry, but, upon many occasions, he also practiced the art of negotiation with his adversaries.

Dulles was, on the whole, favorably regarded by Western observers while he was in office and for some time thereafter; since the Vietnam War, historians critical of him have contended that his insistence on the monolithic unity of aims among Communist states left American foreign policy in an excessively rigid and unyielding position. According to this line of argument, Dulles unnecessarily intensified the Cold War and burdened the United States with commitments to resist Communism on a global scale. For others, however, it is possible to regard Dulles' diplomacy as the expression of views that were held in the United States during a specific period, before Soviet or Chinese aims in the Cold War had become manifest. In this view, Dulles formulated an approach to foreign policy that stated American interests and aims in bold and definite terms and thus answered the anxieties of his times without the actual resort to war.

Bibliography

Berding, Andrew H. *Dulles on Diplomacy*. Princeton, N.J.: Van Nostrand, 1965. Sympathetic recollections of a professional diplomat who for two years was assistant secretary of state under Dulles. Based on Dulles' speeches and the author's lengthy conference notes.

Dulles, Eleanor Lansing. *Chances of a Lifetime: A Memoir*. Englewood

Cliffs, N.J.: Prentice-Hall, 1980. The reminiscences of Dulles' sister, who led a varied life of authorship combined with travel and some diplomatic functions. There are a number of useful passages about her brother's early years and about the crises he confronted as secretary of state.

Dulles, John Foster. *War or Peace*. New York: Macmillan, 1950. A tract for the times, this work sets forth Dulles' views concerning Communism and the relative balance of forces at midcentury. He discusses the extent of Communist aims while expressing his hopes for reversing Soviet and Chinese advances without causing a world war.

Gerson, Louis L. *John Foster Dulles*. New York: Cooper Square Publishers, 1967. Volume 17 of the series "The American Secretaries of State and Their Diplomacy," this is well-rounded and generally sympathetic study of Dulles' diplomacy by a leading authority on American foreign policy. On balance, the author upholds Dulles' judgments on Communism and international security.

Goold-Adams, Richard. *John Foster Dulles: A Reappraisal*. New York: Appleton-Century-Crofts, 1962. This sprightly account, by a well-informed British journalist, sifts apart the problems of substance and style in Dulles' approach to international relations; while critical in some respects, in others, Goold-Adams acknowledges Dulles' strengths as a negotiator.

Guhin, Michael A. *John Foster Dulles: A Statesman and His Times*. New York: Columbia University Press, 1972. A topical examination of Dulles' pronouncements on foreign policy, this work contends that he was neither so inflexible nor so doctrinaire as many have claimed.

Hoopes, Townsend. *The Devil and John Foster Dulles*. Boston: Little, Brown and Co., 1973. A full-scale biography, this work was written at the end of the Vietnam War, and the author implies that Dulles cast American foreign policy in a rigid mold that unduly emphasized anti-Communism. Particular attention is paid to Dulles' positions on Middle Eastern and Asian crises; the moral and religious elements in his diplomacy are stressed and commented upon unfavorably.

Kahin, Audrey, and George McTurnan Kahin. *Subversion as Foreign Policy: The Secret Eisenhower and Dulles Debacle in Indonesia*. New York: New Press, 1995.

Marks, Frederick W. *Power and Peace: The Diplomacy of John Foster Dulles*. Westport, Conn.: Praeger, 1993.

Mosley, Leonard. *Dulles: A Biography of Eleanor, Allen, and John Foster Dulles and Their Family Network*. New York: Dial Press, 1978. A lengthy popular work, somewhat fast and loose in its presentation of facts, which deals as much with Allen Dulles and his career in government intelligence, as with John Foster Dulles' diplomatic work. For all of the Dulleses, matters of personality are emphasized as much as their actual political concerns.

Pruessen, Ronald W. *John Foster Dulles: The Road to Power*. New York: Free Press, 1982. The most detailed single account of Dulles' life before he became secretary of state, this work is written from a new leftist standpoint, but it fully acknowledges the complexity of its subject's character. The contrapuntal influences of his legal career and his religious beliefs are discussed in relation to Dulles' political work and government service from the early years through the onset of the Cold War.

Toulouse, Mark G. *The Transformation of John Foster Dulles: From Prophet of Realism to Priest of Nationalism*. Macon, Ga.: Mercer University Press, 1985. A study of the years until 1952, this work contends, perhaps too strongly, that Dulles' political views were intertwined with his theological outlook. His church-affiliated work during World War II and his relations with religious groups during the early Cold War are explored at length.

J. R. Broadus

DWIGHT D. EISENHOWER

Born: October 14, 1890; Denison, Texas
Died: March 28, 1969; Washington, D.C.

During World War II, Eisenhower served with distinction as Allied Commander for the invasions of North Africa, Italy, and France. He won the presidential elections of 1952 and 1956 and guided the country through eight years of peace and prosperity.

Early Life

Although born in Texas, where his parents lived briefly, Dwight David Eisenhower grew up in the small town of Abilene, Kansas. The Eisenhowers were a close-knit family and belonged to the Brethren Church, part of the heritage of ancestors who had immigrated to Pennsylvania from Germany during the eighteenth century. The third of seven sons (one of whom died as an infant), Dwight Eisenhower enjoyed a secure childhood, completed high school, and worked in a creamery for two years before entering West Point on the basis of a competitive examination. West Point appealed to him because it offered a free college education.

As a cadet, Eisenhower excelled briefly at football until a knee injury ended that career. He proved a conscientious but not exceptional student and was graduated sixty-first in a class of 164. At graduation in 1915, he stood five feet, eleven inches tall and weighed 170 pounds. His classmates remembered and respected "Ike," as did his boyhood friends, as likable, honest, and confident, a person with a quick temper but a quicker infectious grin. He had an expressive face, blue eyes, and light brown hair that thinned and receded when he was a young man.

Eisenhower's early military years were uneventful except for his marriage in 1916 to Mamie Geneva Doud of Denver, Colorado. The two had met in Texas during his first assignment at Fort Sam Houston. They became parents of two sons, the first of whom died as a child.

Life's Work

During the 1920's and 1930's, Eisenhower demonstrated exceptional organizational skill and an ability to work with others. In 1926, Eisen-

Dwight D. Eisenhower *(Library of Congress)*

hower, who had been merely an average student at West Point, finished first among 275 in his class at the army's elite Command and General Staff School. When General Douglas MacArthur served as the army's chief of staff, Eisenhower assisted him, and then served as his senior assistant in the Philippines. MacArthur once evaluated Eisenhower as the most capable officer in the army.

Eisenhower's personality and his performance during maneuvers in the summer of 1941 impressed the army's chief of staff, General George C. Marshall. Both in 1941 and in 1942, Eisenhower won two promotions, jumping from lieutenant colonel to lieutenant general. In June, 1942, Marshall appointed Eisenhower European Theater Commander. The next year, as general, Eisenhower became Supreme Allied Commander and won fame as the leader of the multinational invasion of Europe in June, 1944.

After accepting Germany's surrender, Eisenhower served as the army's chief of staff. He retired in 1948 and became president of Columbia University. His book *Crusade in Europe*, published the same year, sold millions of copies and gave him financial security. Two years later, President Harry S Truman recalled Eisenhower to active duty as Supreme Commander of the North Atlantic Treaty Organization forces.

In May, 1952, Eisenhower retired from the army to seek the Republican Party's nomination for president, an office leaders in both parties had urged upon him for years. With his decisive victory in the November election, Eisenhower embarked upon a second career, one even more important than the first.

As president, Eisenhower set his primary foreign policy objective as maintaining the international role the United States had assumed during the previous decade. More specifically, he intended to end the fighting in Korea, reduce military spending, and lessen the intensity of the Cold War while still adhering to the policy of containment. Militarily, Eisenhower pursued a policy of strategic sufficiency rather than superiority. This policy, as well as a reduction of the capacity to fight limited wars, made possible cuts in the defense budget.

In 1953, Eisenhower approved an armistice in Korea and the next year rejected the advice of his secretary of state and the chairman of the Joint Chiefs of Staff, among others, and refused to intervene in the French war in Indochina. The United States took the lead, however, in establishing the Southeast Asia Treaty Organization as an attempt to accomplish in a region of Asia what the North Atlantic Treaty Organization had accomplished in Europe. During this same period, Eisenhower also approved Central Intelligence Agency covert activity that helped overthrow the governments of Iran and Guatemala and thereby contributed to the growing acceptance of undemocratic action in the name of freedom.

In 1955, he helped terminate the post-World War II occupation of Austria and then, at Geneva, Switzerland, became the first president to meet with Soviet leaders in a decade. That same year and again in 1956, Eisenhower reacted to crises in the coastal waters of the People's Republic of China, in Hungary, and in Suez in a manner that helped prevent these crises from escalating into greater violence.

On the domestic side, Eisenhower followed a moderate path. He accepted the New Deal programs and even expanded those covering labor, Social Security, and agriculture. Although he cut the budget of the Tennessee Valley Authority and reduced federal activity and regulations regarding natural resources, Eisenhower championed the nation's largest road-building project (the Federal Aid Highway Act of 1956) and federal development of the Saint Lawrence Seaway. He also approved spending increases in health care. Fiscally, Eisenhower cut taxes and controls, and each year balanced or nearly balanced the budget. The nation's gross national product, personal income, and house purchases all climbed. Inflation proved negligible, averaging one and a half percent per year. Fundamental to Eisenhower's public philosophy was his belief that only a sound economy could sustain a credible, effective foreign policy.

In the presidential election of 1956, Americans gave Eisenhower a second, even greater, landslide victory over his Democratic opponent Adlai E. Stevenson, despite Eisenhower's major heart attack in 1955 and his operation for ileitis in 1956. Voters approved his moderate policies and, like the friends of his youth and the military personnel with whom he worked, responded positively to his famous grin. His dislike of politics and his lifelong refusal to discuss personalities in public also struck responsive chords. Even his hobbies of golf, fishing and hunting, bridge and poker, and cookouts embodied widespread American values.

Eisenhower's second term continued the basic policies and themes of the first. He steadfastly resisted demands from Democrats and from conservative Republicans to increase defense spending, although he expanded the ballistic missile program after the Soviets launched the world's first human-made earth-orbiting satellite (*Sputnik*) in 1957. In

1958 (in Quemoy) and in 1958-1959 (in Berlin), Eisenhower again handled crises with deliberation. After he hosted the visit of Soviet leader Nikita Khrushchev, Eisenhower looked forward to a Paris summit meeting in May, 1960, and to a visit to the Soviet Union as his final contribution to promoting peace. On the eve of the conference, the Soviets shot down an American spy plane over Soviet territory. The U-2 incident, named after the plane, ruined the conference, canceled Eisenhower's planned visit to the Soviet Union, and dashed his hopes to improve relations between the two superpowers.

Domestic highlights of Eisenhower's second term included his ordering troops to Little Rock, Arkansas, to maintain order while the high school racially integrated its classes. In the same year, 1957, Eisenhower signed the first civil rights act in eighty-two years. Important symbolically, the act produced little change in the lives of black Americans. The same proved true of another civil rights act in 1960. In response to *Sputnik*, Eisenhower established the National Aeronautics and Space Administration (NASA) and approved the National Defense Education Act, providing the first substantial federal aid to higher education in almost a century.

Criticism of Eisenhower dealt mostly with three subjects. First, he refused to exercise any public leadership in response to Senator Joseph McCarthy's excessive unsubstantiated accusations of disloyalty directed against numerous Americans, including General George C. Marshall. Second, after the Supreme Court ruled in 1954 that separate-but-equal facilities were unconstitutional, Eisenhower refrained from lending his moral or political support for implementation of the ruling or for promotion of civil rights in general. The third area of criticism concerned his sparse defense budget and the limited range of responses it permitted in time of crisis. Eisenhower's confidence and public support, however, kept him from altering his positions because of such criticism.

In his presidential farewell address, Eisenhower warned the nation of the threat to democracy from the influence of the military-industrial complex, which benefited from massive military budgets. He retired to his Gettysburg, Pennsylvania, farm and wrote his memoirs. Most contemporary observers agreed that, had the Constitution permitted and had he been willing to run, Eisenhower easily would have won a third term.

Summary

Eisenhower, the career military officer, curtailed defense spending, pursued a foreign policy that emphasized conciliation rather than conflict, and presided over eight years of peace. An advocate of gradual domestic change, Eisenhower watched his most prominent appointee, Supreme Court Chief Justice Earl Warren, use his position and influence to bring sweeping changes to society. As a Republican president, Eisenhower, who disliked politics and favored limitations on the terms of senators and representatives, proved the most able politician of his generation. He adhered to definite policies, faced a Democratic Congress for six of his eight years in the White House, and suffered domestic and foreign setbacks, yet he gave the country eight years of economic growth and prosperity and left office with undiminished popularity.

Eisenhower obviously was a capable, complex man, but the key to his success seems to have been his ability to radiate straightforward honesty and uncomplicated common sense. The events of the decades following his presidency—the international arms race, war, riots, Watergate, inflation, declining standard of living, and uncontrollable budget deficits—have greatly enhanced respect for Eisenhower's accomplishments. Indeed, according to many, he has joined the ranks of the nation's ten greatest presidents.

Bibliography

Ambrose, Stephen E. *Eisenhower: Soldier, General of the Army, President-Elect, 1890-1952*. New York: Simon and Schuster, 1983. The most comprehensive book covering Eisenhower's life and career before he entered the White House. Based on an unequaled mastery of archival material, Ambrose provides an insightful and readable narrative. The book is especially strong on the influences that shaped Eisenhower's personality and career. The book's highlight is Eisenhower's tenure as Supreme Allied Commander during World War II.

_____. *Eisenhower: Soldier and President*. New York: Simon and Schuster, 1990. Condensed version of Ambrose's 1983 work.

_____. *Eisenhower: The President*. New York: Simon and Schuster, 1984. This authoritative volume presents a detailed chronology of Eisenhower's presidency. The coverage of personalities and events, both foreign and domestic, is broad. Ambrose, the leading Eisenhower scholar, concludes with a favorable assessment of his subject. He awards higher grades in foreign than in domestic affairs.

Bischof, Gunter, and Stephen E. Ambrose, eds. *Eisenhower: A Centenary Assessment*. Baton Rouge: Louisiana State University Press, 1995.

Burk, Robert F. *The Eisenhower Administration and Black Civil Rights*. Knoxville: University of Tennessee Press, 1984. The most important book about Eisenhower and civil rights. Although Burk concentrates on events, he also discusses Eisenhower's attitudes and beliefs. The bibliographical essay is especially valuable.

Divine, Robert A. *Eisenhower and the Cold War*. New York: Oxford University Press, 1981. A clear, brief summary of several problems and themes in Eisenhower's foreign policy. In four essays (dealing with the presidency, Asia and massive retaliation, the Middle East, and Russians), Divine offers a favorable view of Eisenhower and of his handling of international crises.

Eisenhower, David. *Eisenhower: At War, 1943-1945*. New York: Random House, 1986. This massive study (nearly a thousand pages long) provides an indispensable account of Eisenhower's wartime leadership. The author (who is the grandson of his subject) emphasizes Eisenhower's awareness of long-range strategic considerations that would shape the postwar era.

Eisenhower, Dwight D. *The Eisenhower Diaries*. Edited by Robert H. Farrell, New York: W. W. Norton and Co., 1981. This 445-page volume presents the diary that Eisenhower started in 1935 and continued sporadically until late in life. Among other things, the diary records Eisenhower's frustration with individuals whom, as a matter of policy, he refrained from criticizing publicly. Farrell's introduction is excellent.

Greenstein, Fred I. *The Hidden-Hand Presidency: Eisenhower as Leader*. New York: Basic Books, 1982. This influential revisionist book examines Eisenhower's leadership techniques. Drawing heavily from the files of the president's personal secretary, political scientist Greenstein explains Eisenhower's behind-the-scenes domination of his administration. In doing so, he also reveals much about Eisenhower's personality.

Griffith, Robert. "Dwight D. Eisenhower and the Corporate Commonwealth." *American Historical Review* 87 (February, 1982): 87-122. A long, interpretative article that analyzes and synthesizes the components of Eisenhower's political philosophy (view of society, responsibility of government, role of economics) and the influence of this philosophy on his domestic and foreign policies. Griffith also describes the influences that shaped Eisenhower's philosophy.

Mayer, Michael S. "With Much Deliberation and Some Speed: Eisenhower and the Brown Decision." *The Journal of Southern History* 52 (February, 1986): 43-76. An assessment that portrays Eisenhower's civil rights record as more complex and, at times, more ambiguous than previous scholars have judged it to be. This article is broader in its concerns than the title suggests and is valuable for its account of Eisenhower's view of equality and blacks.

Pickett, William B. *Dwight David Eisenhower and American Power.* Wheeling, Ill.: Harlan Davidson, Inc., 1995.

Reichard, Gary. *The Reaffirmation of Republicanism: Eisenhower and the Eighty-third Congress.* Knoxville: University of Tennessee Press, 1975. A careful study of Eisenhower's relationship with Republicans in Congress during his first two years in office, the only period of his presidency during which the Republicans controlled Congress. By focusing on key domestic and foreign policy issues, Reichard evaluates Eisenhower as a party leader and as a Republican.

Keith W. Olson

DIANNE FEINSTEIN

Born: June 22, 1933; San Francisco, California

In each of her elected offices from the presidency of the Board of Supervisors of San Francisco to U.S. Senator from California, Dianne Feinstein has been a pioneer, the first woman to hold that position.

Early Life

Dianne Goldman was born in San Francisco, California, on June 22, 1933, to Leon Goldman, a Jewish physician, and Betty Rosenburg Goldman, a Catholic woman of Russian descent. Dianne endured a difficult childhood that could have irreparably scarred her but instead left her resilient and strong. An alcoholic who was ill with a brain disorder that was not diagnosed until much later, Betty Goldman was frequently abusive toward her daughters, and Dianne assumed a protective role for her two younger sisters. Her father, a busy physician, was a sustaining force in Dianne's life as well as a highly respected member of the community. The poles of opposition that dominated Dianne's childhood were reflected in her concurrent attendance at temple services and the Convent of the Sacred Heart High School, where she was graduated in 1951.

One of the stabilizing forces during Dianne's youth was her uncle, Morris Goldman, who moved in with the family and introduced Dianne to the workings of government by taking her to meetings of the San Francisco Board of Supervisors. Often critical of the board's actions, he urged his niece to get an education and do the job better. She determined while still in high school to pursue a career in government service. In preparation, Dianne attended Stanford University. During her senior year, she served as vice president of the student body.

After graduating from Stanford with a bachelor's degree in history in 1955, Dianne accepted an internship in public affairs with the CORO Foundation and spent a year studying public policy. In her subsequent position as an administrative assistant for the California Industrial Welfare Commission, she met and married Jack Berman, a lawyer, but the marriage lasted less than three years. With her nine-month-old daughter, Katherine Anne, Dianne started anew. Governor Edmund S.

Brown, having been impressed by Dianne when she was a high school friend of his daughter, sought her out to serve on the California Women's Board of Terms and Paroles, a position she held from 1960 until 1966.

Dianne's second marriage in 1962 to Bertram Feinstein provided stability in her personal life. Her second husband encouraged her continued involvement in public activities. Dianne Feinstein's interest in the justice system broadened with positions on the Committee on Adult Detention and the San Francisco Mayor's Commission on Crime. Her experiences in these jobs further prepared her to seek elected office.

Life's Work

Dianne Feinstein's election to the San Francisco Board of Supervisors in 1969 marked the beginning of her noteworthy career as an elected public official. As one of the first San Francisco politicians to use television extensively for campaigning, Feinstein received more votes than any other candidate for supervisor. Thus, she became president of the Board of Supervisors for 1970-1971, the first woman to serve in that position.

Despite Feinstein's popularity as a supervisor and as president of the Board—serving a second term as president from 1974 to 1975, and being reelected for a third term in 1978—life was not without its setbacks for her both professionally and personally. After losing two bids for mayor in 1971 and 1975 and coping with her husband's long bout with cancer and subsequent death in April of 1978, Feinstein was so emotionally bereft that she contemplated a full withdrawal from public life. Only hours after making such a pronouncement to reporters, however, Feinstein found herself acting mayor of San Francisco. The assassination of Mayor George Moscone and Supervisor Harvey Milk thrust Feinstein abruptly into the forefront of San Francisco government and placed her once again in a pioneering role as the first woman to serve as the city's mayor.

The dignity and poise with which she handled the crisis evoked strong support for Feinstein from her constituency. Running a city with as many diverse groups as San Francisco possessed was not easy. Feinstein prided herself in being a centrist, however, and immediately demonstrated her intention to be an activist mayor. She established such early priorities as reducing response time for police and firemen, revitalizing public transportation, and improving garbage pickup. To ensure the success of her endeavors, Feinstein raised taxes when necessary, leading some critics to label her as a "tax and spend" Democrat while others complained about her lack of a long-term plan.

Feinstein remained politically popular, winning her second full term as mayor with 80 percent of the vote. By law, however, she was unable to seek a third term and began exploring the possibility of running for governor of California. Although the office of mayor in San Francisco was nominally nonpartisan, Feinstein's allegiance to the Democratic party was widely known, and she had been seriously considered for the 1984 Democratic vice presidential nomination. Although Democratic challengers faced a difficult battle for the governorship (which had been dominated by Republicans), especially a candidate without a statewide political base or network of support, Feinstein believed that the time was right and committed herself to a campaign for California governor.

The early stages of Feinstein's campaign for the Democratic nomination for governor were fraught with problems in staffing. Feinstein was also troubled by physical problems that left her without adequate energy and forced her to undergo major surgery in July of 1989. Her opponent, California Attorney General John Van de Kamp, had pulled far ahead of her in the polls by late fall, and her campaign was so underfunded that her staff contemplated the possibility of her withdrawal. At that point, however, Feinstein responded by conferring with her staff to devise a strategy to revitalize her campaign. Her third husband, Richard C. Blum, an investment banker whom she had married in 1980, provided strong financial support for Feinstein's advertising campaign on television. The most effective commercial centered on her ability to handle crises, as illustrated through dramatic black and white footage of Feinstein's announcement of Moscone and Milk's deaths. This sympathetic portrayal of Feinstein's leadership ability was a major influence in her come-from-behind victory over Van de Kamp.

With the momentum of a strong primary victory, Feinstein moved into the general election against the Republican candidate, Senator Pete Wilson. The election was especially significant to both parties because the victor would oversee reapportionment of the seven new congressional districts that were to be created in California as a result of the increase in population measured by the 1990 census. Republicans were thus pouring in considerable money, and Feinstein again found herself confronting the difficulties of raising money and reaching voters statewide.

In addition to promoting government reform, Feinstein campaigned on issues related to the environment and abortion rights. Although Feinstein had identified herself as unequivocally pro-choice in the primary, most feminist leaders, including the state chapter of NOW, had endorsed her opponent, Van de Kamp. Even in the general election, feminist supporters were unenthusiastic, and some analysts suggested that her lack of ties to women's groups ultimately cost Feinstein the election.

Once again, the Feinstein campaign relied heavily on television advertising and centered on the slogan "tough but caring." During the last weeks of campaigning, the race became extremely close, but Feinstein eventually lost by 3.46 percent of the vote. Campaign manager Bill Carrick attributed the loss to a failure to produce commercials that attracted voters, citing the difficulty of presenting a woman candidate as tough enough for the job without creating a sense of hardness that alienates voters.

Undaunted by the loss, however, Feinstein proclaimed that public service had been and would continue to be her life. Indeed, she moved almost immediately into a campaign for the Senate, announcing in early 1991 her intention to run in the 1992 election for Pete Wilson's former seat, then being filled by Wilson's appointee, Republican John Seymour. Some political analysts questioned Feinstein's decision to run for the remaining two-year term rather than for the full six-year term to succeed retiring Senator Alan Cranston. Although Feinstein may have hoped to preempt the Democratic field with her early move and avoid an expensive primary campaign, that did not occur, and state controller Gray Davis provided strong opposition.

Because she had proved herself a viable statewide candidate in the 1990 race for governor, however, Dianne Feinstein found fund-raising easier and she had to rely less on her husband for campaign financing. Nevertheless, the issue of finances plagued the early part of her campaign when the California Fair Political Practices Commission filed an $8 million suit for campaign reporting violations in her race for governor. The suit was eventually settled for $190,000 with both sides agreeing that unintentional errors in bookkeeping and reporting had occurred.

Following a decisive victory in the Democratic primary, Feinstein entered the general election alongside noted feminist politician, Barbara Boxer, who had won the Democratic nomination for the second Senate seat. Feinstein's male Republican opponent was John Seymour, who was known for his support of feminist causes over the years. As a result, Feinstein, who had generally not emphasized women's issues in previous campaigns, began aggressively stressing such feminist issues as abortion rights, family leave, child support, and domestic violence. A prominent campaign phrase also played on the fact that only two members of the U.S. Senate were women: "Two percent may be okay for milk, but it isn't for the U.S. Senate."

When critics complained about her record on women's issues while she was mayor, Feinstein admitted she had been wrong in refusing to sign a 1983 resolution commemorating the tenth anniversary of *Roe vs. Wade*, but noted she had consistently been pro-choice. She also defended her veto of a comparable worth plan in 1985 by arguing that it was inadequate and by emphasizing that she had written a better proposal which passed the following year.

With her subsequent election to the Senate, Feinstein again broke new ground. She and Boxer became the first female senators from California, the first Jewish senators from the state, and the first all-female delegation to the U.S. Senate. Analysts indicate that major factors in Feinstein's victory were her plan for improving the economy (especially reducing military spending in order to increase funding for environmental protection projects), the desire to initiate change in Washington, the anger over the Senate's treatment of Anita Hill during the confirmation hearings of Clarence Thomas to the U.S. Supreme Court, and the related desire to see more women in the Senate. In 1994, she easily won her primary campaign for reelection, but faced stiff competition and numerous negative campaign advertisements from her Republican challenger, Michael Huffington.

Summary

In many respects, Dianne Feinstein's life has been one exploring new territory for women. In each of her elected positions, she has been the first woman to hold that office, a situation often fraught with difficulties. Feinstein has acknowledged feeling that she is constantly being tested because of being "first," yet she has successfully met the challenges in each position. Having begun her quest for political office prior to the full flowering of the feminist movement, Feinstein established her position in the world of politics independent of women's groups and without a feminist agenda. Subsequently, however, she embraced women's causes and made them a significant part of her life's goal, to contribute to humankind through government service.

Bibliography

"Feinstein, Dianne." *Current Biography* 56, no. 8 (August, 1995): 22-28.

Leavitt, Judith A. *American Women Managers and Administrators*. Westport, Conn.: Greenwood Press, 1985. Provides brief but basic biographical data through Feinstein's career as mayor of San Francisco.

Morris, Celia. *Storming the Statehouse: Running for Governor with Ann Richards and Dianne Feinstein*. New York: Charles Scribner's Sons, 1992. The most valuable source of information available on Feinstein. Although the work focuses on her unsuccessful bid for governor in 1990 (in contrast to Richards' successful bid), it also presents essential biographical details of her earlier personal and professional life.

Stall, Bill. "Battle with Wilson Left Feinstein Tougher, Quicker." *Los Angeles Times*, April 28, 1992, p. A1. A good analysis of the Feinstein campaign for Senate.

Wilkinson, Tracy. "Senate Races Offer Stark Contrasts on World Affairs." *Los Angeles Times*, September 20, 1992, p. A3. Provides Feinstein's views on major issues during her campaign for Senate.

Witt, Linda, Karen M. Paget, and Glenna Matthews. *Running as a Woman: Gender and Power in American Politics*. New York: Free Press, 1993. A journalist, a political scientist, and a historian collaborated on this narrative overview of the experiences of female candidates in American politics. Written from the vantage point of 1992's "Year of the Woman," this work contains useful information on Feinstein's political career at the state and national level, including a telling assessment of her appeal among women voters.

Verbie Lovorn Prevost

MILLARD FILLMORE

Born: January 7, 1800; Summerhill, New York
Died: March 8, 1874; Buffalo, New York

In 1850, President Fillmore pushed for legislation designed to resolve a deadlock between Northern and Southern states over the admission of California to the Union and extension of slavery into new territories. Fillmore's support of the compromise legislation cost him the Whig presidential nomination in 1852; it also may have postponed the Civil War for a decade.

Early Life

Millard Fillmore was born January 7, 1800, in a log cabin on the farm in Locke township, New York, that his father, Nathaniel, and his uncle Calvin had purchased in 1799. Nathaniel and his wife, Phoebe Millard Fillmore, had come to the western frontier from Vermont, prompted by the prospect of more fertile land in the Military Tract set aside by New York State after the American Revolution in order to pay bonuses to veterans. In time, there were nine children in the Fillmore family; Millard was the second child and first son.

In 1815, Millard Fillmore was apprenticed to a wool carder and cloth-dresser at New Hope, near the farm in Niles, New York, that Nathaniel Fillmore had leased after title to the property in Locke proved invalid. He attended the district school in New Hope, teaching there and in Buffalo schools after 1818, and there he met his future wife Abigail Powers. Fillmore spent the years between this first acquaintance and their marriage, on February 5, 1826, establishing himself as a lawyer. He studied law from 1820 under Judge Walter Wood in Montville, New York, and in 1822 began work as a clerk in the Buffalo, New York, law firm of Asa Rice and Joseph Clary. Even though he had not completed the usual seven-year period of study, Fillmore was admitted to practice before the Court of Common Pleas and opened his own law practice in East Aurora, New York, in 1823. He moved to Buffalo in 1830 and in time went into law partnership with Nathan K. Hall and Solomon G. Haven.

Fillmore's appearance and public manner marked him for a career in politics. Just under six feet tall, he had broad shoulders, an erect carriage, and bright blue eyes. His hair was thick and yellow, but by middle age it had turned snowy white. His voice was deep and masculine. Never an orator like Daniel Webster or Edward Everett, both of whom served him as secretary of state, Fillmore struck juries and audiences as carefully prepared, sincere, and unaffected. An associate of Thurlow Weed in formation of the Anti-Masonic Party, he was elected three times to the New York State Assembly (1829-1831). Fillmore's chief accomplishment in the legislature was authorship of a law eliminating the imprisonment of debtors and providing for a bankruptcy law. Characteristic of his mature political style was the careful balancing of individual and business interests that this legislation achieved.

Life's Work

Since the chief impetus behind the formation of the Anti-Masonic Party was reelection of John Quincy Adams and defeat of Andrew Jackson in the election of 1828, the party lost strength when Jackson was elected, although it retained local influence chiefly in New York, Pennsylvania, and New England. Fillmore was elected to the House of Representatives as an Anti-Mason (1833-1835), but he followed Thurlow Weed into the newly formed Whig party in 1834. Subsequently, he was sent to Congress as a Whig (1837-1843) after William Henry Harrison was elected president in 1840. Fillmore served as chairman of the House Ways and Means Committee, and in that position he engineered congressional approval of protective tariff legislation in 1842.

Mentioned as a senatorial or vice presidential candidate prior to the 1844 election, Fillmore accepted Weed's advice—perhaps intended to keep the vice presidential prospects of William H. Seward alive—that he run for governor of New York. He was defeated by the popular Democrat Silas Wright but came back in 1847 to win election as New York's comptroller. Fillmore and Seward were both favorite son prospects for the Whig vice presidential nomination in 1848. The presidential candidates were Henry Clay, General Winfield Scott, and General Zachary Taylor. When the convention chose Taylor, and some delegates objected to Abbott Lawrence of Massachusetts as his running mate, the antislavery Clay delegates put their votes behind Fillmore and assured him the vice presidential slot. He was not assured of influence within the Taylor Administration itself when, having won

Millard Fillmore *(Library of Congress)*

the election, the new president took office in 1849. William H. Seward, Weed's ally and the newly elected senator for New York, worked to minimize Fillmore's influence on the new president. Unable to control party patronage in his home state, Fillmore was limited chiefly to his constitutional duty of presiding over the debates of the United States Senate.

California had petitioned for admission to the Union. There were thirty states at the time, fifteen slave and fifteen free, and California would tip the balance in the debate over slavery. The same issue complicated discussion of territorial governments for Utah and New Mexico, acquired at the end of the Mexican War, and an outstanding Texas-New Mexico border dispute. Abolitionists and Free-Soilers campaigned to limit the expansion of slavery into new states and territories, even trying to prohibit the slave trade in the District of Columbia, while Southern political leaders argued for the extension of slavery and for more vigorous enforcement of laws requiring the capture and return of fugitive slaves.

Senator Henry Clay, the support of whose delegates at the Whig convention of 1848 had assured Fillmore the vice presidential nomination, proposed an omnibus package of compromise legislation to deal with these issues. President Taylor, though a slaveholder from Louisiana, indicated that he would veto the bill if it extended slavery into the territories gained from Mexico. He also claimed he would use federal troops to resolve the Texas-New Mexico boundary dispute. Initially, Fillmore supported Taylor's position on Clay's omnibus bill, but, in 1850, he advised the president that he would vote to accept the package if required to cast a tiebreaking vote in the Senate. Fillmore never had to cast that vote. Taylor became ill after attending ceremonies at the Washington Monument on July 4, and died on July 9, 1850, making Millard Fillmore the thirteenth President of the United States.

After taking the oath of office and accepting the resignations of Taylor's entire cabinet, Fillmore moved to occupy a pro-Union political position. He appointed Daniel Webster as secretary of state and John Crittenden as attorney general, and he filled the rest of the cabinet with equally moderate men. Fillmore repeatedly insisted that slavery was morally repugnant to him, but he also said that he intended to be the president of the entire United States. He was prepared to make compromises in the interest of national unity. When Senator Stephen A.

Douglas, a Democrat, took over Senate management of Clay's stalled "omnibus bill," Fillmore indicated his willingness to sign the provisions of the omnibus as separate pieces of legislation. Between September 9, and September 20, 1850, he signed five measures designed to hammer out a compromise between Northern and Southern interests. California was admitted as a free state; Utah and New Mexico were given territorial status, with the citizens eventually to determine the status of slavery there; and Texas was compensated for the loss of territory in the adjustment of its border with New Mexico. Fillmore also signed a tougher law dealing with fugitive slaves and another prohibiting the slave trade, but not slavery itself, in the District of Columbia.

This reversal of Taylor's position achieved a political solution to a conflict threatening to erupt into military action. Fillmore had to send troops into South Carolina to deal with threats of secession and threatened to use them in the North to enforce the Fugitive Slave Act before there was general acceptance of these measures. While moderate men of all political parties supported Fillmore's position, both the Southern and New England factions of his own Whig party blamed him for those parts of the compromise package of which they disapproved. Therefore, Fillmore did not get the Whig presidential nomination in 1852 and retired to Buffalo in 1853, turning over the powers of the office to the Democrat Franklin Pierce.

In the face of the virtual dissolution of the Whigs as a national political party, Fillmore accepted the presidential nomination of the American, or Know-Nothing, Party in 1856. He attempted to distance himself from the proslavery, anti-Catholic, nativist principles of the party and to run his campaign on the Unionist basis he had advocated while president. The strategy did not work. In a three-way race against Democrat James Buchanan and Republican John C. Frémont, Fillmore came in a poor third.

With the election of Buchanan in 1856, Fillmore's national political career came to an end. Abigail Powers Fillmore died in Washington, District of Columbia, on March 30, 1853, only a few weeks after her husband had left the White House. On February 10, 1858, Fillmore married Caroline Carmichael McIntosh, a widow, in Albany, New York. He died in Buffalo, New York on March 8, 1874; Caroline McIntosh Fillmore died there on August 11, 1881.

Summary

During the Civil War and in the years following, the popular press depicted Millard Fillmore as a Southern sympathizer. He supported the candidacy of General George B. McClellen in 1864, and he also expressed approval of Andrew Johnson's efforts to achieve reconciliation with the South at the war's end. Properly speaking, Fillmore's positions were not so much pro-Southern as conservative, exactly as they had been when he accepted the compromise legislation of 1850 in the name of preserving the Union. His role in passage of that legislation was the central achievement of his term as president.

Fillmore's initiatives in foreign policy were modest, but they too reflected his unwillingness to adopt extreme positions. Fillmore resisted moves to annex Cuba and Nicaragua; he expressed disapproval of Austria's handling of the Hungarian uprising led by Lajos Kossuth, and he blocked French attempts to make the Hawaiian Islands a protectorate. Fillmore's administration moved to normalize relations with Mexico and opened negotiations to build a canal connecting the Atlantic and Pacific oceans through Nicaragua. He sent Commodore Matthew Perry on his mission to open the ports of Japan to merchant ships of the United States.

Like Taylor, Pierce, and Buchanan, Fillmore's reputation has been affected by the failure of nineteenth century American politics to avert the Civil War. The administration of each of these presidents struggled to control the forces that led to military conflict. The legislation passed in 1850 was the most significant attempt to defuse the sectional conflict, and Millard Fillmore's role in its passage is his chief claim to historical importance.

Bibliography

Barre, W. L. *The Life and Public Services of Millard Fillmore*. New York: Burt Franklin, 1971. Reprint of a campaign biography originally published in 1856, Barre's book provides an undocumented contemporary account of Fillmore's life and tenure as president.

Fillmore, Millard. *Millard Fillmore Papers*. Edited by Frank H. Severance. 2 vols. Buffalo, N.Y.: Buffalo Historical Society, 1907. Reprint. New York: Kraus Reprint Co., 1970. These volumes contain the only printed collection of Fillmore's public papers.

Goodman, Mark. *High Hopes: The Rise and Decline of Buffalo, New York.*

Albany: State University of New York Press, 1983. While Goodman's book deals with Fillmore only in passing, it contains a fascinating account of local reactions to his 1856 campaign as the presidential nominee of the American, or Know-Nothing, Party.

Holt, Michael F. *The Political Crisis of the 1850's.* New York: John Wiley and Sons, 1978. Reprint. New York: W. W. Norton and Co., 1983. Holt argues that disintegration of the Whig-Democrat two-party structure was a cause and not an effect of the political crisis of the 1850's.

Potter, David M. *The Impending Crisis, 1848-1861.* Edited by Don E. Fehrenbacher. New York: Harper and Row, Publishers, 1976. This excellent history of the period places the various conflicts Fillmore dealt with squarely within the ideological framework of Manifest Destiny.

Rayback, Robert J. *Millard Fillmore: Biography of a President.* Buffalo, N.Y.: Henry Stewart, 1959. The book explains the complex factors that drew Fillmore into the Anti-Masonic Whig and American parties and the effects of these associations on his political career.

Schelin, Robert C. "A Whig's Final Quest: Fillmore and the Know-Nothings." *Niagara Frontier* 26, no. 1 (1979): 1-11. Schelin focuses on Fillmore's 1856 campaign for president against the background of Whig decline and Know-Nothing appeals to prejudice.

Smith, Elbert B. *The Presidencies of Zachary Taylor and Millard Fillmore.* Lawrence: University Press of Kansas, 1988.

Snyder, Charles M., ed. *The Lady and the President: The Letters of Dorothea Dix and Millard Fillmore.* Lexington: University Press of Kentucky, 1975. The correspondence of Fillmore and Dix, the chief nineteenth century American advocate for reform in the treatment of the mentally ill; gives insight into Fillmore's personality as well as his actions as a public official and political candidate.

Robert C. Petersen

GERALD R. FORD

Born: July 14, 1913; Omaha, Nebraska

Becoming president after Richard M. Nixon's resignation in disgrace, Ford restored integrity to the office of President of the United States and a sense of decency and unity to the nation.

Early Life

Gerald Rudolph Ford, Jr., was born July 14, 1913, in Omaha, Nebraska, the son of Leslie and Dorothy King. When the boy was two, his parents were divorced and his mother presently married Gerald R. Ford, Sr., who adopted her son as his own. Jerry Ford grew up in the conservative environment of Grand Rapids, Michigan, in a warm family in which the emphasis was on integrity and hard work. These traits helped Ford, Sr., to maintain his paint manufacturing business through the Depression of the 1930's, which must have been a lesson for his sons. A good student in high school, Jerry was also an exceptional athlete both in high school and at the University of Michigan, where he earned a B.A. degree in 1935 with a B average. He then enrolled in the Yale Law School, also working full-time at Yale as a football and boxing coach. He earned his law degree in 1941, also with a B average, despite his full-time work. By this time he was more than six feet tall, powerfully built, with ruggedly handsome features which allowed him to model sports clothing in *Look* magazine. As years passed, his full blond hair slowly receded from his forehead.

Admitted to the Michigan bar in 1941, Ford and a friend founded their own law firm. Ford specialized in labor cases, always important in Michigan. When the United States entered World War II, he entered the navy as an ensign, on April 20, 1942. After a year of giving aviation cadets physical training, he went first to gunnery school and then to the *Monterey*, a new, small aircraft carrier in the Pacific. He received the highest ratings possible for an officer while serving in ten battles and through one of the worst typhoons in history, his commander describing him as an "excellent leader . . . steady, reliable, resourceful." He was released from active duty early in 1946 with the rank of lieutenant commander and returned to Grand Rapids. There Gerald Ford, Sr., had

Gerald R. Ford *(Courtesy Gerald R. Ford Library)*

become Republican Party chairman for Kent County, elected by re-formers who wanted to clean up the local political machine. There, too, was Republican senator Arthur Vandenberg, a leader of the Senate's internationalists and a believer in a bipartisan foreign policy. Young Ford's military experience had convinced him that prewar isolation-ism had been disastrous. He also believed in honest government and ran for the local seat in the United States House of Representatives in 1948, campaigning hard and winning the Republican nomination with 62.2 percent of the vote, and the general election with 60.5 percent. The same year, on October 15, he married Elizabeth "Betty" Bloomer; they had three sons and a daughter.

Life's Work
Gerald Ford represented Michigan's Fifth District for more than twenty-four years, never winning less than 60.3 percent of the vote in general elections and usually winning far more. In the House, he served on the Central Intelligence Agency and Foreign Aid subcom-mittees of the Committee on Appropriations and was soon regarded as an expert on drafting defense budgets. Such budgets are infinitely

complex; his expertise made him one of the significant members among the 435 representatives. Hoping to become Speaker of the House one day, he turned down chances to run for the Senate or for governor of Michigan.

With the election of Dwight D. Eisenhower to the presidency in 1952, there seemed a chance of an era of Republican control of government, but Eisenhower's popularity did not have enough impact on congressional elections. Apart from 1953-1955, Ford always served in a Congress with Democratic Party majorities. His record was one of enlightened conservatism with some liberal tendencies, supporting foreign aid and military appropriations, the reform of House rules, civil rights bills, and caution in government spending. In 1966, Americans for Democratic Action rated his voting record liberal sixty-seven percent of the time. By the 1960's, he was making hundreds of speeches each year to raise money for Republican candidates.

He also began to have formal leadership roles, being elected chairman of the Republican caucus in the House in 1963 and serving on the Warren Commission to investigate the assassination of President John F. Kennedy. In 1965, he was the House Republicans' choice to become the new minority leader, replacing the older, more conservative, and less effective Charles Halleck of Indiana. This meant that if the Republicans had won control of the House, Ford would have become the Speaker. As minority leader, Ford listened to the views of congressmen of all opinions, respected others' principles, accepted differences, and tried to avoid enforcing party loyalty on every vote. He helped to shape legislation in fields ranging from education to crime control. He became a national figure and a leading spokesman for his party on major issues. He continued to support civil rights legislation, tried to keep government spending down in President Lyndon B. Johnson's Great Society programs, and supported Johnson's actions in Vietnam.

Ford had first visited Vietnam in 1953, becoming a "hawk" in his support for American intervention. In the 1960's he urged more effort to win the war, not less, telling a group of Nixon campaign strategists in 1968 that the proper response to that year's "Tet" offensive was to Americanize the war. He later defended Nixon's bombing of Cambodia and served as a channel to the House for the views of the Administration. Critics accused him of being an unthinking "hawk" who merely reacted patriotically rather than analyzing the problem.

His loyalty to an administration already haunted by "Watergate" probably made Ford Nixon's choice for vice president under the Twenty-fifth Amendment when Spiro T. Agnew, under indictment, resigned the office. Allegedly, Nixon's first choice had been John Connally, a recent convert from the Democratic Party, but the Texan was too controversial to win congressional confirmation. The Senate confirmed Ford by a vote of 92 to 3; the House, by 385 to 35. As vice president, Ford remained doggedly loyal to Nixon while the Watergate cover-up became ever more obvious, but with the House Judiciary Committee about to vote articles of impeachment, the president resigned. On August 9, 1975, Gerald Ford became president, an office he had never contemplated holding or even seeking.

His presidency was made difficult by the lack of time for a proper transition, such as occurs after an election, and by the presence in the White House of many Nixon men whose loyalty remained to their old leader. Some critics and even some friends asserted that Ford was not really in command of his administration. Moreover, he inherited an economy caught in the grip of "stagflation" (recession accompanied by inflation, supposedly an impossible combination) and the aftermath of both the Vietnam War and the Watergate scandal. He did have widespread public approval, but that dropped from seventy-one percent to fifty percent, according to the Gallup poll, after he gave Nixon a pardon. Yet, this was something that Ford believed he "must" do in mercy to Nixon and his family and to end a "nightmare" for the country. He also divided his own party by naming the often controversial Nelson Rockefeller, governor of New York for several terms, as vice president.

The Ford Administration was unable to end either the recession or inflation, in part because of a difficult global economic situation and in part because of advisers' belief that "tight money" and a "slump" would soon end inflation. The slogan Whip Inflation Now (WIN) and presidential exhortations became subjects of ridicule. Ignorant of foreign policy matters, Ford was virtually the captive of the able but egocentric Henry A. Kissinger, who served as both secretary of state and presidential adviser. Ford's "summits" with Soviet leaders accomplished little but to associate the United States with the Helsinki Accords on human rights and Eastern Europe, which left that region under Soviet control without ending Soviet human rights violations.

Worse, South Vietnam fell during Ford's time in office, its impending collapse leading him to ask Congress for massive aid for the Saigon regime, using such 1960's rhetoric as South Vietnam's "fighting for freedom." He was bothered by congressional refusal, apparently not grasping the Vietnam War's impact on the country, which included widespread distrust of Saigon.

In 1976, Ford was defeated for reelection by Democrat Jimmy Carter, former governor of Georgia. Probable reasons include Carter's imaginative and relentless campaigning, Ford's choice of the capable but then acid-tongued Senator Robert J. Dole of Kansas as his running mate, and voters' perception of Ford himself as a good man but an inept one. Retiring from the presidency on January 20, 1977, Ford wrote his memoirs, in 1981 represented the United States at the funeral of assassinated Egyptian President Anwar el-Sadat, along with fellow former Presidents Nixon and Carter, and later joined Carter in sponsoring conferences for serious discussion of major international issues.

Summary

Gerald Ford's presidency was that of a man of integrity, character, and modesty, in important contrast to his imperious predecessors of questionable honor, Lyndon B. Johnson and Richard M. Nixon. Johnson and Nixon had divided the nation; Ford sought to heal it and to some extent succeeded. Americans were relieved to find an honest man in the highest office and also to find that the "imperial presidency" of Johnson and Nixon was not permanent. Ford thus redressed the balance in American public life, making the president once more a part of the federal government rather than its tyrant. Voters also, however, perceived him as less than imaginative and forceful in a time of economic trouble; at such times Americans have customarily demanded strong leadership. Ford's speaking style, adapted to pretelevision party rallies, made him seem inarticulate, even fumbling, when exposed to the new medium nationwide and to comparison with anchormen and actors. The length of his presidency and his impact on the country were thus limited by his own characteristics.

Bibliography

Cannon, James M. *Time and Chance: Gerald Ford's Appointment With History*. New York: HarperCollins, 1994.

Ford, Gerald R. *A Time to Heal: The Autobiography of Gerald R. Ford*. New York: Harper and Row, Publishers, 1979. Like the man himself, calm, unpretentious, straightforward; the honesty contrasts sharply with memoirs of Lyndon Johnson and Richard Nixon. Ford admits some mistakes but does not go beneath the surface to analyze his motives and decisions.

Greene, John Robert. *The Presidency of Gerald R. Ford*. Lawrence: University Press of Kansas, 1995.

Hartmann, Jerry. *Palace Politics: An Inside Account of the Ford Years*. New York: McGraw-Hill Book Co., 1980. Ford's chief of staff's revealing if egocentric account, emphasizing the interplay of personalities between the Ford men and the Nixon men. Blames the failures of Ford's presidency on the held-over Nixon staff members.

Hersey, John. *The President*. New York: Alfred A. Knopf, 1975. A brilliant writer's diary of a week in Ford's presidency, well illustrated, but useful mostly for personal glimpses of Ford interacting with others. Avoids policy issues.

Mollenhoff, Clark R. *The Man Who Pardoned Nixon*. New York: St. Martin's Press, 1976. An investigative reporter's harshly critical account, accusing Ford of deception behind his promises of openness. Includes attacks on Ford's appointments, policies, and use of executive privilege.

Reeves, Richard. *A Ford, Not a Lincoln*. New York: Harcourt Brace Jovanovich, 1975. The most informative critical book, analyzing Ford's personality and political techniques, including the best explanation of the Nixon pardon. Reeves finds Ford decent but ignorant, overdependent on his staff, not really a leader.

Sidey, Hugh. *Portrait of a President*. New York: Harper and Row, Publishers, 1975. Evocative of the "feel" of the Ford presidency through pictures and tales of Ford's dealing with his staff and with congressmen, voters, and chiefs of state.

Vestal, Bud. *Jerry Ford, Up Close: An Investigative Biography*. New York: Coward, McCann and Geoghegan, 1974. A friendly account of Ford's early years, family, schooling, navy service, years in Congress, and the vice presidency. One can see emerging the kind of president Ford would be.

Robert W. Sellen

BENJAMIN FRANKLIN

Born: January 17, 1706; Boston, Massachusetts
Died: April 17, 1790; Philadelphia, Pennsylvania

Franklin helped shape most of the important political, social, and intellectual developments in eighteenth century America. He became a veritable symbol of America by the end of his life, both at home and abroad, and he remains an influential folk hero.

Early Life

Among Benjamin Franklin's English ancestors, one had owned a bit of land only twelve miles from the English ancestral seat of the Washingtons. His father, Josiah, had repudiated the Church of England and removed from England to Boston in the 1680's; his mother's forebears had arrived somewhat earlier. When Franklin was born on January 17, 1706, the modest household was already teeming with children, for he was a tenth son—and, incidentally, the youngest son of the youngest son for five generations back. The salient facts of Franklin's life were extraordinary from the start.

Although his father was a struggling tradesman (a candle maker and soap boiler), there was much in the way of reading, thinking, and discussing as well as hard work in his home. Franklin learned to read when very young, and by the age of twelve he had progressed through the Bible, the works of John Bunyan, Plutarch's *Parallel Lives* (105-115), and certain essays of Daniel Defoe and of Boston's Cotton Mather. He had very little formal schooling, and his family could not afford to send him to Harvard College.

Instead, an effort was made to bring him into the family business. He disliked the work, and he hated the smell. At that point, an older brother, James, returned from London, where he had been trained as a printer. Thus, the restless, bright, bookish twelve-year-old Benjamin Franklin was apprenticed to his high-spirited brother, who in 1721 started a newspaper, *The New England Courant*. It was the fourth newspaper in the colonies. These years were supremely important in shaping the man who later became so famous. He learned a trade which would bring him profits and prominence. He had access to many books, especially those loaned by patrons and friends. He discussed and debated matters with men who loitered in the shop and also with friends after hours. The principal subjects were the two which would be commonly avoided centuries later: religion and politics. He worked hard at learning to write and he experienced the thrill of seeing his first piece, an anonymous letter to the editor, in print. When the pugnacious James got into trouble with the authorities and was jailed, his brother, then sixteen, functioned as the editor.

The brothers often quarreled and the younger Franklin, a mere apprentice, was often treated severely. He resented this and decided to run away. He arrived in Philadelphia in October, 1723, munching on a

Benjamin Franklin *(Library of Congress)*

large roll, with one Dutch dollar and a copper shilling in his pocket. The scene became a memorable passage in the memoir he later wrote, which included the fact that his future wife happened to see him and laughed at the ridiculous sight he made. He soon found work, for he was an excellent printer, and he soon found adventure as well. An eccentric governor of the province, William Keith, proposed that Franklin go to England to purchase equipment for a new printing business which Keith hoped would outdo all competition. He would send letters of credit and letters of introduction.

Franklin was in London by Christmas, 1724, but no letters came from the governor. The eighteen-year-old did find work, however, in a printing house, and as always he read intensively and grappled with ideas. After setting type for a religious book, he became convinced that the author was all wrong. In response, Franklin composed and printed a pamphlet which set forth a radical refutation. He later regarded this as a mistake, but it did gain him some attention and some new acquaintances, a few of them prominent writers of the day.

Franklin returned to Philadelphia in 1726, and he was soon employed again in his old shop. Before long, he left it to form a new business with a partner, on credit. By dint of very long hours of work, ingenious planning, and excellent workmanship, they survived—barely. Then the partner wanted to leave, and Franklin, borrowing money, bought him out. By July, 1730, he was the sole proprietor of a promising business, which included the printing of a newspaper begun the year before, *The Pennsylvania Gazette*. Six weeks later, he married Deborah Read, the daughter of his first landlady. Though she was uneducated and ignorant (thus never an intellectual companion), she was frugal, industrious, and loving. Franklin, at twenty-four, had become a solid Philadelphia burgher.

Life's Work

The foundation of Franklin's renown was his success as a businessman. Both he and Deborah worked very hard, and they lived frugally for some time. It was, however, more than routine drudgery, for new projects were always appearing: Franklin established a stationery shop; Deborah collected and prepared rags for the papermakers; he imported books in both English and foreign languages; he printed almanacs for those who compiled them—and then decided to compile

his own. *Poor Richard's Almanack*, begun in 1732 and published between 1733 and 1758, was ultimately to become the best known of the
many which were printed in eighteenth century America. Franklin
enjoyed borrowing and reworking phrases from his reading and sometimes wrote new adages, which delighted his readers. For many, he and
his fictional wise man, Richard Saunders, became one. The central
themes of Richard's concern were thrift, industry, and frugality, and
Franklin at the time appeared to be practicing what "Poor Richard"
preached.

Political connections quickly became an important feature of Franklin's business success. He printed much of the provincial government's
work: laws, records of legislative voting, and even the new paper
currency in favor of which Franklin had argued in his first political
pamphlet, *A Modest Enquiry into the Nature and Necessity of a Paper
Currency* (1729). He became clerk of the Pennsylvania Assembly in
1736. The following year, he secured an appointment as postmaster for
Philadelphia, a position which gave him immediate access to the latest
news—very helpful in his newspaper business. Later, he was deputy
postmaster general for all the colonies (1753-1774), and under his
administration the governmental department showed a profit. He was
always heavily involved with public affairs and often managed to
influence their course.

It was during his years as a businessman that Franklin's remarkable
flair for civic improvement by private initiative appeared. In 1727, he
founded a discussion group, or club, of tradesmen, clerks, and mechanics, which he called the "Junto." Often Franklin would first pro-
pose to his friends at the Junto for discussion an idea for a public
project, and then follow his proposal with an article in his newspaper.
Soon the project would be under way. He was prominent in the founding of a circulating library, a fire company, a hospital, and an academy
which evolved into the University of Pennsylvania, among many other
projects. Ever the keen observer of daily life in his beloved city, he was
always alert to possibilities for improvement.

Franklin was also a particularly astute observer of nature itself, and
this ultimately led him to the forefront of certain branches of the
science of his day. On an early transatlantic voyage, he kept careful
records of temperatures, of the flora and fauna of the sea, of the
positions of the moon and the stars; later he made a map of the Gulf

Stream. He believed that knowledge must be useful, and actual inventions came out of many of his studies, including the improved Franklin stove, bifocal spectacles, a glass harmonica (a musical instrument for which even Wolfgang Amadeus Mozart wrote music), and other lesser gadgets. His main interest, though, was electricity. His famous kite experiment in 1752 demonstrated the identity of lightning and electricity and gave him an international reputation. He was, as always, interested in practical application, which in this case became the lightning rod. Nevertheless, he was also responsible for naming the concept of polarity, negative and positive, to describe the behavior of electricity.

In 1748, Franklin was able to retire from business, expecting to devote himself to his favorite scientific pursuits. Public affairs, however, became the dominant force throughout the remainder of his life. When the threat of war with France led to a gathering of delegates at Albany in 1754, Franklin was there representing Pennsylvania. He proposed a plan for an inter-Colonial union which the Albany Congress approved, only to see it rejected by both the various Colonial governments and the imperial authorities in London. Franklin always believed that if these governments had not been so shortsighted, the American Revolution might have been avoided. In 1757, as a result of a quarrel between the Pennsylvania Assembly and the proprietors of the colony, he was sent to London as spokesman for the Assembly, the members of which wanted the authorities there to intervene. In this he achieved a partial success. While in England, he received honorary degrees from St. Andrews and Oxford. He was very happy in England and seriously considered a permanent move, but he came home to Philadelphia in 1762.

Another political quarrel in Pennsylvania led to Franklin's return to England in 1764, where he soon became involved in efforts to forestall the new imperial policies toward the Colonies, which Americans regarded as outrageous. For ten years, Franklin was torn between his profound pride in America and things American, and his enthusiasm for English culture. As the foremost American of his day, he was looked to for the preservation of American rights: He became an agent for Georgia, New Jersey, and Massachusetts, as well as the Pennsylvania Assembly. As Anglo-American relations deteriorated, Franklin revealed in private his growing conviction that the American colonists' claims were sound and that their resistance was justified, while he continued to make every diplomatic effort possible for accommodation.

Early in 1774, however, news arrived of the destruction of tea at Boston Harbor: the "Boston Tea Party." This was quickly followed by a mighty personal attack on Franklin, occasioned by his part in obtaining and circulating certain letters written by Governor Thomas Hutchinson of Massachusetts, the contents of which inflamed opinion against Hutchinson and led to a petition for his recall. Franklin was dismissed by the royal government from his postal appointment and subjected to a searing public humiliation before a committee of the Privy Council (January, 1774). For another year he tried in many ingenious ways to achieve a reconciliation, but to no avail. He sailed for America in March, 1775.

When Franklin arrived home, the Continental Congress, which had first convened during the preceding fall, was now into its second session at Philadelphia. The deliberations were now becoming extremely anxious because the unthinkable had happened: Actual fighting had broken out with British soldiers at Lexington and Concord. Franklin was made a member of the congress the day after he arrived, and he immediately undertook important work. He drew up a plan of Colonial union—something similar to an early version of a national constitution. He organized a post office and became postmaster general. He served on a number of important committees, including one which in 1776 was to draft the Declaration of Independence. He was, at the age of seventy, the oldest signer. Toward the end of that year, he was sent by the congress, along with Arthur Lee and Silas Deane, to solicit French support for the American cause.

Franklin was well-known in France. He had visited that country before, but more important was his reputation as a scientist, writer (Poor Richard's witticisms had been translated), and apostle of the latest ideas of the Age of Reason. He played the part well, with fur hat and simple clothes, a genial manner, and appropriate *bons mots*, and he exuded the spirit of liberty—a veritable backwoods Socrates spreading the truths of nature. Following the American victory at Saratoga (October, 1777), the French became receptive to American suggestions, and by February of 1778 France had become a formal ally. This meant that France was now at war with Great Britain.

Franklin became the sole American ambassador in September of

1778 and, as always, found many interests beyond his principal work. He managed, nevertheless, to keep Franco-American relations good; France provided America with material aid, an army, and, in the crucial autumn of 1781, a navy. After the British defeat at Yorktown (October, 1781), peace negotiations with Britain began. Franklin was joined by John Adams and John Jay in the final talks, but on several occasions the wily old Philadelphian's role was decisive. It was an excellent treaty for Americans, gaining them a formal acknowledgment of independence and generous boundaries.

When Franklin returned to Philadelphia in September, 1785, he was nearly eighty years old. Yet he was chosen president of the executive council of Pennsylvania, and he became the president of an antislavery society. He was chosen as a Pennsylvania delegate to the Philadelphia Convention, which drew up the United States Constitution in 1787, and he gave his prestigious support to its ratification. His last public act was signing a petition to Congress for the abolition of slavery. He died on April 17, 1790.

Summary

Franklin's life was so varied and his achievements so diverse that it seems as though there were several Franklins, though one tends to overlap the other. The most familiar is the successful businessman who rose from humble circumstances to dine with kings, substantially by his own efforts. His life symbolized the rags-to-riches success of a self-made man, a theme of great importance in American thought. His version of his life, as presented in the didactic *Autobiography* (1791) and in the sayings of Poor Richard, stressed thrift, industry, and frugality—important elements of his own Puritan heritage, rendered in secular, easily understood forms. His zest for useful knowledge became the main style of American science and technology, yet he had great respect for learning and for intellectual curiosity, and he believed that educational opportunity was indispensable for a great future nation.

He was civic-minded from the start. He demonstrated what could be done by private, voluntary community effort to care for human needs, but he also stressed the importance of alert participation in the prevailing political system. His style was egalitarian, tolerant, and democratic before such a style was expected and common; yet he understood well the importance of dignity and deference in human

affairs. Americans, during his later years, repudiated kings and heredi-
tary aristocrats, but they also yearned for heroes. Franklin provided
them with a hero unlike any other known before.

Bibliography

Aldridge, Alfred Owen. *Benjamin Franklin: Philosopher and Man*. Philadelphia: J. B. Lippincott Co., 1965. An effort to explain Franklin's
human qualities as much as his achievements, this is a judicious,
authoritative biography by one who has done much to expand
knowledge of Franklin and who has written extensively about him.
Some unconventional frankness, but without debunking.

Cohen, I. Bernard. *Benjamin Franklin's Science*. Cambridge, Mass.: Harvard University Press, 1990.

_____. *Franklin and Newton*. Cambridge, Mass.: Harvard Univer-
sity Press, 1966. In this reprint of the excellent 1956 study of eighteenth century scientific thought, Cohen, distinguished historian of
science, places Franklin in the context of prevailing notions about
scientific method; he appreciates Franklin as a scientist without
overstating the case. Especially good depiction of human qualities
which affect scientific work.

Conner, Paul W. *Poor Richard's Politics: Benjamin Franklin and His New
American Order*. New York: Oxford University Press, 1965. System-
atic discussion of Franklin's political ideas. This is a thoughtful,
well-informed book, filled with materials regarding Franklin's intellectual world. Strong effort to arrive at balanced judgments about
Franklin as a thinker.

Crane, Verner W. *Benjamin Franklin and a Rising People*. Boston: Little,
Brown and Co., 1954. Succinct, extremely informative, and reliable.
Neither very short nor very long, this book gets to the essentials
about Franklin in a commonsense way reminiscent of the good Dr.
Franklin himself. Especially strong on philosophical, social, and
political ideas.

Franklin, Benjamin. *The Autobiography of Benjamin Franklin*. Edited by
Leonard W. Labaree et al. New Haven, Conn.: Yale University Press,
1964. Franklin's memoirs (the word "autobiography" was not used
in the eighteenth century) have been printed a bewildering number
of times, and most readers may well believe that they are familiar
with them. It is one of those classics, however, which deserve re-

peated readings, even though it presents only one of the several Franklins.

Granger, Bruce I. *Benjamin Franklin: An American Man of Letters.* Ithaca, N. Y.: Cornell University Press, 1964. Skilled presentation of Franklin's literary achievements. Each chapter is devoted to a kind of writing, such as essays, letters, almanacs, and so on. Strong claims are made for Franklin, many of them persuasive.

Jennings, Francis. *Benjamin Franklin, Politician.* New York: W. W. Norton, 1996.

Lopez, Claude-Anne. *Mon Cher Papa.* New Haven, Conn.: Yale University Press, 1966. Unusually charming account of Franklin's life in France during the American Revolution by one of the editors of the Franklin papers. The author does a good job of dispelling some of the myths and the nonsense about Franklin and the ladies and makes a strong case for his greatness as a diplomat. A very entertaining book.

Middlekauff, Robert. *Benjamin Franklin and His Enemies.* Berkeley: University of California Press, 1996.

Stourzh, Gerald. *Benjamin Franklin and American Foreign Policy.* Chicago: University of Chicago Press, 1954. Searching, learned analysis of some major features of Franklin's thought. This account begins with a review of prevailing currents of thought in the eighteenth century, featuring the Great Chain of Being, the belief in progress and in reason, and other basic notions; then it proceeds with the way Franklin developed such materials in the course of his diplomatic career.

Van Doren, Carl C. *Benjamin Franklin.* New York: Viking Press, 1938. Magisterial biography, massive and still impressive. This is the kind of book to which one might turn for reliable information about nearly anything regarding Franklin's life. An excellent literary achievement containing profound, extensive scholarship.

Wright, Esmond. *Franklin of Philadelphia.* Cambridge, Mass.: Harvard University Press, 1986. A lively, well-written biography. Much new knowledge about Franklin has come to light since Van Doren's biography, and even since that of Aldridge, and this work incorporates it gracefully. In some ways, Wright says, Franklin was " the most modern-minded of all the Founding Fathers."

Richard D. Miles

JESSIE BENTON FRÉMONT

Born: May 31, 1824; near Lexington, Virginia
Died: December 27, 1902; Los Angeles, California

As the daughter of a powerful senator and wife of an explorer and general, Frémont participated in Jacksonian politics, the opening of the West, abolitionism, and the Civil War. In her behind-the-scenes work, she challenged the constraints of nineteenth century roles for women.

Early Life

Jessie Ann Benton was born on May 31, 1824, at Cherry Grove, her mother's family plantation near Lexington, Virginia. She was the second daughter of the five children born to Thomas Hart Benton and Elizabeth McDowell Benton. Her father had moved as a young man from his native North Carolina to Tennessee, where he became a friend and protégé of Andrew Jackson. In 1815, Benton migrated to St. Louis, Missouri, where he practiced law and was elected the new state's first senator, in 1820. In 1821, Benton married Elizabeth McDowell, whom he had courted for six years. Elizabeth's Scotch-Irish Presbyterian family had settled in a Blue Ridge mountain valley near Lexington, Virginia, in 1737, and had become prominent in local and state politics.

As Jessie grew up, the family moved between households in St. Louis, Cherry Grove, and Washington, exposing the curious child to an array of personalities, from Washington insiders to southern aristocrats to rough frontiersmen. Jessie was privately tutored in languages, piano, history, and classics. Her father's favorite child, she was taken along to the Capitol and White House, where she absorbed the elder Benton's democratic convictions. A champion of the common people, her father advocated western expansion and opposed the extension of slavery.

Jessie displayed a willful and independent spirit, which her father encouraged as long as she was a child. As she approached womanhood with no sign of diminishing assertiveness, he realized that allowing her to exercise her mind and personality freely had ill prepared her for the submissive role expected of nineteenth century women. At age fourteen, Jessie was sent to Miss English's Female Seminary in Georgetown, a fashionable finishing school which she despised.

In 1840, Jessie met John Charles Frémont, a handsome young officer with the Army's Topographical Corps. Frémont had all the qualities of courage, impulsiveness, and willfulness that would make him a great explorer and attractive to the ladies, including sixteen-year-old Jessie. Her father was alarmed, since Frémont lacked the status and wealth that Benton thought important in a suitor for his daughter. Frémont was the illegitimate son of a French immigrant and had been reared in poverty by his mother in South Carolina. Despite efforts by her father to prevent a romance, Jessie eloped with the dashing Frémont on October 19, 1841. Eventually reconciled to the marriage, Thomas Hart Benton welcomed his new son-in-law as a willing partner in his campaign to open the West to American expansion, and in his daughter Benton recognized a talented and driven helpmate who would advance Frémont's career.

Life's Work

Unable to participate in politics in her own right, Jessie Benton Frémont devoted her considerable energies to promoting her husband's career. Like her father, she believed fervently that the destiny of the United States was to expand across the continent. John Charles Frémont shared this goal and embodied the resolve necessary to achieve it. Through Benton's influence and his own credentials as an explorer, Frémont was appointed to head a series of expeditions to chart the West. The first of these assignments sent Frémont into western Wyoming in 1842, where he surveyed South Pass and climbed one of the highest peaks of the Wind River range. Upon his return, Jessie helped him write the report of the expedition which was published in 1843. While the scientific observations were John Frémont's, the dramatic flair and poetic touch added by Jessie made the report a romantic adventure story. Their collaboration produced results reflecting the strengths of each, although the credit reverted to John. Jessie, like other women of the day, measured her own success by her husband's triumphs.

At the start of John's second expedition in 1843, an incident occurred which revealed Jessie's capacity for audacious actions on her husband's behalf. While John was preparing to leave Missouri, Jessie intercepted a message from the War Department instructing Frémont to return to Washington. Withholding the order, Jessie sent word to John to set out immediately on his journey. The expedition, which traveled to Oregon and California, was a huge success. The report, written by Jessie from John's dictation, sold in the tens of thousands and served as a guidebook for settlers moving West on the Oregon Trail.

In the meantime, Jessie began to raise a family. A daughter, Elizabeth Benton, was born in 1842. Jessie saw two children die before their first birthdays: Benton (1848) and Anne Beverley (1853). Two healthy sons were born: John Charles in 1851, and Frank Preston in 1854.

John Charles Frémont's third expedition altered the fate of the family. Ending up in California in 1846, John was on hand to participate in the Bear Flag Revolt, an uprising in which American settlers seized power from Mexican officials prior to the actual outbreak of war between the two countries. Caught in a dispute between superior officers, Frémont disobeyed a direct order and was sent East for court-martial. Jessie went in person to President James K. Polk to argue vigorously in her husband's defense. The court found John guilty and recommended his expulsion from the Army, though Polk rescinded the dismissal. The Frémonts refused to accept clemency, however, and John resigned in indignation from the Army. Embittered, the Frémonts moved to California, where John had purchased an estate called Las Mariposas near Yosemite Valley.

Life was rough in California during the Gold Rush, with occasional food shortages and few reliable servants available. The rewards, however, greatly outweighed the inconveniences when several rich veins of gold were discovered on Las Mariposas. Despite legal disputes over the title of the estate, the Frémonts found themselves millionaires, able to travel to Europe as celebrities in 1852. After returning to America in 1853, John headed yet another western expedition, while Jessie settled the family in New York.

In 1856, the new Republican Party chose John Charles Frémont to run for president. The Frémonts favored the Republicans' free-soil position of prohibiting slavery in the new territories of the West. For the first time in American history, the candidate's wife figured prominently in the presidential campaign. Republican banners proclaimed "Frémont and Jessie" and "Jessie's Choice," with illustrations of the attractive Jessie and her handsome husband. While in public she played the decorous role expected of her, behind the scenes Jessie masterfully managed John's campaign. She helped to write his campaign biography, read and answered all of his mail, and received his visitors. Her prominent role was criticized by Frémont's opposition, yet it also galvanized women into political activity as never before. Women attended political rallies, and a few went on the lecture circuit for Frémont and free-soil. Although Frémont lost the election, the strong Republican showing in the party's first national election revealed the rising strength of the free-soil movement and the growing rift between North and South.

Jessie, exhausted from the campaign and upset over her father's refusal to endorse Frémont for president, reluctantly followed her husband to California once more. Her depression was compounded by her father's death in April, 1858.

When the Civil War broke out in 1861, Abraham Lincoln appointed John C. Frémont as Union commander of Missouri. Jessie joined her husband in St. Louis, acting as his unofficial adviser and assistant. Beset with shortages of men and supplies and surrounded by Confederate sympathizers, John had difficulty controlling the state. Largely as a military strategy, Frémont proclaimed the emancipation of all slaves belonging to disloyal Missourians. When a storm of protest erupted, Jessie traveled to Washington to plead John's case personally with President Lincoln. Speaking forcefully and emotionally, she antagonized Lincoln and failed to help her husband. John lost his Army command and retired to New York to wait out the war. In an effort to save her husband's reputation, Jessie wrote *The Story of the Guard: A Chronicle of the War* (1863), a book about John's exploits.

After the war, a series of financial disasters eroded the Frémont fortune, and by 1873, the family was destitute. Jessie wrote to support her family, contributing reminiscences and fiction to magazines such as *Harper's, Century*, and *Atlantic Monthly*. She produced a number of books based upon her travels, adventures, and acquaintances, including *A Year of American Travel* (1878), *Souvenirs of My Time* (1887), *Far-West Sketches* (1890), and *The Will and the Way Stories* (1891).

In 1887, the Frémonts moved to Los Angeles. After John died in 1890, Jessie continued to work on her memoirs and other writing and lived with her daughter Elizabeth, who acted as her nurse and companion until Jessie's death in 1902.

Summary

The life of Jessie Benton Frémont reveals the limited roles allowed women of the nineteenth century and the efforts they made to find fulfillment within those narrow boundaries. Reared by an indulgent father who encouraged her natural curiosity and independence, Jessie never comfortably fit into the passive role then commonly expected of women. While she did marry and raise a family, she acted out her own ambitions through her dynamic husband. She promoted his career by capitalizing on her own attributes, winning influence for him by calling upon her own political connections. She transformed his dry scientific reports into romantic adventure stories with her skilled pen. When he stumbled, she stepped beyond accepted propriety of the time to defend him brashly in front of presidents. When his ineptitude in business bankrupted the family, she quietly but competently went to work to bring in an income.

Jessie Benton Frémont often felt frustrated with the limited roles available to women. When she could, she gave generously to support the suffrage movement. She lamented that as a woman, she was not taken seriously in politics. Nevertheless, she did help to expand the opportunities for women through her example of feminine brilliance and assertiveness. Her role as the active wife of the presidential candidate in the 1856 campaign inspired women to demand the right to participate in politics. Like others of her generation, she responded to the Civil War with patriotism, public action, and compassion.

Bibliography

Chambers, William Nisbet. *Old Bullion Benton, Senator from the New West: Thomas Hart Benton.* Boston: Little, Brown, 1956. Though somewhat dated, this work is still the most thorough biography of Jessie's father, Thomas Hart Benton. Useful for Benton and McDowell family background, political context, and relationship between Benton and John Charles Frémont.

Frémont, Jessie Benton. *The Letters of Jessie Benton Frémont.* Edited by Pamela Herr and Mary Lee Spence. Urbana: University of Illinois Press, 1992. A delightful collection of letters written by Frémont which gives first-hand insight into her personality. The editors have written an excellent biographical sketch of Frémont and have provided detailed chapters introducing each section of her life.

Herr, Pamela. *Jessie Benton Frémont: A Biography*. New York: Franklin Watts, 1987. An up-to-date biography of Jessie Benton Frémont that makes valuable use of letters and papers of the Frémont and Blair-Lee families. Highly readable account of Frémont placed within the political and social context of her time, reflecting new scholarship on women.

Nevins, Allan. *Fremont: Pathmarker of the West*. Reprint. Lincoln: University of Nebraska Press, 1992. This reprint of a classic biography of John Charles Frémont portrays him in heroic proportions. This work also gives Jessie Benton Frémont deserved credit for contributing to John's career. Useful for meticulous detail on both John and Jessie's lives, though poorly documented.

Stone, Irving. *Immortal Wife: The Biographical Novel of Jessie Benton Fremont*. Garden City, N.Y.: Doubleday, Doran, 1944. A fictionalized account of Jessie Benton Frémont's life. Despite its fictional format, Stone's novel is based upon the papers and published works of Frémont, thus ensuring a relatively high degree of factual accuracy.

Lynne M. Getz

John C. Frémont

Born: January 21, 1813; Savannah, Georgia
Died: July 13, 1890; New York, New York

John C. Frémont's exploits as an explorer helped to propel the American people westward toward Oregon and California. When the continental nation he helped to create was faced with civil war, he fought to maintain the Union and end slavery.

Early Life

When John Charles Frémont was born on January 21, 1813 in Savannah, Georgia, his parents were not married. In 1811, Ann Beverly Whiting had left her elderly husband John Pryor to run away with Charles Frémon, a young French emigrant who taught dancing and French. For several years the struggling Frémon family traveled the South, but after the father died they settled in Charleston, South Carolina, where John Charles grew to maturity.

At age fourteen, Frémont clerked in the law office of John W. Mitchell, who soon sent the young man to Dr. John Roberton's academy. In 1829, Frémont entered the junior class of the College of Charleston. Showing promise, he nevertheless fell behind in his studies from a lack of diligence as well as the distraction of a young love. In 1831, the faculty reluctantly dismissed him for "incorrigible negligence," three months short of his graduation.

In 1833, saved from obscurity by Joel Poinsett, former minister to Mexico, Frémont taught mathematics on the USS *Natchez* on a South American cruise and then earned an appointment in 1835 as professor of mathematics in the navy. He nevertheless declined this position to join Captain William G. Williams in surveying part of a proposed railroad route from Charleston to Cincinnati. This first assignment earned for him a second as Williams' assistant in 1836-1837, surveying the lands of the Cherokee Indians in Georgia. Frémont showed little concern for the forced removal of the Cherokees across the Mississippi, but he did discover a longing to pursue a life in unexplored lands.

With the help of Secretary of War Poinsett, Frémont was assigned in 1838 to assist Joseph Nicolas Nicollet, a respected French scientist mapping the region between the Mississippi and Missouri rivers. He was commissioned a second lieutenant in the United States Topographical Corps and from Nicollet received valuable experience in frontier survival, as well as rigorous training in mapmaking and scientific observation. As Nicollet's protégé, Frémont stood ready to replace the gravely ill scientist on future missions.

Bright and inquisitive, Frémont already possessed the knowledge of surveying, mathematics, and natural sciences, as well as the impulsiveness, that would shape his later career. Bearded and slightly but sturdily built, he was able to endure great physical and personal hardships. His dark hair, olive skin, and piercing blue eyes attracted the friendship and affection of men and women alike. In 1841, he won the lifelong admiration and love of the young and talented Jessie Benton, acquiring not only a bride but also another powerful benefactor in her father, Senator Thomas Hart Benton of Missouri.

Life's Work

Frémont received his first independent assignment in 1841 to survey the Des Moines River region. On his return, he secretly married Jessie, soon benefitting from his family connection with Senator Benton: Advocates of American expansion, led by Benton, were eager to encourage emigration to the Oregon country, and Frémont was thus given command of his first western expedition, assigned to examine part of the trail to Oregon while gathering information useful to emigrants and the government.

In Missouri, Frémont enlisted Kit Carson as his guide and set off from the Kansas River in June, 1842. Following the Platte to the Sweetwater River, he went on to cross the Rocky Mountains at South Pass in Wyoming, later describing the route as no more difficult than the ascent up Capitol Hill. He then explored the headwaters of the Green River in the Wind River Range, unfurling an American flag atop one of its loftiest peaks. Returning, Frémont led six men in a collapsible boat down the Platte. When the current became swift and dangerous, he rashly decided to run the rapids, resulting in an accident that destroyed much of his equipment and part of the expedition's records.

Frémont's second expedition of 1843-1844 was more ambitious. With a large, well-equipped party (including an unauthorized howitzer cannon), he was to complete his survey of the overland trail all the way to Oregon. Setting off in May, the explorer first sought a new pass through the Colorado mountains but soon rejoined the Oregon Trail. Crossing at South Pass, he pushed on to the British forts in the Oregon country, finally reaching Fort Vancouver on the Columbia. On this expedition, Frémont made the first scientific investigation of the Great Salt Lake; his reports inspired Brigham Young to lead his Mormon followers to settle there and make the region bloom, as Frémont had predicted.

From Oregon, Frémont embarked on a perilous journey southward, exploring and naming the Great Basin and then attempting a risky winter crossing of the Sierra Nevada into California, successfully leading his men to Sutter's Fort in the Sacramento Valley. Inspired in part by American interest in the Mexican province of California, Frémont's adventures intensified American passions to possess this valuable Pacific prize. Returning via the old Spanish Trail, Utah Lake, and Bent's Fort on the Arkansas River, Frémont emerged in August, 1844, a national celebrity.

With Jessie's valuable help, Frémont prepared reports of his first and second expeditions that captured the excitement and promise of the new land. Congress ordered the reports published for public distribution, providing emigrants a guide for western travel. The popular reports helped to dispel the notion that the Plains region was an arid wasteland, showed the Oregon Trail passable, and praised the fertile valleys of Oregon and California.

With a well-armed party of sixty men, the brevet captain's third expedition would place him in California just as relations with Mexico worsened. Starting in June, 1845, the party followed the Arkansas and then crossed the central Colorado Rockies. Frémont paused to examine further the Great Salt Lake, then led his party across the desert to the west. While the main party followed a safer route, Frémont led a smaller group directly across the Great Basin and then attempted another winter crossing of the Sierra. Encountering less difficulty than on the previous trip, he arrived once again at Sutter's Fort, eager to play a role in California's future.

Frémont's formidable force earned the suspicion of Mexican officials, who ordered the party to leave the province. Although war with Mexico was months away, Frémont defied the order, raised the American flag, and prepared for a confrontation. When none developed, he slowly moved toward Oregon but retraced his steps after the arrival of a messenger from Washington. Marine Lieutenant Archibald Gillespie had carried important dispatches to Consul Thomas O. Larkin at Monterey, directing him to conciliate the native Californians to accept American rule. Gillespie repeated these instructions to Frémont and relayed news of trouble with Mexico. Frémont misinterpreted the government's instructions to mean that he should return to California and act to protect American interests there. After a bloody clash with Indians, he returned to the Sacramento Valley, assuming command of the "Bear Flag" revolt of American settlers in June, 1846.

Frémont's actions secured northern California for the United States, but were contrary to the government's wishes to win the province peacefully with the aid of its citizens. Once hostilities with Mexico began, American naval forces seized the ports of Monterey and San Francisco in July, 1846. Frémont's frontiersmen and settlers then formed the "California Battalion" to assist Commodore Robert F. Stockton in securing southern California. San Diego and Los Angeles were quickly occupied, but a revolt by Californians forced the Americans to retake the south. Assembling a large force in the north, Frémont arrived too late to join in the battle for Los Angeles, but he did accept (without authority) the Californians'surrender at Cahuenga.

In January, 1847, Stockton appointed Frémont governor of California. This position embroiled the current lieutenant colonel in a bitter dispute over proper authority between the Commodore and General Stephen Watts Kearny, who had arrived from Santa Fe only to be bloodied by Californians at San Pasqual. As governor in Los Angeles, Frémont recognized Commodore Stockton's authority while unwisely resisting General Kearny's commands, resulting in his arrest and return east virtually a prisoner. In a celebrated court-martial defense, he won public sympathy, but in January, 1848, was found guilty of mutiny, disobedience, and conduct prejudicial to military order. He was sentenced to dismissal from the service. President James K. Polk disallowed the mutiny conviction but upheld the lesser charges while suspending the punishment. Frémont spurned Polk's gesture and resigned his commission instead, ending his career as an explorer for the United States Army.

To regain his injured honor, Frémont organized a privately funded fourth expedition in late 1848. Intended to locate suitable passes for a central railroad route to the Pacific, the expedition attempted a mid-winter passage of the severe San Juan Mountains in southern Colorado. Disregarding the advice of mountain men and perhaps misled by his guide "Old Bill" Williams, Frémont plunged into the snowy mountains, only to find disaster. Cold and starvation eventually took the lives of ten of his thirty-three men, while a few survivors may have resorted to cannibalism. Frémont withdrew to Taos, New Mexico, sending a relief party to his surviving men. With a smaller party, he pushed on to California by the Gila River route, arriving in early 1849.

Frémont's fortunes revived once more as gold had just been discovered in California. In 1847, he had directed Consul Larkin to buy a tract of land near San Francisco; instead Larkin had secured a large grant in the interior. At first apparently worthless, the Mariposa grant yielded immense wealth in gold and became the Frémonts' California home. Then in December, 1849, Frémont was selected one of California's first United States senators, serving a short term from 1850 to 1851 as an antislavery Democrat.

Not chosen to lead one of the five government parties surveying the best route for a Pacific railroad, Frémont in late 1853 undertook his fifth and final expedition to prove the superiority of a central route. On this venture, Frémont found less hardship in attempting another winter crossing of the Colorado mountains. Crossing into Utah, however, his men were again on the brink of starvation, whereupon he swore them not to resort to cannibalism. The party was finally saved in February, 1854, when it arrived at a Mormon settlement in Parowan. The route was not adopted for the Pacific railroad.

As tension grew between North and South, Frémont emerged as a candidate for president in 1856, first for the Democratic party and then for the newly organized Republican party. Hostile to slavery, he favored the Republican position, opposing slavery's westward expansion, and in June, 1856, accepted the first presidential nomination of the young party. In the general election he faced both Democrat James Buchanan and the candidate of the Know-Nothing Party, Millard Fillmore. The "Pathfinder" made few campaign utterances, but his illegitimate origins and false campaign charges that he was a Catholic virtually overshadowed his opposition to the spread of slavery to Kansas. While he carried eleven free states, lack of campaign organization and money in critical states such as Pennsylvania and Indiana probably cost him the election. Perhaps Frémont was not the best man to lead his nation in time of crisis, but his popularity helped to establish the Republican party and thus contributed to the election of Abraham Lincoln four years later.

After his disappointing defeat, Frémont temporarily retired to private life, absorbed in developing the Mariposa, by now encumbered with debt. When the Civil War erupted in April, 1861, he was in Europe on business. Born a Southerner, he did not hesitate to support the Union in its greatest crisis. On his own authority he purchased arms and ammunition for the Union in England and France, and then returned home to accept an appointment as a major general commanding the Western Department based in St. Louis.

Beginning in July, 1861, Frémont's challenging task was to pacify the divided state of Missouri while raising an army to undertake an offensive down the Mississippi. He received little support from Washington, and his duties were overwhelming. While he reinforced the strategic Illinois town of Cairo, he did not act quickly enough to aid Nathaniel Lyon, who was defeated and killed at Wilson's Creek on August 10. Charges of favoritism and corruption in government contracts haunted Frémont's command, but most controversial was his sudden order of August 30 declaring martial law in Missouri, threatening to shoot captured guerrillas, and freeing the slaves of rebel masters.

While antislavery advocates praised Frémont's emancipation edict, Lincoln feared its effect on the border states and directed him to modify the order. The general stubbornly refused to heed Lincoln, forcing the president to reverse the measure publicly. With Frémont's command assaulted by powerful political enemies, Jessie went east to present his case, but her stormy interview with Lincoln did more harm than good. As Frémont sought to lead his troops to victory in southwestern Missouri, Lincoln removed him from command of the Western Department in November, 1861.

Outcry over Frémont's removal induced Lincoln to appoint him in March, 1862, to command the newly formed Mountain Department, designed to capture an important railroad at Knoxville, Tennessee. Abandoning this effort, Frémont was also outmarched by Stonewall Jackson in the Virginia Valley Campaign of 1862. At the battle of Cross Keys on June 8, Frémont proved ineffective against Confederate troops, and when Lincoln added Frémont's force to the command of John Pope, Frémont asked to be relieved. In 1864, Frémont was nominated to the presidency by some Democrats and radical Republicans dissatisfied with Lincoln. At first accepting the nomination, he soon feared a Democratic victory and withdrew from the race, helping to ensure Lincoln's reelection.

As the war came to an end, Frémont lost much of his wealth as well as control of his beloved Mariposa. His ambitions turned to railroad finance, as he still hoped to realize his dream of a Pacific railroad. He became involved with unscrupulous business associates, however, squandering the remainder of his fortune and a good portion of his reputation when the Southwest Pacific failed in 1867 and the Memphis & El Paso did so in 1870.

From 1878 to 1883, Frémont served as governor of Arizona Territory. With Jessie's help he wrote his memoirs, published in 1887. Belated gratitude from his nation came in April, 1890, when he was restored to his rank as major general and placed on the retired list with pay. Death came in New York in July, 1890, from a sudden attack of peritonitis.

Summary

Frémont's exploits as an explorer exemplified the restless energy and unbounded ambition of mid-nineteenth century America. Proud and self-reliant, Americans resented restraints and the rulings of authority. Frémont's career also reflected the lack of discipline and wisdom born of experience that led the young and sometimes careless American people into such tragedies as the brutal treatment of American Indians, the war on Mexico, and the spilling of brothers' blood in the Civil War. Like his nation, Frémont climbed heights of adventure and opportunity, but also found failure, conflict, and injustice.

Frémont never claimed to be a "Pathfinder"; his mapping expeditions usually followed paths already worn by fur traders and early emigrants. Yet his romantic journeys spurred American expansion to the Pacific, his reports encouraging western emigration while providing travelers with useful information. Frémont's mapping and scientific work rivaled that of earlier explorers, improving knowledge of the vast interior region from the Rockies to the Sierra, while helping to clarify the true natures of the Continental Divide and the Great Basin.

As politician, soldier, and financier, Frémont found less glory. His unauthorized actions in the California revolt remain controversial, while his service during the Civil War provoked charges of political opportunism and military ineffectiveness. His mining and railroad schemes typified the boom period of American industrial expansion, but left him almost destitute. His death in 1890 coincided with the end of the romantic age of the American West, where he left his name and his mark.

Bibliography

Allen, John Logan. "Division of the Waters: Changing Concepts of the Continental Divide, 1804-44." *Journal of Historical Geography* 4 (October, 1978): 357-370. This article helps to clarify Frémont's contributions to geographical knowledge of the American interior.

Dellenbaugh, Frederick S. *Frémont and '49*. New York: G. P. Putnam's Sons, 1914. An old but detailed account primarily of Frémont's expeditions. The author traces the explorer's routes and includes several useful maps.

Egan, Ferol. *Frémont: Explorer for a Restless Nation*. Garden City, N.Y.: Doubleday and Co., 1977. By focusing on Frémont's career to 1854, this work praises his accomplishments more than most.

Frémont, John Charles. *Memoirs of My Life*. Chicago: Belford, Clarke and Co., 1887. Frémont's own memoirs are the only source for much of the available information on his personal life as well as his career. An intended second volume was not published.

Goodwin, Cardinal L. *John Charles Frémont: An Explanation of His Career*. Stanford, Calif.: Stanford University Press, 1930. This is perhaps the most critical account of Frémont's life. It views the explorer as a "drifter" who entered into corrupt financial dealings.

Harlow, Neal. *California Conquered: War and Peace on the Pacific, 1846-1850*. Berkeley: University of California Press, 1982. Much of this work examines Frémont's controversial role in the California conquest. It also discusses his dispute with Kearny and subsequent arrest.

Jackson, Donald, and Mary Lee Spence, eds. The Expeditions of John Charles Frémont. 3 vols. Champaign: University of Illinois Press, 1970-1984. This multivolume collection of documents is an invaluable source of information for Frémont's expeditions. It includes his reports, important correspondence, and the record of his court-martial.

Nevins, Allan. *Frémont: Pathmarker of the West.* 2 vols. New York: Frederick Ungar Publishing Co., 1961. Perhaps the best study of Frémont, this work by a famous American historian portrays the explorer as a flawed hero of American expansion.

Rolle, Andrew. "Exploring an Explorer: Psychohistory and John Charles Frémont." *Pacific Historical Review* 51 (May, 1982): 145-163. This article presents an interesting if speculative psychological interpretation of Frémont's often erratic career.

Volpe, Vernon L. "The Frémonts and Emancipation in Missouri." *Historian* 56, no. 2 (Winter, 1994): 339-355.

Vernon L. Volpe

ALBERT GALLATIN

Born: January 29, 1761; Geneva, Switzerland
Died: August 12, 1849; Astoria, New York

Drawing upon the social philosophy of the French Enlightenment, Gallatin contributed, as secretary of the treasury to the administrations of Presidents Thomas Jefferson and James Madison, to the fiscal stability of the new nation and, as the first president of the American Ethnological Society, to the development of American anthropology.

Early Life

Abraham Alfonse Albert Gallatin was born January 29, 1761, in Geneva, Switzerland. Both his mother, née Sophie Albertine Rolaz, and his father, Jean Gallatin, died when Albert was an infant, so his care was entrusted to a distant relative of his mother, Mlle Catherine Pictet. The Gallatin family, part of the Geneva aristocracy and supplier of lords and councillors to the city-state, saw to it that young Gallatin was provided an excellent education. Despite access to the rich cultural heritage of his family, who counted Voltaire as a close friend, and a fine education at the academy, from which he was graduated in 1779, Gallatin resisted the aristocratic trappings of his family and identified with a growing number of students who supported Jean-Jacques Rousseau's Romantic call of "back to nature."

When his grandmother successfully gained for Gallatin an appointment as lieutenant colonel in the army of her friend Frederich, the Langrave of Hesse, then preparing to fight as mercenaries for England against the American Colonies, Gallatin rebelled and with a friend fled Geneva at the age of eighteen for America. He arrived in Massachusetts in 1780 and, without much money, set off for the frontier of Maine. After spending a year there, he returned to Boston, where he eked out a living as a tutor teaching French to students at Harvard College. Finding the atmosphere in Boston too cold for his tastes, Gallatin moved to the back country of Pennsylvania in 1782. Through business dealings, he acquired land in the region and, as a good Romantic, settled down to devote his life to farming. At one point, Gallatin hoped to establish a Swiss colony on the American frontier, but these plans

Albert Gallatin *(Library of Congress)*

came to nothing. Gallatin was successful as neither farmer nor land speculator. Personal tragedy also touched him when his wife of a few months, Sophia Allegre, whom he had met in Richmond, Virginia, died at his farm, Friendship Hill. Despondent, Gallatin contemplated returning to Geneva, but an inability to sell his farm and the fighting in Geneva triggered by the French Revolution caused him to remain in America.

His intelligence and gregariousness led him to politics, first in Pennsylvania as a member of the Harrisburg conference of 1788, which met to consider ways in which the United States Constitution could be strengthened, and then as a member of the convention that met in 1789-1790 to revise the Pennsylvania constitution. In 1790, he was elected representative of Fayette County to the Pennsylvania state legislature.

Life's Work

Gallatin had three careers: politics, business, and science. Although he believed that his investigations in science, rather than his work in government, would cause his name to be remembered in history, the reverse, ironically, proved to be the case. Western Pennsylvania elected Gallatin twice to the state legislature, and then he was elected by the legislature to the Senate of the United States. There, his eligibility was challenged because he had not been a citizen for nine years. Removed from the Senate, Gallatin returned to Pennsylvania, taking his new bride Hannah, daughter of Commodore James Nicholson of New York. His stay in Pennsylvania proved short, for in 1794 the voters of western Pennsylvania sent him to the House of Representatives, in which he served three terms. A Republican, Gallatin defended the farming interests of western Pennsylvania; at the same time, his grasp of international law and public finance and his reasoning ability and cogent arguments made him a valuable legislator at a critical time in America's early history.

In May of 1801, Thomas Jefferson appointed Gallatin secretary of the treasury. Gallatin held this post through Jefferson's two administrations and through part of James Madison's first administration. Accusations that his financial policies hindered American efforts to fight the British in the War of 1812 prompted Gallatin to leave the treasury in 1813 and accept an appointment as a special envoy to Russia, which had offered to mediate the conflict between Great Britain and the United States. Great Britain, however, refused to accept mediation and, thus, frustrated Gallatin's mission. Rather than returning to the treasury, as Madison expected, Gallatin chose to remain in Europe in diplomatic service. So began Gallatin's career as diplomat.

Along with John Quincy Adams and Henry Clay, Gallatin drew up the Treaty of Ghent, which ended the War of 1812. With the work on the treaty concluded, Gallatin, Adams, and Clay traveled to England and negotiated a commercial treaty with the British. On his return to the United States, Gallatin accepted the post of minister to France, which he held from 1816 to 1832. Upon his return from France, he intended to retire from government service and to devote the rest of life to being a gentleman farmer at Friendship Hill, but, although Gallatin was increasingly upset with the emphasis on gain in American politics, he allowed his name to be put forward for vice president. Henry Clay's ultimate acceptance of the nomination allowed Gallatin happily to withdraw his name. Life at Friendship Hill proved boring for the Gallatins after seven years in Paris, and so Gallatin once again accepted diplomatic assignment, his last, in 1826, as minister to England.

The America to which Gallatin returned in 1827 seemed foreign to him. The robust activity of Jacksonian America seemed to make a shambles of the Jeffersonian idealism to which Gallatin subscribed. So disorienting did the new United States seem to him that he seriously considered leaving the country and returning with his family to Geneva. Although he did not return to Europe, he did retire from government service, beginning a new career in business.

Gallatin moved to New York City, where John Jacob Astor urged him to accept the presidency of Astor's new National Bank. In this position, which Gallatin held from 1831 to 1839, he not only wrote on fiscal reform in articles such as *Considerations on the Currency and Banking System of the United States* (1831) but also protested slavery, the annexation of Texas by the United States, and the war with Mexico. In addition, he found time to indulge his interests in ethnology and, especially, linguistics.

While Gallatin had been living in Paris, he had made the acquaintance of the famous German scientist Alexander von Humboldt. Gallatin's knowledge of several European languages and his interest in linguistics complemented Humboldt's study of linguistics and American Indian languages. Humboldt prevailed upon Gallatin to write on Indian languages, and thus, even before Gallatin left public service, he had begun his scientific career. His first major publication in this field was *A Synopsis of the Indian Tribes Within the United States East of the Rocky Mountains and in the British and Russian Possessions in North America* (1836), followed by *Notes on the Semi-Civilized Nations of Mexico, Yucatan, and Central America* (1845) and *Indians of North-west Amer-*

ica (1848). Besides writing in the field of ethnology, Gallatin served as president of the American Ethnological Society, an organization he helped to found in 1842.

Summary

Although sometimes indulging in Romantic notions, Gallatin was first and foremost a gentleman of the Enlightenment. With his superb forensic skills and his ability to remain calm under personal attack, Gallatin proved a consummate politician, negotiator, and diplomat. His brilliance of mind led Jefferson to rely on Gallatin not only to oversee national finance but also to proofread his speeches and act as personal confidant. As secretary of the treasury and disbursing agent, Gallatin assumed a major role in promoting the exploration of the West and settlement of the Western frontier.

Governed by an Enlightenment philosophy that emphasized idealism and humanism in politics, learning, and society, Gallatin became uncomfortable with the raw commercialism of Jacksonian America, which seemed to him to promote only the base side of human potential. By the time of his death, Gallatin was out of step with his time: an Enlightenment figure in Jacksonian America. Yet for many he remained the Enlightenment conscience of America's idealistic beginnings.

Bibliography

Adams, Henry. *The Life of Albert Gallatin*. Philadelphia: J. B. Lippincott Co., 1880. Still a classic account of Gallatin's life. Henry Adams, the grandson of John Adams, provides an intimate glimpse into Gallatin's life and values and places both in the context of Gallatin's European experience and a rapidly developing American society.

Allen, John Logan. *Passage Through the Garden: Lewis and Clark and the Image of the American Northwest*. Urbana: University of Illinois Press, 1975. Logan's work discusses Gallatin's economic contribution as secretary of the treasury and his intellectual contribution to the exploration of the West.

Balinky, Alexander. *Albert Gallatin: Fiscal Theories and Policies*. New Brunswick, N.J.: Rutgers University Press, 1958. An extensive study of Gallatin's theories and policies on public finance.

Bieder, Robert E. *Science Encounters the Indian, 1820-1880: The Early*

Years of American Ethnology. Norman: University of Oklahoma Press, 1986. Contains a chapter on Gallatin, his study of American Indians, and his place in the early development of American ethnology.

Gallatin, James. *The Diary of James Gallatin, Secretary to Albert Gallatin, a Great Peace Maker, 1813-1827*. Edited by Count Gallatin. New York: Charles Scribner's Sons, 1931. A highly intimate and entertaining account of Gallatin's years in Paris and London, written by his son, who served as Gallatin's secretary.

Kuppenheimer, L. B. *Albert Gallatin's Vision of Democratic Stability: An Interpretive Profile*. Westport, Conn.: Praeger, 1996.

Smelser, Marshall. *The Democratic Republic: 1801-1815*. Edited by Henry S. Commager and Richard B. Morris. New American Nations Series. New York: Harper and Row, Publishers, 1968. Mentions Gallatin in the larger context of the growth of the American republic.

Walters, Raymond, Jr. *Albert Gallatin: Jeffersonian Financier and Diplomat*. New York: Macmillan Publishing Co., 1957. Walters differs from Balinky in emphasizing Gallatin's Jeffersonian ties and diplomatic career.

White, Leonard D. *The Jeffersonians: A Study in Administrative History, 1801-1829*. New York: Macmillan Publishing Co., 1951. Now dated but still useful in its consideration of Gallatin's administration of the treasury.

Robert E. Bieder

JAMES A. GARFIELD

Born: November 19, 1831; Orange Township, Ohio
Died: September 19, 1881; Elberon, New Jersey

During his almost two decades, first as congressman, then briefly as president, Garfield played a key role in every issue of national importance. As party leader, he helped resolve the factionalism within the Republican Party and enabled the Republicans to lead the United States into the twentieth century.

Early Life

James Abram Garfield was born in a log cabin on November 19, 1831, to Abram and Eliza Garfield, members of the Disciples of Christ church. Abram died in 1833, thus leaving Eliza a widow, the sole provider for her family.

Next to hunting, reading was young Garfield's greatest interest. He liked history and fiction, especially stories of the American Revolution and stories of the sea. At the age of sixteen, Garfield went to Cleveland, where he was shocked and disappointed by a drunken captain to whom he had applied for work. On that same day, August 16, 1848, Garfield secured a job as driver with his cousin on a canal boat that carried goods between Cleveland and Pittsburgh. After six weeks of working on the canal, Garfield became quite ill and returned home. During his recuperation, his mother and Samuel Bates, a schoolteacher, convinced Garfield of the importance of education.

Garfield enrolled and studied at Geauga Academy in Chester, where he became the academy's prize Latin student. Originally, Garfield planned to spend the winter months at the academy and the spring and summers on the canal, but after he absorbed himself in his studies, he decided to forget the canal life.

In the fall of 1851, Garfield enrolled in the newly established Western Reserve Eclectic Institute at Hiram, Ohio, where he plunged into his studies with a fierce determination to excel. Garfield's popularity and prominence at the Western Reserve Eclectic Institute were based on his scholastic ability as well as his physical prowess. His commanding physical appearance—he stood almost six feet tall, with broad shoulders and a massive head topped by a shock of unruly tawny

hair—and his ability to outrun and outwrestle his schoolmates instilled automatic respect. This, combined with his serious demeanor,
which gave an impression of quiet dignity, and his unaffected friendli-
ness contributed to Garfield's popularity. Enjoying success as a debater, Garfield discovered that he possessed the ability to sway an
audience, and the oratorical techniques which he learned during this
period prepared him to become one of the most effective political
speakers of his time.

James A. Garfield *(Library of Congress)*

In 1853, Garfield began preaching at neighboring churches. The following year, having completed his studies at the Eclectic Institute, he enrolled in Williams College. There, he was elected president of two major campus organizations—the Philogian Society, a literary society, and the Equitable Fraternity, an organization designed to combat the influence of the Greek fraternities. In addition, in spite of his Campbellite beliefs, Garfield was elected president of the Mills Theological Society, a Calvinist organization. He was also elected editor of the *Williams Quarterly*, a pioneer college journal of exceptional quality, to which he contributed extensively. Indeed, Garfield never lost an election at Williams College, nor any election in which he was a candidate for the rest of his life. On August 7, 1856, he was graduated from Williams College with honors in a ceremony that included his delivering an oration on the conflict between matter and spirit.

Life's Work

As an inspiring and electrifying evangelist, Garfield preached continually during the last of the series of so-called Great Awakenings—periodic religious revivals that had begun in the Colonial era. In 1857, at the age of twenty-six, Garfield was elected president of Western Reserve Eclectic Institute, defeating his former teacher, the institute's oldest and most distinguished faculty member. As president, Garfield made the Eclectic Institute the educational center of the region, changing a sectarian academy into an institution that welcomed students of all denominations.

He believed the curriculum should reflect the trends of the time and serve as a medium through which students could prepare for successful living. He sponsored teacher-training workshops and seminars on teaching methods and school administration, and he prepared a series of lectures on American history, a subject which had not been included in the curricula of American colleges.

Garfield did not confine himself to administrative duties; he taught a full load of classes in a style designed to encourage students to think independently. Garfield's kindness and immense vitality, his readiness to praise, his deep concern for the overall welfare of his students, his enthusiasm, his ability to introduce his students to the meaning of education and the high ideals of life, and his participation with them in the extracurricular activities, especially athletic events, inspired great loyalty. The Eclectic Institute prospered under Garfield's leadership. On November 11, 1858, Garfield married Lucretia Rudolph, daughter of Zeb Rudolph, a pioneer Hiram Disciple and one of the school's most prominent trustees.

On August 23, 1859, based on his prominent background and popularity, the Republican Party of the Twenty-sixth Ohio Senatorial District nominated him for the state senate, a seat he handily won, October 11, 1859. This feat ultimately led him to the center stage of the national political arena. Garfield distinguished himself on a number of key issues, especially those pertaining to slavery and the impending crisis—the Civil War. He stood strong against slavery and, shedding his pacifism, believed that war was the best solution to the problem of slavery. When the war began, he took an active role in raising troops, influencing the governor of his state to appoint him lieutenant colonel in the Twenty-fourth Ohio Infantry; later, he was put in charge of the Forty-second Ohio Volunteer Infantry as a full colonel. Learning about Garfield's commission, the young men of Hiram, who held Garfield in the highest esteem, enthusiastically joined the Forty-second Ohio Volunteer Infantry to follow and fight with their hero.

At the outset of Garfield's military service, General Don Carlos Buell assigned him command of the Eighteenth Brigade and gave him the responsibility of planning the campaign to drive the Confederate army out of eastern Kentucky. In spite of the fact that Garfield had no military education or military experience, he accepted the task, presenting a plan which Buell accepted. Under Garfield's leadership, the Confederate forces were driven out of Kentucky.

Assuming control of the administration of eastern Kentucky, Garfield pursued a policy of reconciliation. Promoted to brigadier general, he served outstandingly as chief of staff under General William S. Rosecrans, commander of the Army of the Cumberland. Garfield reached the peak of his military career in the Chattanooga campaign, fighting in one of the epic battles of military history, the Battle of Chickamauga. Garfield's outstanding achievements in the Kentucky campaign led his friends and the Republican Party of the Nineteenth Congressional District to nominate him as their representative to Congress, September 2, 1862. While still in the army carrying out his military duties and without participating in the campaign, he won the right to represent the Nineteenth District by an impressive victory, in the congressional election of October, 1862.

Beginning with the election of 1862, Garfield easily won nine consecutive terms, splendidly serving the people of the Nineteenth District for the next eighteen years as chairman of the Military Affairs Committee (in which capacity he was the first to introduce a bill that proposed an ROTC program for the colleges), chairman of the Banking and Currency Committee, and chairman of the powerful and prestigious Appropriations Committee.

When the Democratic Party won a majority of the seats in the House of Representatives in the congressional election of 1874, Garfield assumed the leadership of the Republican minority in the House. Having lost his chairmanships, he skillfully and relentlessly spoke out against the policies of the Democratic Party. As a member of a bipartisan committee selected to investigate the 1876 presidential election in the state of Louisiana, Garfield submitted a thorough report based on data presented to him by the election board and interviews he held with those who participated in the election and those denied participation, especially voters who were terrorized by white secret societies such as the Ku Klux Klan, the Knights of the White Camellia, and the Rifle Clubs. His report helped influence the election board to nullify Samuel Tilden's majority, and Rutherford B. Hayes was granted the electoral votes of Louisiana.

The 1876 election ended in an intense controversy involving the returns of Florida, Louisiana, and South Carolina. This situation produced a political stalemate that set the stage for a potential crisis that might have led the opposing parties back to the battlefields in a new civil war. Garfield served as a member of a special Electoral Commission to elect the president and participated in the historic conference that led to the compromise between the leaders of the Republican Party and the Southern Democrats. These actions resolved the impending crisis, and Hayes became the nineteenth president of the United States.

On March 29, 1879, Garfield established himself as the outstanding leader of the Republican Party when he delivered one of the most dynamic speeches in the history of Congress. The Democrats' dogged advocacy of the principle of states' rights motivated Garfield to present his greatest speech—a speech that upheld the principle of federalism and inspired the Republicans to quit squabbling and act together as a strong united party. This speech influenced his state's legislature to elect him to serve in the United States Senate, and ultimately led to his nomination and election as President of the United States.

In 1880, Garfield was elected to serve as a delegate to the Seventh National Nominating Convention of the Republican Party, which met in Chicago. He came to the convention without any intention of seeking the nomination, but because of his great popularity, he was considered a darkhorse candidate. On the thirty-sixth ballot, the deadlocked delegates chose Garfield, hoping that he could unify the party. In a move that displeased a large number of Republicans, but as a means of placating the highly disappointed Stalwarts, who had supported Ulysses S. Grant for a third term, the imperious political boss of the New York Republican Party, Chester Alan Arthur, was selected as the party's candidate for vice president.

In November, Garfield's ability to control the various factions of his party and brilliantly manage his campaign, resulted in his winning the presidency in the closest presidential election of the century. In view of the fact that he did nothing either before or during the convention to obtain his party's nomination (he strongly opposed the effort that culminated in his nomination) and the fact that his party had all but self-destructed since the assassination of President Abraham Lincoln, Garfield achieved a magnificent victory.

On July 2, 1881, only a few months after his inauguration, Garfield was shot by a crazed office-seeker, Charles Guiteau. He died on September 19, 1881.

Summary
Garfield's election to the presidency was the crowning achievement of a spectacular and glorious career that began as the driver of a towboat on the Ohio Erie Canal. His was a classic American success story, brought to a tragically premature end.

The legacy of Garfield's brief term suggests what he might have accomplished had he lived to complete it. He laid the foundation for the development of a more independent and vigorous presidency that proved vital for a nation destined to become one of the most powerful nations in the world. The Pendleton Act of 1883, which led to the end of the spoils system in the federal government, was the logical conclusion of his efforts.

Bibliography

Booraem, Hendrik. *The Road to Respectability: James A. Garfield and His World, 1844-1852*. Lewisburg, Pa.: Bucknell University Press, 1988.

Brisbin, James S. *From the Tow-Path to the White House: The Early Life and Public Career of James A. Garfield*. Philadelphia: J. C. McCurdy and Co., 1880. A flattering campaign biography, written in a romantic style shortly after Garfield's nomination. Although hurriedly written, Brisbin's work vividly recounts the story of a leader who exemplified fundamental American values. Includes illustrations.

Caldwell, Robert G. *James A. Garfield, Party Chieftain*. New York: Dodd, Mead and Co., 1934. An exhaustive scholarly chronicle of the life of Garfield that, in effect, summarizes American political history from 1861 to 1881. Includes an excellent bibliography.

Clark, James C. *The Murder of James A. Garfield: The President's Last Days and the Trial and Execution of His Assassin*. Jefferson, N.C.: McFarland, 1993.

Doenecke, Justus D. *The Presidencies of James A. Garfield and Chester A. Arthur*. Lawrence: University Press of Kansas, 1981. This is one of the volumes of the American Presidency Series, intended to present historians and the general public with interesting, scholarly assessments of the various presidential administrations. Includes excellent notes and bibliographical essays.

Hinsdale, Mary L., ed. *Garfield-Hinsdale Letters: Correspondence Between James Abram Garfield and Burke Aaron Hinsdale*. Ann Arbor: University of Michigan Press, 1949. The correspondence between James A. Garfield and his lifelong friend, Burke A. Hinsdale, a former pupil of Garfield, superintendent of Cleveland's Public School System, outstanding teacher at the University of Michigan, and president of Hiram College. The letters between Garfield and Hinsdale discuss the various issues that confronted America between 1857 and 1881, as well as the most popular books of the period; they also reveal the writers in their lighter moods. Their correspondence, which began when Hinsdale was nineteen and continued until Garfield's death, provides graphic self-portraits of Garfield and Hinsdale, and is a significant resource for scholars of Garfield.

Leech, Margaret, and Harry J. Brown. *The Garfield Orbit*. New York: Harper and Row, Publishers, 1978. An absorbing story of the life of Garfield, showing him as a man of complex and contradictory character, in whom ambition and desire warred with firm principle. The book reveals more of the man and less of the vital issues that he confronted. Includes a Garfield genealogy; a selection of Garfield's letters; notes and references; sixty-three illustrations, mainly photographs and sketches; and maps of the Western Reserve and the military campaigns of Garfield during the Civil War.

Riddle, Albert G. *The Life, Character and Public Services of James A. Garfield*. Chicago: Tyler and Co., 1880. This is a classic biography of Garfield that covers the period from his birth to his nomination as the standard-bearer of the Republican Party.

Smith, Theodore Clark. *The Life and Letters of James Abram Garfield*. 2 vols. New Haven, Conn.: Yale University Press, 1925. Smith's biographical study is principally based on Garfield's own words contained in his letters, journals, school and college notes, speeches, and memorabilia. The author's masterful selection and arrangement of the materials produces the effect of Garfield himself interpreting his life.

James D. Lockett

ULYSSES S. GRANT

Born: April 27, 1822; Point Pleasant, Ohio
Died: July 23, 1885; Mount McGregor, New York

Grant became the preeminent general of the Civil War, demonstrating the persistence and strategic genius that brought about the victory of the North.

Early Life

Ulysses S. Grant, born Hiram Ulysses Grant on April 27, 1822, in Point Pleasant, Ohio, was the eldest child of Jesse Root Grant and Hannah Simpson Grant. His father had known poverty in his youth, but at the time of his first son's birth, he had established a prosperous tannery business. In 1823, Jesse moved his business to Georgetown, Ohio, where Grant spent his boyhood. He received his preliminary education at Georgetown, at Maysville Seminary in Maysville, Kentucky, and at the Presbyterian Academy, Ripley, Ohio. He did not show special promise as a student and lived a rather ordinary boyhood. His most outstanding gift turned out to be a special talent with horses, enabling him to manage the most fractious horse. He also developed a strong dislike for work at the tannery and a lifelong fondness for farming.

Jesse Grant secured an appointment for his son to the United States Military Academy at West Point in 1839. His son did not want to go but bowed to parental authority. Concerned about the initials on his trunk, "H.U.G., " he decided to change his name to Ulysses Hiram Grant. Arriving at West Point, Grant had his first skirmish with military bureaucracy. His congressman, evidently confusing Grant with his brother Simpson, had appointed him as Ulysses S. Grant. The army insisted that Ulysses S. Grant, not Ulysses H. or Hiram Ulysses, had been appointed, and eventually Grant surrendered. Grant wrote to a congressman in 1864: "In answer to your letter of a few days ago asking what 'S' stands for in my name I can only state *nothing*."

He was graduated in the middle of his class in 1843. While at West Point, he developed a fondness for novels and showed a special talent for mathematics. Appointed a brevet second lieutenant in the Fourth United States Infantry, Grant served with distinction in the Mexican

Ulysses S. Grant *(Library of Congress)*

War (1846-1848). He fought in the battles of Palo Alto, Resaca de la Palma, and Monterrey under the command of Zachary Taylor, "Old Rough and Ready." Taylor impressed Grant with his informal attire and lack of military pretension, a style which Grant later adopted. He participated in all major battles leading to the capture of Mexico City and won brevet promotion to first lieutenant for bravery at Molino Del Rey and to captain for his behavior at Chapultepec. Although he fought with distinction, Grant believed that the Mexican War was unjust and later said that he should have resigned his commission rather than participate.

Grant married Julia Dent, the daughter of a St. Louis slaveholding family, on August 22, 1848. He had been introduced to his future wife in 1843, by her brother, a West Point classmate, while stationed at Jefferson Barracks, Missouri. The Mexican War, however, interrupted their romance. The Grants had four children, Frederick Dent, Ulysses S., Jr., Ellen Wrenshall, and Jesse Root, Jr. A devoted husband and father, Grant centered his life on his family. Indeed, the many surviving letters to his wife during absences caused by a military career provide the most poignant insights into the man.

Ordered to the Pacific Coast in 1852 with his regiment, Grant could not afford to take his wife and children. He grew despondent without his family, decided to resign his commission in 1854, and returned to live on his wife's family land near St. Louis to take up farming. For the remainder of Grant's life, rumors that he had been forced to resign on account of heavy drinking followed him. The next seven years were difficult for Grant. His attempt at farming did not work out, and he tried other occupations without real success. Finally, in 1860, he moved his family to Galena, Illinois, to work as a clerk in a leather-goods store owned by his father and operated by his two younger brothers.

Grant had never been a strident, political man. His father had been an antislavery advocate, yet Grant married into a slaveholding family. At one time, he owned a slave but gave him his freedom in 1858 at a time when Grant sorely needed money. His wife retained ownership of slaves throughout the Civil War. When news of the firing on Fort Sumter reached Galena, Grant believed that he had an obligation to support the Union. Because of his military experience, he assisted in organizing and escorting a volunteer company to Springfield, Illinois, where he stayed on to assist Governor Richard Yates in mustering in and organizing volunteer troops. Eventually, Yates appointed Grant colonel of the Twenty-first Illinois Volunteers, a disorganized and undisciplined unit. Grant quickly worked the regiment into shape, marched it to Missouri, and learned much about commanding volunteer soldiers.

Life's Work

On August 7, 1861, President Abraham Lincoln appointed Grant brigadier general, and Grant established headquarters at Cairo, Illinois, an important staging area for Union movement farther south. On September 6, he occupied Paducah, Kentucky, near the strategic confluence of the Tennessee, Cumberland, and Ohio rivers. Grant's first battle followed shortly. He attacked Confederate forces at Belmont, Missouri, with mixed results. He lost control of his troops after initial success and had to retreat when Confederate reinforcements arrived.

Grant gained national prominence in February, 1862, when authorized to operate against Fort Donelson and Fort Henry, guarding the Cumberland and Tennessee rivers, obvious highways into the Confederate heartland. He moved his small army in conjunction with naval forces and captured Fort Henry on February 6 and immediately moved overland against Fort Donelson, twelve miles away. The Confederates attempted to escape encirclement on February 15 in a brief, but bloody, battle. On February 16, the Confederate commander asked Grant for surrender terms. His response brought him fame: "No terms except an unconditional and immediate surrender can be accepted." The Confederates surrendered on Grant's terms, and Lincoln rewarded him for the first significant Union victory with promotion to major general.

Grant's next major engagement, the battle of Shiloh, April 6-7, left him under a cloud. Surprised by Rebel forces, Grant suffered heavy losses but managed to rally his army on the first day. The second day, General Grant counterattacked and drove the Confederates from the field. This bloody engagement cast a long shadow, and Grant faced newspaper criticism, with rumors of his heavy drinking appearing in the press. Major General Henry W. Halleck arrived on the scene to take command of Grant's forces, placing him in a subordinate position with little to do. Grant considered leaving the army. He retained his humor, however, writing to his wife, "We are all well and me as sober as a deacon no matter what is said to the contrary." Halleck, however, was called to Washington to act as general in chief, and Grant resumed command. Although many had criticized Grant, Lincoln refused to relieve a fighting general, thus setting the stage for Grant's finest campaign.

Confederate control of the Mississippi River rested on extensive fortifications at Vicksburg, Mississippi, effectively barring Midwestern commerce. In the fall and spring of 1862-1863, Grant made a number of attempts against this bastion. The overland campaign through northern Mississippi came to grief when Confederate forces destroyed his supply base at Holly Springs, Mississippi, on December 20, 1862. Grant then decided to move down the Mississippi to attack the city. Ultimately, Grant bypassed the city, marching his army down the west bank of the river. At night, he sent steamboats past the batteries to assist in crossing the river from Louisiana into Mississippi. The general then launched a lightning campaign into the interior of the state to destroy Confederate communications before turning back against Vicksburg. Thoroughly confusing his opposition, he won five separate battles and besieged the city on May 19. On July 4, 1863, Grant accepted the surrender of his second Confederate army.

After a brief respite, Grant was given command of all Union forces in the West on October 18 and charged with rescuing Union forces besieged in Chattanooga, Tennessee. In a three-day battle (November 23-25), Grant smashed the Confederate forces and drove them back into Georgia.

In March, 1864, Lincoln promoted Grant to lieutenant general and gave him command of all Union armies. Grant left Halleck at Washington as chief of staff to tend to routine matters and established the beginning of a modern military command system. He stayed in the field with the Army of the Potomac, commanded by Major General George G. Meade. Grant made Union armies work in tandem for the first time. Using the telegraph, he managed troop movements across the country, keeping pressure on the Confederacy at all points. The two major efforts consisted of Major General William T. Sherman, moving against Atlanta, and Meade attacking Confederate forces in Virginia, commanded by the South's finest general, Robert E. Lee.

The final campaign opened in May, 1864, with the battle of the Wilderness (May 5-6). After a series of bloody engagements, Grant maneuvered Lee into Petersburg, Virginia, where siege operations commenced on June 16. While Grant held Lee at Petersburg, Sherman proceeded to gut the South, capturing Atlanta in September, then marching across Georgia and capturing Savannah in December. Grant then planned for Sherman to march his army up through the Carolinas into Virginia. On March 29, 1865, Grant launched his final campaign. He smashed Confederate lines at Petersburg, then tenaciously pressured the retreating Confederates, and accepted Lee's surrender at Appomattox Court House on April 9. Grant's magnanimous surrender terms attest to his humanity and sensitivity. Seventeen days later, the last major Confederate force surrendered to Sherman and the Civil War ended.

Lincoln's assassination on April 14 deeply affected Grant, but he believed that President Andrew Johnson would be able to reestablish the Union on an equitable basis. Grant busied himself with the reorganization of the army, threatening French forces operating in Mexico, marshaling forces to fight Indians, and seeking to avoid political questions. Yet he could not avoid the growing antagonism between Johnson and the radical Republicans. Increasing doubts about Johnson's Reconstruction policy brought the two men into conflict. In the face of growing Southern persecution of blacks, Grant came to believe that blacks had to be protected by the federal government. In 1868, the breach between Johnson and Grant became public, and Grant believed that it was his duty to accept the Republican nomination for president.

A reluctant candidate, Grant easily defeated his Democratic opponent. His military background, however, had left him with a distaste for the hurly-burly of politics, and his two-term presidency (March 4, 1869, to March 4, 1877) had many problems. Already convinced of the need to protect blacks, Grant sought in vain to advance Civil Rights for them. With the Force Acts (1870-1871), he succeeded in breaking up the first Ku Klux Klan, but by 1876, conservative Southerners had regained control and reasserted their dominance.

In foreign policy, Grant did much to normalize relations with Great Britain with the Treaty of Washington in May, 1871, which settled the *Alabama* claims arising out of the Civil War. His stubbornness and persistence, which had served him so well in war, however, proved to be an embarrassment in his unsuccessful attempts to annex Santo Domingo.

Grant made a number of unfortunate appointments to federal office, and official corruption even reached into the White House with the Whiskey Ring Scandal. Although Grant was not personally involved, these scandals tainted his second term. Plagued by corruption and politics, Grant resisted attempts to draft him for a third term in 1876.

After the presidency, Grant made a two-year journey around the world, indulging a passion for travel developed early in his life. This triumphant tour brought him worldwide renown. Restless after returning to the United States, he unsuccessfully sought a third term in 1880. He then moved to New York City to pursue business interests in connection with his son, Ulysses S. Grant, Jr., and became a silent partner in Grant and Ward. Ferdinand Ward turned out to be a swindler, and in 1884, Grant found himself penniless.

To support his family, Grant decided to write his memoirs. At about the same time, Grant learned that he had contracted cancer of the throat. He completed the manuscript only days before his death, on July 23, 1885. This work has become a literary classic and is recognized as one of the best military memoirs ever written.

Summary
Grant's boyhood had been ordinary, showing nothing of the extraordinary man he would become. He had not sought a military career and did not like things military. He detested military parades, disliked military dress, and rarely carried a weapon. He left the army in 1854 and suffered through seven years of disappointment. The outbreak of Civil War, for all its national trauma, rescued Grant from a life of obscurity.

This seemingly common man turned out to have a genius for war unmatched by his contemporaries. Grant perhaps had an advantage in that he had time to learn gradually the art of war. Grant made mistakes, learned from them, and never repeated them. He grew into the responsibilities of higher command. He also understood volunteer soldiers and their motivations for fighting.

Grant's military writings are extraordinary. His instructions are clear, brief, and to the point. Subordinates made mistakes, but not because of ambiguity of instruction. Grant became the finest general that the Civil War produced, indeed, the greatest American military figure of the nineteenth century.

The Grant presidency had many shortcomings. Not a politician, Grant never really understood presidential power and its uses. In this sense, he was a nineteenth century man: He believed that Congress decided policy and the president executed it. Had Grant viewed the presidency in the same manner that he perceived military command, his two terms might have been far different.

Grant returned to wartime form in the fight to complete his memoirs. This literary classic is really a gift to the ages as he again demonstrated that he was truly an extraordinary American.

Bibliography
Catton, Bruce. *Grant Moves South*. New York: Little, Brown and Co., 1960. This biography of Grant, covering his early Civil War career, is thoroughly researched and superbly written.

_____. *Grant Takes Command*. Boston: Little, Brown and Co., 1969.